PORTRAITURE

Also by S.R. Osborn

Song of Earth
Inquiry into the Sun
Memories of the Ocean

PORTRAITURE
S R OSBORN

iUniverse, Inc.
New York   Bloomington

PORTRAITURE

iUniverse books may be ordered through booksellers or by contacting:

iUniverse
1663 Liberty Drive
Bloomington, IN 47403
www.iuniverse.com
1-800-Authors (1-800-288-4677)

ISBN: 978-1-4401-1395-6 (sc)
ISBN: 978-1-4401-1396-3 (ebk)

Cover graphic by Ron Heck.
Reprinted by permission of Mari Andrus, with thanks.

Printed in the United States of America

iUniverse rev. date: 01/26/2009

For Daphne, with the desire to be near

Contents

▼

Acknowledgements

A very special *Thank You!* to the muses who have inspired the author's most important works: Angelina Fiordellisi, Founder and Artistic Director of the Cherry Lane Theatre, New York City, for a generous heart, opportunity, and electricity when most needed; diva Shirley Be, of the Chamber Music Conference of the East, Bennington, VT, for Beauty, the cello, and laughter; Elizabeth Weinreb Fishman, Associate Dean of the Columbia University Graduate School of Journalism, for brightness of being and intensity of happiness; and those who remain unnamed but without whom this collection of portraits could not have been completed; all, proof that Divine Mother indeed takes human form. And deepest gratitude to the Metropolitan Museum of Art and its branch, the Cloisters Museum and Gardens, for a second home.

Unmanifested

From the unmanifested Night, is born to Man, Interpretation's final stand. Delight not, Muse, if the Beginning ends the End; remotely decorated, superbly held in fray, the jittery resolutions of Beauty in one day. What must forcèd be delay? if to push a corpus in a way that may, please a heart's desire, lead no less a year of want. Taxing Romance, all fury aside, Beauty took a turn. In defeatist's memory trial, the heart of Love gave smile. All pleasant growths from the bough of the feminine; and rightly so, fairer sex made gain, drew response in difference, opposèd men, to angelic cares from heaven's end—where begins this world of flesh and scares. The Grace's loveliest self, svelte stature, unreflected and interior-generated shone, yet sheen of the Unseen. Giddily willing to be duped and engaged, situations must just lit enraged—for Love having fallen, renounced a pearly gate, to play posthaste... ephemeral, noumenal, transcendental—Light dressed in the human garb of Night. Sure cousin, and in retrospect, to remnant soul set free from the grasp of Finity—where during yesterday's tomorrow, before that rolling of the di, locomotion and transformation spilled from the flapping of aetherial wings. Sneaking in on moonbeams, Loveliness came to rule: journeyed, storied Self, enacted this local play; men meet woman, and divine endings from before, timeless foundations for resultant beginning love affairs. Sacred structure of an eternal script, the Descended reascend by glorious spiral turns of lives lead. Majestic occurrence of due blessings, but mostly great joy in opportunity, to have a gifted part in this grandest cosmic show.

Feast of Lost Remembrance

The heavy, damp, night air condensed upon the lover's breath, exhaling at the moon, from a mountaintop rest stop, beneath the stars of early June. Two were one and happiness, and so the half moon was a full sun, and darkness was no less than a day for play. Comfortable in a long-lost love found, indeed tight in sleeping bag, two peas for a pod. Trust must just be, in the upside to infinity, in rebirth for true lovers on earth, an odd quality. Strength to fire hearts' desires beyond the funeral pyres, and link to a new life incomplete of you; forgotten, you, remembered by an ache, deep within the lake of being, or that faculty that finds the 'I' in 'my'...*equally weighted, and food enough for two, a feast of lost remembrance; lover complete, having eaten.* Contribute a murderer to a loving throw, such as this, and the Fates hiss; lion of a love, misses. Adamant volume of youthful missus tosses into the sanity, a depraved humanity, such that the death occurs, by ambitious confidence, of the one love twixt these two, in that another love has risen above; then the decline and the end, of what might have been. Terrible love assassin; greed? or just the need to sow the wildly seed? based upon the thoughts that *know* fresh love comes 'round, again, and again, and again. *So why the need for a permanent plan at 21? Wonder has just begun!*

CATHERINE

Strong woman hiding child, passed in heavenly mild, in enclosure surround, a pod for two peas, to please within a moment. White light of pure will, pushes to top the holy hill, crownèd bolding, holding spills, of glory, painted grace for anything but, when winding up, when lover winding up. Cold distance, though, when memory cannot know, what it knows. Brown-gray eyes, peer up to distant, intimate inner skies, not touchable with a thousand tries, so down she falls, to a gentle kiss upon the lips, *Love, you are so near, but what destruction has separation won? that love berefts the one held dear.* The shimmering lake that upon the surface skates, the light that with angels make love, brightness from above, that becomes the alighted dove—Peace has descended, that the ice that must be defended, the wife, the designation that had become from the registration—a blurt and a signature, so, still stood two who, were marred—married—in the moment, buried in constant the comments, hurriedly said on hearts that bled, so death of affection may ensue—perfect infection-blessed dissection of the distillation, of poison on perfection. The frequency vibration of enamored coloration of the two—a conversation never ensued by mouth, but passing twixt the feelings of the sacred tryst; man, woman, the love they make. In brief, that third being very mortal; for as susceptible so, to time's weapons—only seconds in passing. And so how the treasure mounts, in the little lives the lovers lead, where heartbeats count; each one the last, what Essence outlasts, the distractions, the wrong commitments long enough for growth of love true? Turning loose, Catherine, from Joy.

Regarding Ice

The maiden fair, stood tall and strong, golden hair waving shoulder long; light blue irises a reflection of ice and water and sky, melded into her from Northern climes. Frozen, seeming, in any moment, a yogi in her divinely still grace—the only movement her silent chanting lips, and the rustling of the feathers of her invisible wings in the unseen yet always present Summer breeze, circulating around her. And in a passing moment, the next, she smiles from beneath a laser gaze, and then the Northern ice melts, the waves of motion return, and she breaks free from the ongoing instance of living in the regimented, self-possessed existence. Deep concentration marked her character; thoughts mounted high atop the spine. She maneuvered through reality sublime, navigating expertly hooks and oxbows, shallows and rapids, automatically piloting the sky lines—sleepwalking yet awake—more for boredom at minutia than for competence's sake. The great grace in motion, the Winter flowing toward home; her sparkling brightness, wavelets cupping each the sun, the cascading on the run, into the falls, into the falls, into the falls. She stood in absolute stillness at first meet, gazing as if at the forest ever green, in February, beneath a heavy snow. The quiet, the solitude, she stores for limited release, later.

THE BLEWING BACK

Madonna paused from lightening stance, and beheld the lover, deep entranced—and with a presser beam, blew back, to a distance safe, where the hook of desire could not take stake, in a heart already reserved for others' take, yet the force of attraction countered her intended action, and the rebounding energy pushed—shoved—back the *labour of love*. As though a field of force concealed her horse power, she roiled with restraint, and were it not for invisible constraint, that explosion long past due would have fired into a hand hungrily placed upon the cheek, guiding four lips to softly meet, in remembrance of, and in the submission of apparent recognition. Madonna and her lover bathe in instantaneous grace; gift of existence that no separation is permanent in time, and the gale of attraction lifts joinèd souls to action, finding the benefaction of company in each other in eventuality. The brown iris, the generator of the beam; the white of the eye, the light that defeats that which would ask a marriage to die. The endless span of love.

DAUPHINE

A slight irritant in the night, to blight in a spot, the sunshine within her, burning bright. Svelte, she moved, a fluid taken form, a lovely contained spill. An abundance of positivity, strained against a lifetime of collecting negativity, and shooting it to the stars; though not in entirety, complete, for some of the darkness is found sticky, and resistant to rejection. Ready wit for sanity, she lends a helping hand, a fiery compassion she offers on loan, and holds in terms of love, with the magnet of the soul. She giggles, reminiscent of the girl within, no longer alive, and as such, a ghostly countenance haunts the woman resurrected. Dancer on the aires, she alights to find the earthly rarities, to touch disparities, each as much: the living to the dead, the light and the dark, the love and the hate—the composition of the race. As she danced, one foot in heaven, one foot in hell, the outline fine of a dagger to tell, of those she had saved from, or had sent back to, that hell. And then she dissolves into indifference toward love, having had her fill, she looks toward the Above; Abode Beyond the Hall, from where she worked untouchable; so many stories to tell, one to hear.

MAGNIFICENT MORNING

A sense that one had beaten Spring, by extending Fall a month into Winter's reign. The fragrant flowers were yet on notice, that, loh, a minor mandate would be lift, before the snowfall would reclaim all, that breathed. As particular green, battling a cancerous auburn at the edges of the leaves, shimmered, wavered, before the flooding sun, creating emeralds by the treefulls, in the gentle breeze. Strange peace had calmed the usual war, Nature had waged heretofore—the death and life. The coming and the going, in the night. The heightened level of color saturation, animation an aliveness permeation; permutations of consciousness to keep awareness in the thoughtfulness of each little leaf, blade of grass, bird song replete, with a month of dawns. Then complete, concentrated upon that distant glow of dawn, when the dark deep of Night, has all but blinded the inner sight, and but for the dim spark of stars, the Day would be too far away to stay with any sense of surety, that it did indeed exist, beyond the mental tryst: alternation, concept, affirmation. A prison, then, when held at bay, from the bounty of true reality, found in the magnificent morning.

Rainbow's End

Svelte, she elegantly leapt to the wall, brown eyed cat of grace, reaching for a sword to place, twixt the moon and the cartoon life she lead. *Shine on, brightest star, Luna loved you the most, by far*, in terms of light dispersed in Night; its light equals night. The blend of almandine, at her iris, encircled by black, at the perimeter, holding hostage that which would become color, not in this life but in some other. That circumscription, then, marked the life of an earthbound desirous of an infinite heaven. From absence of color to a rainbow bridge, Bifrost rocket to Valhalla, carries two who share the lover's view—the sense of weightlessness and combination of coupling to Joy, as though the toy most precious and they the eager child, who knows nothing less than play. Tender lips that, upon a kiss, inebriate: a day trip whilst standing, still in place. A shared breath, an exhale into an inhale, neither knows when either falls, the dying pale. Time, suspended, casts these two lovers in the day that never ended; descended serendipitously, lasted for a moment, for ever! Then devolves to the warmth of a friendship's hand, catch as catch can, maybe never, again, the flush, the rush, the hush, the hush.

HAPPINESS

The astral shine on the face of the maiden doing time, in Life's unsatisfactory! beacons in the Night, *soul of sweet delight*. Banner in the sun, body nearly done, quivering with earthly ways; shivering for a moment of connected cold, when the flesh had fallen, old, only to then remember light, was borne of One before the sight, was split 'to two, for eyes fallen down the line. Irregardless of the buoyant solids that which is worn to warn: too warm! The electric biplasmic smile, peeled away to bone reveals, some subtler energies for real, that project and be the model for the transparency; potency in potentiality, just heavier than air, the veriest of skin, that keep the blood from pumping out, and that without from caving in. For such precarious sincerity, to mug the day of hilarity, may thug-away from posterity, an newly happiness earned.... in contrariety, of life among the wagèd masses, blazed upon the lightless days; dazed then by that maiden-holds brightness, being the onliest glow, that of the corpus in tow. What heart-centered kindness throws, cautions to the breeze, so that the maiden smiles with ease, in happiness.

MOONLIGHT

September glory! How the moonlight falls, square upon your rounded shoulders bare. To see you withdrawn in heavy thought, attendant to writing words quite few, gives a lover pause....But kisses on your neck so soft, nonetheless interrupt, but give your breast no despair. Long and fair, arms and legs everywhere, but gracefully played. And when you lift eyes of brown, to gaze upon the moonèd bay, where a broken reflection of the lunar shore, true but wavering in the ripples laboring, under the evening breeze; a startled recognition showed, for the former lover Death had moved the unaware; this sacred secret of Histories' writ: that lovers betrothed in moonlight will in years hence betray, and belong to another, after a death's bewildering slumber. But spectacular moments lived, yet, in wanting memory, which is the actors' forgiven, until the source of happiness, dissolved—the lover in love with another. Then in love, perhaps addressing this, in mystery, she scribes slowly some ode to love, a prayer to the heaven's up, but then admits, again, to quit, frozen in the moment by tender kisses on the lips, and, thus, again forgets. *Were this cycle not such a tragedy, perhaps even worse, death might ensue for the hilarity, of it—to begin brand new, and yet to in reality be, a child of never-ending, cyclic infinity.*

Glory, or Jackie Mayer

In a space between the sea, sky, and lake coast, the white highway runs East and West, mostly. A virgin yellow sun bears down, and reflecting off the sea to the sand aside, deflects from there the cotton clouds, back into the blue skies; and this cycle splits the prismatic yellow, and gifts that remarkable white light, which bars the hold of Night and ensures that *sailors delight*, which red gust beforehand, sends them in confidence and good grace to foreign lands, and Peace descends beneath the clouds, which ne'r fails to meet, the lover of peace. Saturating, rejuvenating mirth stakes a claim, makes joyful what life otherwise progresses in vain, in pain. Laughter never far away. And silence, in the balmy Summer night, gives birth in moments, to love-children thoughts of bliss, feelings of flight, hanging low in the gravitational slow on aetherial speedors. A land without threat, and white and black both share the aires complete, without incident. And, here, two sail across a bay, on starlit waters, aboard a labouring boat, yet quiet cutting the near-midnight, glasslike waters, from barely a wind. Caramel eyes, and coal blue hair—had Snow White adorned the despairèd? with her gentle kiss at midnight there, at sea on the Bay of Sandusky. A marriage made by proximity, between object and adoration, but thru mutual confiscation of desires! or that weightless part of the being, that typical dons the angel's wings; pure in the August moon, cupped a trillion fold in the spreading waves, Her romance gave glory to the days, in Sandusky.

Floral

Emanation of the flagrant vagrants, so beautifully sewn and strewn, by waysider renewed; holy highway imbued by a walking sort; her perfume transpossessing, volt electric-waft transporting to an ancient irreducible few, where a love long lost would appear clear and evident, and so dear, in rarity—appearance in arrearage, due to the disappearance of the manifested two, daffodils who in stem and petals drew, beginning, often, end after beginning, again and again and again. A music in the ear, a rejoicing of a yesteryear, long forgot then remembered, again: a green wool lawn, and standing upon, those hard to find stems—for the blending-ins again' the grass. But the blossoms on about, the vast casting of the Everlasting; what *portion* of the soul, does Spirit not encompass whole? and so the person—the maidens such as these, traveled this way, before the days were bred. Lit by lightening at the back of the head, drunken; then, arisen from the dead, an Easter Lily! Inebriated in so much contact contraction—becoming whole, the missing pieces caving in; the heart, the core, again. At last, Feeling; a thud, the oxygen charge in the venous blood, the soft touch of the warm, feminine hand, of one who had been loved from above, and recognized; nurture onward a hurt, as the light of recognition was not returned. And how to say to one of two, that of those least remembered, most surrendered to, the delight of paradise was the smell of you.

EVE

From the first bite—an apple in the Night—the flesh of white, bare to beneath the bright red site....And the pursuant shock, at the speed of transportation back to that childhood tree, to the youthful body. The sunlight, the orchard and green grass, the field of brown wheat. The Summer breeze blowing parallel to South Main Street. Never wish to dwell upon the wishing well, draining of time waning to tell, of past mysteries sublime, days of heaven; days of hell, might the physical body snap? at the length of the going back; cross time and what fixed to the mind. Penetrating seems by razor beam, sweet in light sugar coats. The dread of night, of visions lost to the fright; spent, dead to rights. Having left, and paradise put to test, may only be a pause, then, on the advancing date to Infinity, and permanency, herald, red, the apples of the head—that shrank the form to photons' packet, blossoms on the morn; where in transparency, the visible is not what's seen....it's feeling that paints these reds and greens. A broken heart, then, with the fragment's piece, reality in a memory shreds, transcends, mends. Then Eve gifts the red apple, again. The caramel in her eyes, defends desire, makes, maybe, the fleeting joy of touching her way in the consummation's fire.

Sphere of the Fire Tree

Near December, in a warm Fall, the firelight of night, descends upon trees tall, and, burning though not consuming, even the sky cloudy stoops to witness the oddity. As seen from morning's window, the fiery orange catching at the green, end the sunless, raining scene, near artificial with stillness and color. The mystery of the Animae, which lurks, hidden away. The incendiary nature of that which upholds Nature, energizes from the vibrationless realm, to roam among the visible, yet remains unseen, and indivisible. Variations on a rainbow solid, dipped in leafèd stolids, the burning of each tree of fire, every sphere a lick lofting higher, 'til entering at a lower heaven, where *thoughts* of color, to the earthly trees, a bread its leaven. Thus rain soaked, light poked, burning bright, harbinger of the days of night, to come in the Winter's blight, when fled to source the blues and the reds consumed at last in the drop from branch to ground; life bled. Filed by a Hand, away, until the start, again, on a Spring day, in future, though not so far away, in time, in place. A sprout green.

MISSION HILLS

With great grace she gave an invitation to drink. Endowed with alienable rights, the maiden could choose her sights, on admirers. Svelte at her limbs, an ensemble of coordinated, angelic caving ins, upon her Self—Mother of Kindness, hugs, embraces with blindness, so that her ways are mere expressions of a nature her own. And over a warm cup, there a communion lay, was made to stay, in an aetherial way; encyclical, then, to feather high in the mind's sky, ne'r to be forgot, a bird beautiful to call to land in future days, when such a sight must needs be welcomed home to alight, a bright star in the deep of night. To recognize—the native genius of similars: the giggle of playfulness, the confidence and contentment of the self, if not the flaunting of the admirable loveliness. A home is found, in short, in the presence of another, and the imagination makes of alienation from happiness a feeble construct, feebler still, concept. The night sky above the hills, communicates by cool breeze the lightlessness below the bespeckled dark. Water, hill, and night unite beyond sight into togetherness of world, cosmos, lovers. Then the cool breeze gave way to warmth. Touched deeply in California.

Light Rain in Late Fall

The curative to the dreary day, the gentle mist that warmly falls, and the maiden who withstands it all, with indifference. The calculation of emotion to give or to take, the essence of the day to make; brake what would to break, and have broken be the way to live. And, so, in command, she plans. Among colors of outrageous trees, wild leaves from some world other, that tumble on the evening breeze, and in just a few days, are all fallen down. She stands before the barren limbs, and adjusts her collar against the winds, thinking that the onset of night, of Winter, will tax the wanèd will, commissioned at distant stars, resigned to a cubby of the Evermore. Methodically, she predisposes to examining the academics, who, may ne'r do well toward her and, by nibbling at the base of her indifference, taketh away the gain of her rainy day. Stuck, then, in thinkingness for the duration of the sustenance of the nation; stark contrast, trees with leaves having fallen, in the faintest often breeze that, turning frozen bade farewell to Fall, and until Spring only snow would fall, and what this message brings, rings truth to all—clerical transformation by transmutation is the natural experience; the water drop becomes the snowflake; the snowflake begets the mist; the mist condenses to the raindrop old.

THE DESERT

Wastelanded Netherland, *en place twixt air and sand*, Hope in future obscurity? safety in former firmity. The giving up to get, the remembering to forget, to make a chance on love, to take a stance upon a dove, being intimate with the aires, casting aside all fears for all but things of earth; the feeble and the steele, the make-believe and the real; in blindness, unseen remains the day, so, in default Night rules as it may. To grasp, then, at Darkness, without fingers, delivering mere pokes, while withdrawing no content subject to qualitative tactile inquiry is to lead a dubious life. Doubting, then, the constituency and therefore the constancy of men—the foothold taught into what? Naught nary, wanting, tarry, *en place twixt air and sand*? convincing, then, the lover's touch when up, again. The Unseen Hand not borne of men. Not such, the Vagrant Much, that grants the flowers their fragrance, and fits life to the lovely wife. Admire the gorge, which presents too great a leap for a single step, and, yet, too deep to repel and ascend the opposite side of it, then. And what laughter have the gods? to suspend humanity midway between either end.

Caramel Nordic

Madonna reached; it took a team to teach, portraits how to hang. Her slender hand, raised as if to land, upon the subject's face, so that, as if she had known them quite well, if not intimately. In a postpartum glow, though removed, a child still haunted her soul, attached an aetheric cold. As she moved gracefully about, there, but also elsewhere, her love pouring out for a little one, beyond. Adverse mystery to view: here but gone.

CHOCOLATE

Love affair with sweetness, richness, darkness. A gift to tempt the not-the-weak—but the strong; garner a rift twixt two planes on heaven, driven insane those who heretofore, there, had been connected. And it is the separation that slays what is to be respected—but is then rejected, for want of positive effects, toward the good of the whole: or that which may leave a bad taste in the mouth. And can it be? that preference for the sweet black sorority may disturb the lighter identity, such that its fraternity may never be of the same composition, again. The imposition on society—a lesser inquisition—may be the aghastness of the palatability of a love for the sweet darkness. The incredible delectable, remarkable softness at the lips, sweetness affirmed at the tongue a moment—or a year—thereafter. The adorable svelte—form upon which to heap affection—love?—or is it a leap to establish a reconnection between the twain interrupted, planes on heaven! Enflight to wholeness, the distance closes, and the aeons' lost souls are found; rejoin upon the sacred ground, homecoming of a cosmic sort.

MADONNA WITH CHILD

Hair brown, teased into a long bob. Decorated thru, with a glow; child in tow. Smiling widely, at the crowd, holding love in a sling. World evolved around this delicate scene, such that spinning on the blur surround, blessed the already-been: that which had come back, again! In the caramel iris, Madonna-painted portraiture of a soul departed after long a stay, after wrong the way, home. And glory to see—so at ease among humanity, a celebrity of happiness. What movie may she enact? The whole cast present in present cast whole into the masses, advocating glassless glasses, invisible from which to drink, sink into entrance into you. Lacking husbandry, the picture perfect in incomplimentary. Corporeal grace, in motion about the place; flit, dance, plie, though babe en arms, transfer from lover to lover via the childhood monkey bar hover—one hand afore, one aft, dangling above the chasm far below, by one hand, when aft releases to project to the other, afore. In the moment, passing, dangling, heaven feel. And under the spell of loss, the childhood fled, as the Christ babe bled; left, the zed of once a lovely nativity. Wisdom masters from far East shores, blessed, no less the love the lover felt, for the madonna. And with the warmth of the hand-in-hand, some slight recompense for the Spirit departed with the Christ—as the maternal lit the dark of Night. And respite, then, upon an iris-windowed beam—the weaponology of the soul—to make friends with such a fearèd defender of the Light, from a distance, may naught tarry at the might, diminish the shining in the light; phosphorescence, and humble holding of the glow, the madonna *glid* across the lobby floor, with youthful aires, invested of the Evermore. Smiling.

FACE IN WINDOW

She bared the maiden's sword: intolerance to her dislikes. And though a face of beauty, a raspy impatience simmered beneath. Strength of only three, this side of reality, she nonetheless lay dormant, yet, choosing the life of silent restraint. A magical intelligence enabled, the way of living. Bright, eyes both collected and reflected a steady, streaming flow of light, within an instant may snap, redirected to an altered course. Perhaps inward toward the Light, perhaps outward onto day's objects: controlled and certain, her senior ways betray her junior days. To consummate a kiss, to pull to materiality all what Spirit might miss, then, leaving in doubt, the maiden and her soul left out, the sharing of the breath twixt two, asudden become most daring, to whomever dons the fairings against the winds of fate, when soul and self remain yet separate for want of sharing. Bewildered, then, the maiden takes comfort in the shadow She, so that she may have the sense of touch, to feel the kiss, some descended notion? allures the mouth to speak in silent gestures, which shout in intensity of feeling, cry without making a sound; for what the soul must teach is much.

Hadrian's Maiden

She stood atop the stonèd wall, admiring the arising sun. Long brown hair set atop her shoulders square, the flow of it an umbrella sheltering the narrow, lower self, draped in cotton dress green, reflective of resplendent eyes emerald, beacons aglow in the misty gray morn, will color the sloping meadows in the afternoon, to contrast the flower rainbows, blooming. Kissing earth, the predawn is yet to give birth to a full-on day when, the solar rays she steals from night to come, bud on her, so that even though she stands atop Hadrian's wall, disconnected, she yet remains among the floral growth of paradise's boast, on the plain below. And cutting the North with the West, from the skyey view, Hadrian slew, by a stony snake, cast into the garden of England. Raising her arms, she breathed in morning. Untouched Mother of Nature, she awaits an unnatural lover she never knew, husband to some other, yet to one who lived long ago, who seemed so familiar. What Force? contorts a mind to build walls with effort irate, meant to make them fall. And so, the stony snake, though a mistake, *in the end at present*, a union to make of human flowers, and so spared the stake, in England's garden with visual interest. Hadrian won, *in the long run so far*, with an accumulation of admirers, and at least one estranged wife, who, in that Force of his efforts, moretheless knew and loved him. The warm breeze of morning now awake greeted her, whispering: *Hadrian, Hadrian, Hadrian.*

WITH VISION

A blessing a maiden lay at the feet—a heart so sweet, that only youth may claim such a confection, affection, *affectation*. Night eyes of India, see long sighs long said by lovers long dead, oh, *the tempestuous, quiet, beautiful lives once lead, together!* Krishna bows on ages, when desire never rests in countless hearts and heads, begging with his own, for such lost souls to hurry home, who makes of the Divine a beggar through time? but all those lovers, of others waylaid in sublime fields lit by lesser suns. The pure face of the maiden India, made erase millennia, of forgetfulness so that tumbling back from annihilation's disgrace, full memory of the sole light illuminating this familiar yet new face. And to not be in the *see*, is to founder perpetually, sargassorily. When night falls in your eyes, sparkling stars rise, constellations ablaze in the firmament of your gaze. Then no more windless daze, to scuttle two ships assail, in theory, only inches from your face, the inspection took place, impromptuly. The mate of afore from India's Southern shore, yet in separation twixt the last and the next first breath. She makes the lover wait, in heartbreak, for now a life ends. With a soft kiss, from the Beloved Friend. Then forgetfulness.

BERNINI RADIALS FROM THE CAVE BENEATH THE STAGE

Poem and Interpretation

Introduction

This piece of *poetica fantasticale* is constructed in several degrees of reference; meaning that at once in the poem Bernini's actual sculpture, *St. Terese in Ecstasy,* is the object of rumination, when at other times the Self of St. Terese, the mystical actor, is at issue; then a moment later the author is the worker in question, in history; and then, perhaps, it is the Cherry Lane Theatre pulling focus, whose stage has become *heaven* above, in relation to the understage room, *cave,* which is the spiritual repository, in the poem, of St. Terese—but which is also, in reality past—the early morning meditation room of the author-worker. The poem, *Bernini Radials from the Cave Beneath the Stage,* coupled with its interpretation, forms in brief an intimate, musical study— if words be notes!—in image and voice morphology, and is a silent ode to Spirit.

Editorial Note

For clarity's sake and ease of reading, and then for referral purposes, the poem is first presented without superscript annotation, which is included in the second version; following which, the poem is then deconstructed—analyzed line-by-line, or at times word-by-word—offering an interpretation of what is to be considered the author's true intention. Invoking the literary Nimble, and honoring the thought stream Flow, directly quoted words or lines are written in italics throughout the interpretation, and the comma plays a major role as Pause. Occasionally, certain words and phrases appear in parenthesis or in singular quotations marks, providing an additional aid to clarification.

Author's Disclaimer

All reference to the nature of saints is but passionate speculation based upon hearsay.

Bernini Radials from the Cave beneath the Stage

Steely bronzèd rays, radiations from the deepest cave beneath the stage, where St. Terese stays, awake in the ecstatic state. Attendant cherubs to keep wet the white of her eyes, rolled back for which to spy, upon the skyèd lair of Otherwhere. Spirit, transmutationed into the sacred station—the alterview, the condensation of the realization: the Light creates the Night. Sourcing, then, on the dewey morn, Terese's child—the Play—is born, in the cave beneath the stage. Soft glow of inner sight, replaced the switched-off bulb, so no darkness fell. In the cosmic whirl, mass, hence matter, twirls, and electrons lob, arch with grace, to the stage above, and animate the works of love, create the breath, the mind the soul—the Alighted Dove, of players. Generator Divine, Terese's finery, heaven shine, the written word, the action's spine, is then heard from the mouths of her immaculately birthèd babes, the sacred clowns, blessing with smiles and frowns, those who then bring the house down. Comfortable, perhaps, in their antique seats anchored atop oak slats, they nonetheless rise to their feet, tap to a musical beat, and applaud. Finding the frequency of the vibration, a visiting scientist may unhide, the animae—the cinematic tide of photons hitching rides—upon Terese's thoughts, which form the days and ways of the plays, having met the stage. Pinging off the house's brass sconce, occasional ray from the cave, making flickering the bulb of supposèd noon, preempting the Sunday matinee. Triangulate to accommodate—in a trapezoidal way—felt drapery, that curtain of the theatre's eye. Stratified shelving according to utility, relegates to posterity, that which awaits day's light, again. Drama of life: comedies of youth, tragedies of old age, on oft a third eve the curtain razed, tore, as if that of the Temple yore—it is the little creations that make the humans more, than the additions and subtractions of the karmic score—telling the story's from the godly half, of That which inhabits the fleshly mass, whose matter is another matter— thoughtless though not ignored, of the Saint. Annunciating upon the street, the glass of a box thrice broken, girded in poplar, hand cut, then bathed in black fish-oil paint, joined at the corners with corrugated teeth, then set in brass, enclosing a flyer told to speak, and commanded to last a decade in weather, in traffic. Carpenter complete, having built the latticed cage, upon Stella's West stoop, to gird for the age, applications of Cherry stain, which father Stefano laid. Communing at dawn, in the deepest cave beneath the stage. Terese then worked thru, with her rays, as Bernini radials, the carpenter who'd made, but never played; from whom this scene is portrayed.

^ABERNINI RADIALS FROM THE CAVE BENEATH THE STAGE

[1]Steely bronzèd rays, [1a]radiations from the [1b]deepest cave beneath the stage, [1c]where St. Terese stays, [1d]awake in the ecstatic state. [2]Attendant cherubs [2a]to keep wet the white of her eyes, [2b]rolled back for which to spy, upon the [2c]skyèd [2d]lair of Otherwhere. [3]Spirit, [3a]transmutationed into [3b]the sacred station—[3c]the alterview, [3d]the condensation of the realization: [3e]the Light creates the [3f]Night. [4]Sourcing, then, on [4a]the dewey morn, [4b]Terese's child—[4c]the Play—is born, in [4d]the cave beneath the stage. [5]Soft glow of inner sight, [5a]replaced the switched-off bulb, [5b]so no darkness fell. [6]In the cosmic whirl, mass, hence matter, twirls, and electrons lob, arch with grace, to the stage above, [6a]and animate the works of love, [6b]create the breath, the mind, the soul—the Alighted Dove, of [6c]players. [7]Generator Divine, [7a]Terese's finery, heaven shine, [7b]the written word, the action's spine, [7c]is then heard from the mouths of her immaculately birthèd babes, [7d]the sacred clowns, [7e]blessing with smiles and frowns, [7f]those who then bring the house down. [8]Comfortable, perhaps, in their antique seats [8a]anchored atop oak slats, [8b]they nonetheless rise to their feet, tap to a musical beat, and applaud. [9]Finding the frequency of the vibration, [9a] a visiting scientist [9b]may unhide, the [9c]animae—[9d]the cinematic tide of photons [9e]hitching rides—upon Terese's thoughts, [9f]which form the days and ways of the plays, [9g]having met the stage. [10]Pinging off the house's brass sconce, [10a]occasional ray from the cave, [10b]making flickering the bulb of supposèd noon, [10c]preempting the [10d]Sunday matinee. [11]Triangulate to accommodate—in a trapezoidal way—[11a]felt drapery, that curtain of [11b]the theatre's eye. [11c]Stratified shelving according to utility, [11d]relegates to posterity, that which

awaits day's light, again. [12]Drama of life: comedies of youth, tragedies of old age, [12a]on oft a third eve [12b]the curtain razed, [12c]tore, as if that of the Temple yore[12d]—it is the little creations [12e]that make the humans more, [12f]than the additions and subtractions of the karmic score—[12g]telling the story's from the godly half, of That which inhabits the fleshly mass, [12h]whose matter is another matter—[12i]thoughtless [12j]though not ignored, [12k]of the Saint. [13]Annunciating upon the street, [13a]the glass of a box thrice broken, [13b]girded in poplar, hand cut, then bathed in black fish-oil paint, joined at the corners with corrugated teeth, [13c]then set in brass, [13d]enclosing a flyer told to speak, [13e]and commanded to last a decade in weather, in traffic. [14]Carpenter complete, having built the latticed cage, upon [14a]Stella's West stoop, [14b]to gird for the age, applications of Cherry stain, which father Stefano laid. [15]Communing at dawn, in the [1b]deepest cave beneath the stage. [15a]Terese then worked thru, with her rays, as [A]Bernini radials, [15b]the carpenter who'd made, but never played; [15c]from whom this scene is portrayed.

BERNINI RADIALS FROM
THE CAVE BENEATH THE STAGE

[1]*Steely bronzèd rays,* [1a]*radiations from the* [1b]*deepest cave beneath the stage,* [1c]*where St. Terese stays,* [1d]*awake in the ecstatic state.*

The setting for this poem is the understage area of the Cherry Lane Theatre, where the author often meditated in the mornings before the workday. It is said that when yogis concentrate single mindedly upon the thought of God—meditation—subtle, high vibrations, [1]*Steely bronzèd rays,* emanate from the point between their eyebrows, the spiritual eye, or the Christ Consciousness center, saturating the photonic-based matter of the surrounding material world with the divine energy of the soul. For the purpose of forwarding the story of this poem, the author has assigned a characterization to the [1]*Steely bronzed rays,* [1a]*radiations from the* [1b]*deepest cave beneath the stage,* particularly that of, in the first degree of reference, St. Terese in Ecstasy, as remarkably sculpted by Bernini, [1c]*where St. Terese stays,* [1d]*awake in the ecstatic state,* and, in the second degree, from the title, [A]*Bernini Radials,* referencing by name the [1a]*radiations.* The author is asking that the reader imagine that St. Terese, as depicted by Bernini, is at prayer always, [1d]*awake in the ecstatic state,* in the room beneath the Cherry Lane Theatre (CLT, hereafter) stage, the [1b]*deepest cave.* The author deviates in description, for mechanical purposes, from the actual sculpture: In Bernini's work, the Divine Light, or Holy Spirit, sources from above and spreads downward and outward upon St. Terese below; in this poem, please imagine the [A]*Bernini Radials,* divine rays, sourcing from Terese's heart and spiritual eye, radiating outward from her Self, her soul light. That material surrounding which, then saturated by her soul light, is the entirety of the CLT physical structure—and all those individuals dwelling and working within.

²*Attendant cherubs* ²ᵃ*to keep wet the white of her eyes,* ²ᵇ*rolled back for which to spy, upon the* ²ᶜ*skyèd* ²ᵈ*lair of Otherwhere.*

²*Attendant cherubs,* depicted in the actual sculpture, are speculated here by the author to be providing the utilitarian function of insuring that Terese's eyes do not dry out, ²ᵃ*to keep wet*…during the long period that they remain open as she concentrates upon God in heaven, the ²ᶜ*skyèd* ²ᵈ*lair of Otherwhere,* focusing the internal gaze upward toward the spiritual eye, ²ᵇ*rolled back for which to spy,* leaving mostly only the whites exposed to the air, and therefore to the drying effect. ²ᶜ*skyèd,* aetherial, 'light' or spiritually blessed. ²ᵈ*lair of Otherwhere,* here refers, in the first degree, to heaven, but also, in the second degree, for the poem's sake, to the stage directly above and the theatre building at large.

³*Spirit,* ³ᵃ*transmutationed into* ³ᵇ*the sacred station—*³ᶜ*the alterview,* ³ᵈ*the condensation of the realization:* ³ᵉ*the Light creates the Night.*

A reference to the physical effect of a saint's presence, and is the girth of the book of Genesis contained in a single sentence: ³*Spirit,* the Holy Spirit, that creative faculty of the Divine that descends from the vibrationless realm to bring into being the physical universe, meaning ³ᵃ*transmutationed into.* A literal work of the Hand of God, ³ᵇ*the sacred station.* ³ᶜ*the alterview,* the awareness or perception held by a saint that it is massless Spirit that is masquerading as a solid manifestation, the physical universe; elaborated in practicum as ³ᵈ*the condensation of the realization.* In Eastern Thought, all is Spirit, and like the images created by a motion picture projector, shadows are born of the intense light, ³ᵉ*the Light creates the Night,* and the dancing interaction between them creates or quickens the drama. ³ᶠ*Night* here is a reference to a single world cycle of: creation, preservation, and destruction; which is a derivation of, in Hindu philosophy, the 'Day of Brahma.'

[4]*Sourcing, then, on* [4a]*the dewey morn,* [4b]*Terese's child—*[4c]*the Play—is born, in* [4d]*the cave beneath the stage.*

[4]*Sourcing, then…*Terese draws upon her deep wisdom, or [4a]*the dewey morn,* the converse of the [3f]*Night,* or delusion—noumenon, that which appears real—and, created in the image of the Divine, she uses her wisdom-based spiritually creative power in service to Drama: [4b]*Terese's child—*[4c]*the Play—is born*; and further, given locale in our poetic setting, in [4d]*the cave beneath the stage,* at the CLT.

[5]*Soft glow of inner sight,* [5a]*replaced the switched-off bulb,* [5b]*so no darkness fell.*

[5]*Soft glow of inner sight,* radiant, divine intuition, literally the 'soul light,' [5a]*replaced the switched-off bulb,* the author often meditated in the darkness ensured by an unscrewed light bulb at the fixture. But the way of a great saint is illuminated by their soul light, even in black caves, [5b]*so no darkness fell.*

[6]*In the cosmic whirl, mass, hence matter, twirls, and electrons lob, arch with grace, to the stage above,* [6a]*and animate the works of love,* [6b]*create the breath, the mind, the soul—the Alighted Dove, of* [6c]*players.*

Activating the drama of the CLT stage, from her prayerful position beneath, Terese the playwright, the creator, and therefore the god, begins to scribe, practice her craft, creating dramatic worlds: [6]*In the cosmic whirl, mass, hence matter, twirls, and electrons lob, arch with grace, to the stage above,* beginning to describe in scientific mechanics the miraculous Essence, the doting origin of the life of the play's characters, and, of human beings: [6a]*and animate the works of love.* That the playwright-creator instills in the created, [6c]*players,* a reflection of their own image, [6b]*create the breath, the mind,* and particularly, *the soul—the Alighted Dove,* or the 'Holy Spirit', again, that creative Force, borrowed, of course, from Christian theology, is a reference to the sacred nature of Theatre, in as much as it is Godlike to create; indeed, in India it is one of the three holiest arts, along with Music and Dance.

[7]*Generator Divine,* [7a]*Terese's finery, heaven shine,* [7b]*the written word, the action's spine,* [7c]*is then heard from the mouths of her immaculately birthèd babes,* [7d]*the sacred clowns,* [7e]*blessing with smiles and frowns,* [7f]*those who then bring the house down.*

[7]*Generator Divine,* soul source, creator of the drama, which is her specialty, [7a]*Terese's finery, heaven shine,* reflecting qualities of Spirit, she wields her pen, [7b]*the written word, the action's spine,* comment on the mechanics of the play, [7c]*is then heard from the mouths of her immaculately birthèd babes,* the pure actors speak the words of her holy creative works, calling them [7d]*the sacred clowns,* a reference to the laughing-crying nature of the circus imp—the epitome of duality and the Human Condition. Her play becomes the power of dramatic expression, influencing, [7e]*blessing with smiles and frowns,* the clown's nature, as a result of the work's existence, and her presence, [7f]*those who then bring the house down,* the patrons, of course.

[8]*Comfortable, perhaps, in their antique seats* [8a]*anchored atop oak slats,* [8b]*they nonetheless rise to their feet, tap to a musical beat, and applaud.*

Patrons who by nature may be complacent, [8]*Comfortable, perhaps, in their antique seats,* at the outset of an heretofore unknown, original work, having heard yet no review, [8a]*anchored atop oak slats,* offering a direct reference to the author's contribution to the maintenance of CLT's historical main house seating (the three-day oak slat installation marathon!). Experiencing the magic of theatre in its range of genres from drama to musical, the patrons remain no longer unmoved, ambivalent, [8b]*they nonetheless rise to their feet, tap to a musical beat, and applaud.*

[9]*Finding the frequency of the vibration,* [9a]*a visiting scientist* [9b]*may unhide, the* [9c]*animae—*[9d]*the cinematic tide of photons* [9e]*hitching rides—upon Terese's thoughts,* [9f]*which form the days and ways of the plays,* [9g]*having met the stage.*

The 'magic' of theatre—that which separates it from the cinema—is that it is a living illusion. Among the patrons in the audience, perhaps a skeptic, or [9a]*a visiting scientist…*is found who yet remains unmoved at the emotional core of being, and who is, perhaps—unmovable—or one stubbornly centered in the intellect or rational mind, [9]*finding the frequency of vibration,* who therefore refuses by default to participate, [9b]*may unhide,* in the group suspension of disbelief, the [9c]*animae,* or subatomic (quantum) mechanics of the 'stuff of life,' here, [4d]*the Play,* [9d]*the cinematic tide of photons…*a reference to the scientific confirmation that at the quantum level (the microverse) all life is found to be a projection of light, which, in the poem, includes even the subtle-life thoughts of Terese, brought to life through the actors and the playwright, [9e]*hitching rides—upon Terese's thoughts,* manifestations of plots, themes, characterizations, styles, [9f]*which form the days and ways of the plays,* including set design, construction and lighting, [9g]*having met the stage.*

[10]*Pinging off the house's brass sconce,* [10a]*occasional ray from the cave,* [10b]*making flickering the bulb of supposèd noon,* [10c]*preempting the* [10d]*Sunday matinee.*

As playwright, Terese takes on responsibility for the play, and here demonstrates, in a very scientific expression, the astrophysics of saintly operation, [10]*Pinging off the house's brass sconce,* in mention of CLT's beautiful antique wall-light pieces, [10a] *occasional ray from the cave,* as regards the conscious cosmic energy that the great ones command, and with which they build; also how Terese 'travels' about the theatre—while yet remaining hidden in her [1b]*deepest cave beneath the stage.* The light of the saint's soul wisdom far outshines that of her creations' 'apparent' (a wonderful astronomical term, addressing the degree of seeming brightness of a star) reality, [10b]*making flickering the bulb of supposèd noon*; in the poem, the sconce light, or the representation of the grosser physical light, pales in comparison to the light of [3]*Spirit.* It is said that the Light of God is a million times brighter than the sun, yet more subtle and non-consuming, does not burn, which manifests in the universe as all that appears real, noumenon, or the [10d]*Sunday matinee,* but is the only actual Reality, phenomenal sublime, and the Original Show, therefore[10c]*preempting…*

[11]*Triangulate to accommodate—in a trapezoidal way—*[11a]*felt drapery, that curtain of*[11b]*the theatre's eye.* [11c]*Stratified shelving according to utility,* [11d]*relegates to posterity, that which awaits day's light, again.*

Following the trajectory of Terese's rays—soul consciousness—emanating from [4d]*the cave beneath the stage,* the poem asks the reader to accompany the saint on a 'flight of fancy': We find ourselves in the angular dressing room of the CLT Studio, referencing the uniquely shaped plywood shelving that the author and a coworker (Chime Serra) constructed, necessary to negotiate a proper fit and maximize the use of the space, [11]*Triangulate to accommodate— in a trapezoidal way*, items, in the author's memory, which were stored, [11a]*felt drapery, that curtain of* [11b]*the theatre's eye*, remarking on the significance of the curtain to the stage—only when opened can the [4c]*the Play* be seen; in another degree of reference, the spiritual eye of the theatre. Continuing on with a simple reference to the mundane subject of storage, though not unimportant in function, especially in New York City, for the value of what is stored: [11c]*Stratified shelving according to utility*, or what is used more often is stored closest to the grasp, [11d]*relegates to posterity, that which awaits day's light, again*; upon the shelves items remain indefinitely, or until needed next time.

[12]*Drama of life: comedies of youth, tragedies of old age,* [12a]*on oft a third eve* [12b]*the curtain razed,* [12c]*tore, as if that of the Temple yore* [12d]*—it is the little creations* [12e]*that make the humans more,* [12f]*than the additions and subtractions of the karmic score—* [12g]*telling the story's from the godly half, of That which inhabits the fleshly mass,* [12h]*whose matter is another matter—* [12i]*thoughtless* [12j]*though not ignored,* [12k]*of the Saint.*

Making a philosophical comment on life, from which all conflict is drawn, [12]*Drama of life: comedies of youth, tragedies of old age*, and a jab at the 'lesser' of Off-Broadway creations that 'have no legs,' as it is said in the business: [12b]*the curtain razed*, has not only fallen, but did so in a destructive manner— for the show has closed, [12a]*on oft a third eve*, after only three performances, the first weekend! Venturing an example from the author's own experience, for example's sake only, without forwarding any opinion on behalf of the playwright, *Stars in their Eyes* comes to mind. Attaching Biblical significance to the very symbolic object, [12c]*tore, as if that of the Temple yore*, a reference to the phenomenon that took place at the exact moment of Jesus the Christ's death, when a great world drama had drawn to a violent conclusion. Transitioning sharply into existentialism, and a reference to the all-important necessity for humans to participate in their own destiny, as actors in a play that they themselves write each day; it is also a reference to the sanctity of divinely endowed human will power, [12d]*—it is the little creations*, acts of free will, which tip the scales in favor of, [12e]*that make the humans more*, the one who consciously struggles against fate, or karma: in the Eastern tradition—the sum calculation by inexorable Justice of every act, good and bad, committed in a human life: [12f]*than the additions and subtractions of the karmic score.* That this segment was strongly connected by the em dash (—) to the previous, implies that, as profound an event as the Christ's crucifixion was, the daily 'crucifixions' of the average individual are not without significance; neither do they pass karmically unnoticed. [12g]*—telling the story's from the godly half, of That which inhabits the fleshly mass*, a comment on the nature of the human condition, or the eternal struggle between flesh and Spirit, stating that of the dual natures of the human being, it is the spiritual portion, the soul, the direct reflection of God, which is endowed with the Godlike ability to create—exemplified in this case as the writing of the play; which underscores the importance of spiritual victories, the ultimate example of which being Christ's victory over death; however, closely following, [12h]*whose matter is another matter*, accentuates that although soul is superior, Spirit, [12k]*of the Saint*, requires nonetheless the inferior personage, described as [12i]*thoughtless*, being of a lesser consciousness, lacking self-awareness, though far from unimportant, [12j]*though not ignored*, as a vehicle through which to literally 'act.'

[13]*Annunciating upon the street,* [13a]*the glass of a box thrice broken,* [13b]*girded in poplar, hand cut, then bathed in black fish-oil paint, joined at the corners with corrugated teeth,* [13c]*then set in brass,* [13d]*enclosing a flyer told to speak,* [13e]*and commanded to last a decade in weather, in traffic.*

[13]*Annunciating upon the street,* launching upon yet another 'flight of fancy,' Terese's cosmic soul rays transport the reader to the exterior of the theatre, the frontage on Commerce Street, next to the stage door, where concentration is requested at the display case, where a story is told of the author's construction of the wooden window frame that replaced the absent, proper brass frame: [13a]*the glass of a box thrice broken*, working as carpenter, repair of the display case was the author's very first task as a CLT employee (though not the very first task at CLT, which was, as a volunteer, the construction of Louis Black's New York City skyline of newspapers that included the World Trade Center twin towers; a delightful project then, but one which would later take on a certain poignancy for the author, for all time) and the glass was broken three times in the process of achieving a perfect fit (though no company money was wasted, as the last two panes were paid for by the author), [13b]*girded in poplar, hand cut, then bathed in black fish-oil* (Rustoleum) *paint, joined at the corners*

with corrugated teeth, a description of the type of wood used and how it was handled, painted, constructed, [13c]*then set in brass*, inserted in place of the original brass window frame, [13d]*enclosing a flyer told to speak*, referring to the posters, [13e]*and commanded to last a decade in weather, in traffic*, a comment on how long the frame has somewhat surprisingly lasted to date, under stressful conditions, ten years and counting.

[14]*Carpenter complete, having built the latticed cage, upon* [14a]*Stella's West stoop,* [14b]*to gird for the age, applications of Cherry stain, which father Stefano laid.*

[14]*Carpenter complete, having built the latticed cage*, the final carpentry project: constructing an air conditioner housing of wooden lattice on[14a]*Stella's West* stoop, the courtyard deck of actress Kim Hunter, a CLT neighbor, [14b]*to gird for the age, applications of Cherry stain, which father Stefano laid,* to protect the bare wood of the lattice from the elements, Cherry stain was applied by Steve Fiordellisi, father of CLT's artistic director.

[15]*Communing at dawn, in the* [1b]*deepest cave beneath the stage.* [15a]*Terese then worked thru, with her rays, as* [A]*Bernini radials,* [15b]*the carpenter who'd made, but never played;* [15c]*from whom this scene is portrayed.*

[15]*Communing at dawn, in the* [1b]*deepest cave beneath the stage*, a reference to the author's morning meditations upon the Divine, or St. Terese, for the poem's sake, before the day's activities, [15a]*Terese then worked thru, with her rays,* a description of the author's then carrying out the day's activities, as the yogis are taught, with a meditation or Holy Spirit-saturated mind, *as* [A]*Bernini radials,* guided by CLT's patron saint, in the poem, endowed with all the power invoked by the sculptor's masterpiece. [15b]*the carpenter who'd made, but never played,* the author, often carpenter at the CLT, was also a former actor who never participated in that capacity in any play in which he had helped to construct; who is also the writer of this poem, [15c]*from whom this scene is portrayed.*

CATHERINE

She descended upon; a light who alighted as a dove, before, from above. Silent and still, though, song and animation played as you swayed. *Do you sing? for when I see you I hear music,* all what heaven brings to eyes' rings. Ears of admirers. Slowly she smiled: full lips ending, parting, speaking; golden hair flowing in the Fall air, wings to uplift or to receive, that shining light, to drink in motion, she predated the moments she gracefully proceeded; head, neck, and spine, aligned to somehow counter time, or the effects of motion. A saint before, a saint, again, expression of love true, on dispatch of the Lover Who lives above all others. A paradox, of dynamic stillness, she drew from the surroundings its breath of life, leaving—but only in imperceptible moments—a dead world devoid of animation; innocent, however, of wayward thought toward her fellow beings and all that lives, she simply existed unawares of her momentous force of gravity, and its ripping effect upon anything composed of light. Hidden remained the rhythm, though, and logic behind, the pattern of the terrible moments when her presence produced destruction. Only the admirer could see and understand the transcendence of the invisible Hand and how It waved and dipped, in conduction.

UPRISING

There is a bullet that lives in the eyes, that is fired when a lover dies, in the moment before the other, beloved. The action of persecution of an act, to later reflect in doubt—did the actor indeed act out? or had the thought of the act more clout? Such that a living life may only be—imaginary? when the key had dissolved in the hand, one that was thought to have been made, really real, in terms of physicality, solidarity, the infinite finity of the seeable and the touchable; but, alas, the only originality and authenticity of the key, lay in the fierceness of the mentality, that at first brought the key to Be. Fading in and out, a merry fantasy! So what then of stability? when Firmity dissolves into infinity, wavelike as if the sea. Drowning then in doubt, the mere observation of the actor acting out, the clouted thought. But then the bullet interned from that lover's eyes, so that in the moment the admirer died, breath removed from lungs, involuntarily in sigh. But then death incomplete, by Darkness' indiscrete, such that in afar recognition of love, peace, the life of the lover was recovered, discovered to be the only reality—death in love. There amidst the chaotic waves, stillness, joy, light, individuals dancing in the spirit of recognition, or power.

Overlapping Dimensions

The maiden stood, a tower glowing, in invisible light. Beacon eyes, searching the night of silence within, though a raging storm without; the protrusion, then, of peaceful origins thrust into calamity, suspended by a feminine Zen, made for a shocking introduction twixt. A gentle nature, on radio control, taking spartan space nearly less than whole, an almost apology—as close as the aetherial assaulting the material can be; a weaponology of infinity, girded by femininity, as disarming as the image suggests, with kindness as final test, passed. Arrested, all admirers falling to within her gaze with the locking eyes, grey pools that drown fools; the lover is already dead. And intelligence subdued, perhaps, the greatest clue, to how your bloodless coo, yet left an admirer already bled and daft at the head. Men turned away, though remained close, holding out your hands, and reaching back, you asked your lover to hold you, remain attached; swaying in ineffable bliss, two turned front to survey all *This*. That love hath made. The fragrance of your hair, aloft the heated midday aires—the strength in measuring the beauty of the blessèd youth.

GILDED GATE OF ELYSIUM

Massive walls gird the horizon of a yellow night, *en perpetuity*; an ageless mortar bonds timeless stones, stacked atop one another, forming hard ladders, though climbless, reaching into the sky. About the boundaries, grew weedless wildflowers, heedless to feet, which ne'r tread thru, the spectral spread of love new, descended and expressed as color alive. And in the wall's midst, a gilded gate, to separate the heroes from the dead, of war's eternal rage—the only page, it seems, quick humanity has yet read. With a thunderous groan, the gilded gate moans, and Elysium welcomes home, a hero once more. In the distance, atop a green hill, a villa for each veteran own, marked by sir name still, before the original going out, first part of the war game. *The soldier departs the family.* Aswooping lane, of dusty fame; flanking which, one field of yellow wheat, and one of yellow corn, both mature and prepared to yield, endless bounty, and thrill to feel, joy to hear, the rustling ears and grains; scenting upon the aires' waft, the pungent proof of life, a celebration of earth giving birth. And before the villa front, beneath white columns tall, ran a tiled roof of red, stood waving the lover, the mother, and the son—once small! Approaching near, the smiles and the tears—the beaming, beautiful faces of adoration, welcoming in reunion. The wife, the meadow flower come to life, with pastoral, astral-colored brights, turn to flame to burn the sane, trapped in the mortal night of the terran plight. Freed, now, in insanity of love—to reason. Her clutching embrace, and pressèd lips—the home fire true—and ancient history, torn twixt two, repaired in the interlocking stares, retold in exact detail, in the radial array of two irises brown, and two of blue. And a mewing cat, too!

Day Brake

Spectacular reversion to nightfall—from the bright of day—in instantaneity, the flipside of the mercury, from hot to cold, dualities' pairs, the favorite of the lower aires, breathed by the arrested. The suddenness, that must, wrests from the arrested, the dying in the day. A great green canvas, of Spring, upon which the leafy Mulberry sings, the grassy sprainèd ne'r complains, whenever the glorious ocean blue is the lesser thing! How heavy the clothing when, the beams of the bereaved become a man, who no longer has use for what fails to hold free the glowing gold of the soul. The spilling, thrilling, shant be contained, without which That that makes the morning rains, that suddenness, hallmark of the miraculousness of That without sin; heaven sending, the moment, within which the capturing begins. A lonely present, so few occupy, for the seeming aloofness yet inaccessibility, though the whole of Everlasting. The flashing, fanning—shimmering—of ephemerality, recedes into a degradation, until, at last, ablation; that rising dawn, the beginning at the end of night, the real displaces the unreal; the infinity of finity, dies, when is both that Everlasting. *So smooth the plane of sea, and still the shearer the waters, the more pale.* That happiness must just rest.

The Harsh and the Warmth

Two maidens at the table laid, prospective pseudo souls betrayed, by faces: harsh and warmth. Challenge then their dearest friend, and what they'd lost, replete, with the sinless kin within....From beneath the mists of concentration, warmth wafted a sweetened musk; when, opposite the beauty, though harsh, revealed her set of tusks—and imagination made her impaling staid, the brunt of confrontation. The black and heavy eyelashes, heaped with paint and tears, though eclipse, no less, grandeur soul, thru warmth, she of tender years. For purposes of imagination, and hopeful change from devastation, harsh may give way to warmth, when depths of soul may render vacancies whole. And in a moment, the harsh maiden blossomed bright and soft, at a kiss of anciency, agency long sought; beaming thru her night—the victory's delight—if but for instantaneous, and fleeting wrought, and sacredly, magically bought gaze, thru the darkest eyes, as though if the night before the dawn—or the smile wide that had been withheld for far too long, obscured. Excellence in reason, analytically sound, she beaconed all the South, and did justice to her species, in the wisdom that left her mouth, breathing and therefore living, of their own. What happy joys finding reason in the harsh—soul flower, former maiden blossoming in the Summer growing season. She grew to love kindness in men.

UNREMARKABLE

Yet another timed-out, motion-filled, goalless work day. Extra losses to measure the stay, in the hours that make up the day. A maiden fled the confines, one flower to the winds of change, tomorrow's harrowing caller, out-loud, flees the academic crowd...as if some disease....Only those on the receiving, paying end are immune. And, so, lonely in the Night, cold. Furrow of the flower's mend, the busted hearts of broken men, in the planting of their love; defend the onerous, and great positive, in the flower, waylaid in her darkest hour—a maiden fairest, to the end! What bold blaring, how thy love is fairing. So that completion is a heaven's send, finds possibility in the earthly man, whipped by desire, the burning of the fires; colors in the blend, to champion the process in the rending—how the corporal pieces became fertilizer for some glorious other beginning. And then that face, that'd done the whipping, departed abruptly and besides the haunting that is left. The admirer escapes, ghost free—though pursued in dreams throughout eternity, and in conscious moments, drafted by the less-than-real. It is the emptiness left by failure to cognize and negotiate the gravity of a given substantive, to the blissful gain, chain of seconds. The blurring of the cosmic whirr, the exemplary event of the consciousness after the heart is rent—the collapse of the mind into devastation, the dwindling! The return to life, and then the ecstatic growth toward tomorrow, in potential.

ADMIXTURE

Some confusion as to the makeup: what part compassion and the heart of love? Some significance to the will o' the ways one lover passes the days. How much mistaken friends, ne'r subtract each other? arriving from mistakes as the former mother, brother, or any other. The Puzzle Divine, whose conjoinèd pieces make refined, gloss the dross, the lacking in lovers lost thru time. White shower down upon them, Crabtree petals in the Spring, pulled aloft in the gentle breeze; see that no boundaries exist in that which is composed of the Sea's float, eminently, on surface, in body beneath, feel yet the original wave in each. Why should the differences exist? when the Sole Originator is also-blinded procreator, at the opposite end! And the knowing not tomorrow's friend, or name, past the present familiar face of fame, in the mirror, is perhaps the cruelest game—that and re-remembering what has been forget! What slight chance is the amiable stranger more former lover than not, of the millions? Eight million incarnations, one Life. One form to the other. And, so, with Your eyes the Crabtree petals are seen to fly, and with Your astral ink, they have been painted pink. That a part may minus from the connected whole, that one pair of eyes see not the entirety of what the minions stole, in glance and then in turn away, is to be deceived, in that gentle breeze.

SHADOW

In the shadow of the German mountain held firm in the meadow's palm, colorful morning flowers, by the praise and glares, of those who find delight, in the upside of the Night: that Darkness resurrects what Dusk had long forget, in the cycling down thru the moments' round, to dawn rises from horizons' planèd, far-stretched ground, from which in the early light, the flowers gather to drink the joy of brand new, unfolded and embracing. Like a penny found, the wildfire burns within the wildflower; the meadow turns, ablazen, with the bright hues—best second to the astral blues!—which are alive and no different, in any moment, from reds and greens—and yet the separateness seems, only a moment lost in Omnipresent's dreams. Despite the age; the youth arranges in the petals of the meadow's floral pages, turned, turned, turned, by the gentle Hand of Ages. Wandering Bavaria, with the humming bees, the heat of August's afternoon, now, among the living colors—is it any wonder that the lover makes the declaration, with none other! Freedom in the informal fields, the wilderness replete, with disorganized, at a glance, perfection, the delicate direction, tread by paradise's trampling feet; from whose steps spring, the infinite rainbow of Spring, with the music, the singing—the accompanying of the swaying fields of morning barley, quietly falling into the shadow of the German mountain.

THE BIRD

....doth paint some consternation, by what its wings do flap—but empty aires save itself, from what its eyes do attack: a rosy portrait of a bug or berry, or all that a flyer might lack. And then if death it meets, eventually, consumed in the flames of desires to be able to change directions thus, so quickly, as though a corner had a request been made, of an errant wheel for steering been waylaid, or as if a string may tug upon thy turning wing—lightness and tightness are of what the thing is made, so that if it'd been blessed with feet, they would no doubt beat sweet and fleet! Such is the nervous knell, in the tolling of its bell....that'd strike the inner ear, and head to heart for the vital start—the quickening for its queried part, to play, in the drama for its day—the tiny sprite, aloft as the bright of night; thus the starry in a hurry, in the reactive *wave*, of avians in the moonglow of early August, divinely suggested in whisper, of un-understandable language, it seems, that the Mother gave to little beasts of the Father's keep, Whose disseminate soul, into a trillion trillion parts, that only in drama, though, to the skies returns to Him made whole. And if but the bug or berry be forget, the flyer would be cheat of desire, and the morning would be hard wrought, from a moon full but starless night before.

DHYANA

All descended of Olympos—the warrior she, unrivaled in expression of symphony, for the music that'd flowed thru her, silently, from Eternity's keep. The slewer of desires, she warped the sacred spire, of admiration for hire, and leant her name, and likeness to the inspiration of would-be kings. Such commotion to the rationale of the tempested and rarely bested self-anointed higher beings. The death to be arranged, of young men left temporarily insane, by the glimpse of garnishment by the garlanded Rememberer of all finer feminine things, as portraited in this young Dhyana, the huntress of he who drinks at the banks of finite springs; with magical embrace, she erases the years from her lover's face, transporting thru space, the mechanism of the reverent in reverie to alight upon some living times, in days gone by—or yet to be—as in sincerity, a Mother Divine melts from space it's time to create a new and magical physics, wherein limits and exactitudes become nursery rhymes. Streaming hair, as if the river's falls, glistening to crash agusted, windblown, upon the squarest shoulder rocks. And, marionette, this dangling fighter swept across the stage, all the rage, and how her kisses leapt! Still image in perfection of frame and heart and intellect, if a Mother Divine, were so inclined to leave entrapt, a soul enlightened by the feminine physicale divine! If some end be must had, then let the lover rest his head, to die at his beloved's bust, after having received the blessing of the gazing-eyes to meet, at length so as to rust, until that inferno had waylaid, of admiration for an Olympos maiden. So as not to disregard, the blatancy in the discard, to steal some final warmth from her lips, before the eminent cold steel, that the victim lover becomes, before her glorious pale, the never-fading capacities, of the fertile memories, that bind compliant that which passion suggests may be the captured best, that timeless essence sublime, of the dangler marionette—the maiden who'd been represent, of Olympos' fine Dhyana; her spine erect, and married off from brand new, so that in proximity, the gravity created the convection-celled atmosphere surround, such that storm-in-gale, revived of her gazèd glorious pale, to awaken the poorest forsaken of the opposite of the female. The nearly violent, in quantity's thrust only, the liquid lair, brushing back her silken hair, before her tall frame followed up aloft, the dangler fleeing the toss, of admiration, save only after confirmation, and passive vindication, for what had been the cause, of so much affirmation, that love had source in the Above. Her slight smile, off the left of center's side, proved the merriment of this Dhyana offering as polite a game, this side of Brahma's Night, and perhaps a reason to greet the dawning light, of the joyous season, of, adventure outside of fright. That rushing wind, warm upon the receptive skin, of what energy, the Cosmic Heart let in, when Infinity finds actuality, in the tiniest human traits, as a pausing moment between two, lovers not familiar with each other, effortlessly beholden and cherished within. Such symmetry between the reflection and the reality, the blueprint and the well-constructed home, one in each detail. Aquamarine irises dance, and spill into a violet hue, of what her energy renewed, in all that lingered nearer the ocean, then, she'd become, to drown or raise, the mouth of admiration's praise, depending on the voice within, saint or sinner, the instant next of kin, thru vibration waves, her ocean converted to glaze, of sorrow or joy; departing in haze or birthing the baby boy in the grown man. And thus the life in death, at this Dhyana's hand.

ASIA

Not yet perfected in the previous round, the madonna has again visited this town! The simple maiden of the milk, familiar to only the cows and meadow flowers, has returned to sheets of silk—and to a finer version of the Grande Bilk! Though the heart is still preserved, for the kindness is yet reserved, in your manner of consideration. There is a pause, though strangers, in the meeting of the moment, where in deep space eyes, the stars glisten with the hinting sunrise, still at the distance. Though refined in the luxury of the time, the heavy air of the sultry fields, lingers between your lips, at the brief still of your exhaling breath. Where the softness of the Winter wheat, recall upon your feet, at the warmer part of Spring. And, though, in the momentousness in the lacking snow, just as the greenery that the season brings, so the mirth in you, rapturously seems, to begin and end nowhere visible in the physical scheme. Between the admirer and thee, because the kindness and the newness in the days' dealing, there must a master or an infant be, guarding your ego gate to *soulternity*. The minus maliciousness, plus the willingness to see, the youth in what the lowly might be. The Distance, Past, call forth from the meadow Spring, when the first were last, as regards simplicity. Bright-colored Summer flowers, day at the sea, a diffident recollection of the lost Future of thee, in the City.

FLASH, SISTER

.

Instantaneously after only a mere thought of beauty, sister flashed aforely, one younger version of that matronly, from the East, the holographic pane, as the maiden took shape, appeared translucently, then solidified into the clear glass break, of the future lifetime in a moment; the heart aches, over a face, that'd inevitably take place. And leverage the joy of love against the pain that those mistakes make, the life portions that they take, tied-up tiny happinesses, in a fired-bake....but the sun side, in the bask of affection, the sparkle in that electrified complexion, on display at the end projection; spiritual crucifixion, in the interim, the graceful body had grown, and so alike the older sister; remarkably so, as if the temporal tempest would redraw, redress, to that former behest, when their souls' visitation upon youth, bilked from flesh its greater truth—two more lives betrayed. The gory glory of the mess made!—lover raged against the bliss of union. And yet the delicate flower flashed, full bloom in a dark night, so that her light might mitigate the damage done to Right. One kiss upon the flower's lips, may transform to young, again, all that had been left for old, in the Satan's cold; transmuted then to gold. From the dream, the accretion disc solidifies, and thru silence the maiden flower makes firmity, beginning with the dark eyes, from that silent start, in *momentmateriality*. Crossroads of mind and heart.

May Pole Summons

Such sour face, the over-flowing, over growing, effects of Mother Divine, in Spring upon the living things. The maiden's blossom as though the flowering Crabtrees, so happy to feel the sun, that joy may leave the sense, that heaven can be found on earth, in certain spirits, usually at the beginning of cycles. Seems at that time, the brightness of the Overmind, is found to cast shadows on the lacking sublime of existence, and then at least for a time, the Physical delivers all the beauty that is promised in the working stage. And for the least of the gods, what a paradise to be, that in finity lay eternity. How can the suffering feel? without the connected hand all the world surreal, in distant lighted land, where angels whirl about, and the dead instantly figure out, a beginning begins, again, and the acceptance of death the greatest sin. *Hath cried as though a child in the night, from the beginning, in anticipation of the end.* And so go the ways of the desiring man, among the flowers in bloom, all the beauty that may spend, the attention units of the golden soul's mind, on the way back home, to the origination of desire misplaced, and all found, then.

Blue Shore and the Walnut Grove

Some misty aire along the beckoning street of sandy wetness beneath a red sun's beat, down upon the heads of paradise's children, on the bodies above their bare feet. Some Grand Sublime had painted beyond the lines, and the resultant beauty had swept the godlets from those feet, by gently lapping waves at journey's end beneath the Summer's heat, their travels gently endured by their own aqueous street. The peace and Fall—diamonds of all the walnut trees, too—due to waves of green, the similar-acting leaves, to the wave. So, far removed from the sea, the gallant grove of walnut trees, and the shining faced you, to compete, with the deer, the remarkable zoo, without years' touch. So, the Infinite Breeze Much, delighted to the trees' green touch. Trampling quietly the under brush; the twigs' muffled snap, the dried leaves quiet, crumpled hush. And in the tree line's edge, two stood to review, reflect upon the dead who never knew, what kindness spread from the lives they'd led. To stand still in the freshly turnèd earth, to face East, bearing upon a barèd foot, the girth, of a child of paradise. The late evening Summer breeze, that tickled the trees, also tussled the hair, and closing the eyes of Maya's lies, so that peace would descend unharassed to its end, the center of the forehead of the children of paradise.

Angel Having Fun

Fire blest what her lips put to test. The elegance in confident youth, when the make believe world had grips upon her; all barriers in humanity, as other academic youths, put an hermetic seal upon the safety of her truth. Yet nibbling away, upon the basement of her stand, then most gracious of self doubts—which she blew away, thru cigarette smoke. Seemingly balanced at crux, between maiden and womanhood, the regressive winding up? blessing, again, as further nonchalant, shotgun looks, which she leveled upon men—unraveling, in her secret technique, their selves, by their selves, then a blast, with the eyes, as she paused in her post-academic life, with lips tied around the cool breath of the cigarette, in early Spring, beneath a magnolia tree, the steps of the academie....for a brief floating thru the early years, the maiden-woman had excuse of bewilderment, and every protection afforded the new and the lovely, in such an egalitarian state, as angel donning flesh, and gifted the test, of awakening desire, and its frightful fires. But behind the blast, from beneath caramel smoking irises the brightest light, though mischievous, of the dawning soul, white, at once glimmering the reflection, also, of the angel, having fun, at play, child of Joy.

Door Cracked Open

The knocking tap, a gently application of wrapping upon the door that'd cracked, open. No voice to cater in, only an minuted, silent entry. To find the maiden within—without the world—staring thru the Eastern wall of the cube, adrift to outer things, yet sailing intently, bent upon some unnoticed sea, graciously caving in upon itself. When contacted regarding the far-off, by a rippling bit, a tiny ripple in the inner-outer connecting current, and back she came. A golden mane unfurled, and she swept the room's space 'round with it, to though a stranger's surprise, to meet. Lock the lover's eye upon it; and fending then, for the Self, as if Beauty might flee to a distant shelf, without it, leaving haunted a rational concrete self, without it—the soul. With in the moments of silence that pursued the lover new, in spite of you. Dare address the softness on the lips, and lacking shock, that her door had opened, and what she must, most just, admit in her eyes of blue. Some moment when ne'r abandoned, the world for the future of only two, to marry in the moment, an infinite true, love, though heavens had shaken a dice in time, and dissolved their connection to a post life, so that in the end the pitiful begin—again! Aghast. The parted lovers had splashed thru the blinding lack-of-substance glue, binding the one to two; looking in, to see the kiss.

.

INTEGRATED

Fascinating familiar at end and in opposition—two heads at a table same. One yet divisible, the crystalline reflection of a stranger known, though in appearance this one still a turning point round about, to remiss the way you see—somewhere in that duplicate image, proof of eternity to amend the Godlike task of tracking down the soul. How endearing to the Maker of lovely days, that one should question One. Was it a tulip? that beckoned a comparison to your face, or perchance the milky aether? a water for Her navigation, so that the Hand of God may enjoy all that can be touched. A calm smile in the sunny room, revealed that you were the light, who steals the morning from the night. By a glisten plank as roadway true, a connector to that viewable; you delved, the shimmer in the sheen, for a moment at redirect, of the beautiful happiness, the reluctant catch.

THE PEBBLES

The soft white above and beneath the gray, the touching stone of cloud, that shields where the maidens play, upon the sands of alterlands—the mysterious endlessness of finity, captured in watery wave, and bamboo tree. Some joy incarnate, to fossil for a future day, when Hate has lost its way, and Death may make the scarcity of everlasting life parlay, to what had heretofore, been eternal night. And the maidens gaze thru the Mayic haze, at each other's form to rest, alight upon, the vision of brighter ways, though dimmer in a reality unimaginable. What filler of gray, provider of blue, Handler of the sands anew, puts upon the collection of souls, as fingers for the hand, to roll then the stones of men, the pebbles, the pebbles, the pebbles. Oh, to be blessed with eyes, to see the maiden's sighs, when at play with one another in the midst of Brahma's day. The multitude of variety, has each a plusses work when most the bested article beams for live display, such that a pebble each, towers unique, for sages of all ages to pick out, upon the vast seashores of time; when the innocents leave the motherland, spewn about by the Hand.

OWNER OF THE PARK

The Maiden in her towering above—the awkward stance, with weight upon one heel, and with flowing dress of white, she spared an endless night, for the glarors in the light bright of day. Turning thirty, she may have run away, from what she wants not—but the light lines of dark surprise, etched deep into the ambient eye's smile, at the mouth—in the mirror it is the not-so-gentle falling out, with Time, to have lost the music to her rhyme, in the depths of the angled lines. The great surprise was the darkness in her eyes—a sunset reverence, put to a blessed test—the angle of her best arrest, the glory of her beauty fest. Some queenly beaming played upon, the dessert of her frowns, and oasis, she, though, in her flowing gown, waving in the dying day's breeze, another round of day. A one-day madonna in a future's love, making her a duplication of the Mother of Love, to a tiny some other. The great mystery of the Lover from above, invested in the brother, sister; divested of the robber, mobber in the discontinuance of sin. And there she bares her thin—the subtlest soul, and what does not pass within. Adsorbent white, purity in the dank, the night, the shimmering, formlessness of Spirit caught by human shape; the wavering white dress, its cape.

REVELATION

The recoverie she pronounced, face to face, and its mechanistic approach was rooted in her present yet distant reverie. From a mountainous region in the West, she, the madonna with children had labored beneath her tests, and the incendiary nature of her relief, foundered in her disbelief, of the task at hand, having separated from the motherland, in the East. And so, as it goes in failure: home to a feast of crows. And, as the high, harsh winds blow, she found herself lakeside, content in the familiar, dismayed at the hard peculiar, of being mismade into a secretary, from the gifted educator of children. To a bystander, her beaming presence: would it were a partial much? and could be called, perhaps, a gush? or spanning radially, the glower of her soul expanding, reaching out to meet, the admirer at her feet. Statuesque and, oh, so brilliantly aflame....The maiden in the madonna, answered yet to the name same! And if life be lived eternally in the softness and forbiddingness in a kiss, then she as if an immortality granting machine worked freely, madly, discretionately— though, dispassionately—acted no lesser a goddess than the mother she. A note must be addended: her charming laughter, a must disarmament, for any peace-loving goddess; the surprise was having gone from lovely secretary to highly educated educator, done with such a pleasantly revelatory banter, that included, no less, the spiritual nature of life at altitude, in the rarified aires of the snow-capped peaks. Sweet lady: your lover at your service at your feet.

SERVER

There, in a tiny sea ville, she moved about in elegance and stillness, unseen in her silence with grace, she moved from point to place, on display. *Would it were another day*, she seemed to say. The light of fatigue, but only a hint, in her otherwise tireless way, due to, perhaps, the weight of her constant kindness, gentleness, the dove who peered at the half-grown field of corn, in contemplation of a run about it. That one might desire the hair of gold, the slight frame with height, the near lankiness of the female athlete in glorious gate, may a statement make of seriousness of the play—having had, or not having—gives cause to return another day. Yet the aethereality of the forms, deemed alive and warm, to the touch, mend minds broken by the much electricality of the revertant court of human parade—a wet shock, in the end. Though some *glory* in self control, the mourners of the mad flight of senses that efficiently disperse the imagery manufactured of the light; long after the fall of night. Upon dispensation of it, the admiration, her face in detail seemed to recede, perhaps in protection of what may grow from seed, of eye contact—the sacred deed. The familiarity with which she passed before, speaking with the voice of the Evermore, in the musicality of symphony, all its parts in harmonic motion, directed in warmth to one goal, reunion with the lover.

DOORWAY IN YOU

From the sneaken, stolen rooftop view, to feel in secret one heartbeat with you, in the night, and seeing together the Main Street lights, running West into the recent dusk. All emphasis, in breath and form, become the lens thru which distant morn, is found approaching, silently. There, a sole togetherness in existentiality is achieved of three: admiration, object, the Thee. Feeling the gentle Spring breeze, brush madly upon an arm, and wisp sadly the strand of hair across a caramel eye, illumined by, intent upon, the shining city lights, spread before the blackened sky. In the early days of love with you, exhilarate at the touch of you, fluster at the thought of you—how happiness could be so close, so real and bright. Beneath the stars, in conspiracy, where to find that doorway to infinity? thru some team effort, to do. That massive third party created of the two, united to the farthest star, the breeze, the view. Where has gone, then, that tiny two? Now only grains of sand on the galactic beach. The soft lips in a slow discrete, called home the stellar voyagers, who withdrew back into the two, waiting upon the rooftop for the return of this joy from such an adventure, in the night.

ANOTHER YOU

You jilted your lover long ago, not with a hasty, 'NO!' but with ever increasing indifference that had matured to dislike. And the nature of taste? that would have affection's grace spewn about a place in yore—when once you peered into the Evermore, with the enthusiastic yet limited wisdom of youth, and the will expended to make up for that deficit. Were you originally lucky enough to find your ducks lined up at 23? Near but never merging, what differential occurred? in the combined vibration? an inharmonic flat and a sharp on the piano keys? But perhaps the Writer Divine had constructed different parts—and a stranger would, in those days—than the one your lover would have preferred; the two worlds near but that had never merged. Your viewpoint on today, may have another way, as the thousand revolutions of your inner sun have writ a constitution anew of, you. And today, after all life's weapons had blasted away, at the old and the becoming you, at the dreams and desires that had panned out few; would your lover meet another you? if starry fortunes might arrange it. Would that piano keys might harmonize and make melody, and two worlds collide into a third, made only of the two, and thusly aligned, heaven might come into view. A rare escape, for how to build? what had nearly never been conceived upon the board, despite the moment that you had your lover adored, that passed, consisting of the plea at telephone's end so long ago, but that was taken only as a message, and that was never returned, until now.

Forgotten Year

Burden of the playered youth—not the seeking but the finding of truth. The forgotten year, or that never was, had been interfered, by the Light above? The romance, initial chance, what love! first love. A happiness not so remote, elation to a doable level, and extendable. So then the up-for-anything caramel eyes, branding high to utmost heights, lovers of delight. Then what glory to be in, accompany, that otherworldly in you. Two who do, and though emotions may divide, mere manifestations inherent of the roles, your tears, and the others' distance. Yet to breathe a single breath, overcomes all put to *tests*, of the *world* below. The softest, warmest, gentlest hand, to touch the soul of Youth. And ban tomorrow for the moment's stead, play the tremors of the dying, if the lovers never lose the head. Your wanting to be, and the allowance to see you being, the better charm of thee. No trivial vibration passing 'tween, for momentous occasions in the *already seen*, past déjà vu, and the fulfillment in the future you. *Today, what would you like to do?* The forgotten year—when said goodbye? and the fingers slipped away? And the breath returned from one to two? Cannot remember the day, when all Love withdrew, so that the Writer of the play, may have His way, His war, His day. What granted the confidence to consider a life apart? as if the unlimited supply of lovers, might forever wander by....your laughter and excellence always were admired, if not in spite of another life desired, and the ability to apprehend it, evidence of the inspired, even as if the fallen-from-a-cliff, had forever silenced, in your disappearance from Iron Gate Lane, that forgotten year.

BESTUBBLED CORN

....as if toward the cendant sun, had run. All the microlife, that ate little except the high Summer rays, perished methodically and finally, with the short days, for the insects' feast upon the night direct. The love cricket, which should have slept, crept into view, and spoke: *How are you?* The shimmering black, and slow-motion acts, bespoke a peaceful being. Introduction to the finalizing space, the time for the summarizing of the race; who had eminent status? but this black bug, and fighting all the while to rise above the fibers of the rug. The bereft, is earth, for the slumbering in its berth, the children of this greatest hour. One viewpoint is the vacant field of bestubbled corn, moist and chilled in the November morn, beneath the sagging pre-snow clouds, backlit by the leafless, darker brown wood—ne'r had understood whom cricket knew—as most had slept before they'd chewed, upon the kernels of Infinite Blue, corn of another matter. And in the lonely hour of two, when nary naught awoke, only dear cricket there who spoke: *Who are you?* And at the crest of dawn, petting morning's fawn, the unblinking bug had demanded a hug. *Shall you not break? beneath the weight of one who stood upon two. Heaven's sake, how can delicateness translate? such that to express all affection due, without the fatality that might ensue, from such a mismatched pair.* You whisper from the Netherwhere, a name, tiny one—and in the still of night, only you to grant fame, for the sleeping and the insane others. Were you not so kind to appear and to play and to say, *What do you make of Her world?* there would be druthers.

Archer, Madonna

In along the inner rail, the rocket sled to the stars prevailed—from a comfort base in at Paradise's gate, she sent invisible hail. The globular clusters, mini-worlds, yet unseen, impale where humans reign in space, or are used to doing so. The caramel iris she kept in pairs, she vacated when she thought of what's gone, beyond the pale, are the heavens' claim. And gifted, devoted, she lay the shell willingly down, an offering to the emptiness surround, that, greedy as joy is happy, would gladly turn a clown—so fool to the surfactants, and glee to make the Darkness drool, for, the capture of another sanity for bereftation among its reign. And the caramel that a pair fell, into the vacant whites, resolutely refutingly denies Night; turned up, the gleam of the beams so bright—the archer madonna drew the bow and slew all fright. And radiale, then, she dreamed of a touch We Unseen, with the glory of the Gemini, the Motivating Thing Absent Abstract, high proportion of signal-to-noise, sub-linear discovery of infinite curvature, or the point singulaire that—grew into everything—the new cosmology of the once-fragile being, sitting in the flickering of the zoetrope, unfurling her rope of hope.

THE FOUNTAIN

Spray from the spinal way—Madonna had just adjust, asana to project into the blue of the altervu to then: *What had become of you?* As if the ocean Self, she sat erect and still, save the countless waves, rolling, rolling, rolling, in the silence of eternal days, shared by the lovers of the same. What sense of the timeless bent? than this force before! Discrimination of Wisdom's fame, pronounced her character of the *going out*, lay waiting for supp in the river lining the lower eyelids, upon which floats the caramel moons, glistening as though a thousand watery hands, outstretched to receive the Source of up. What wondrous golden behave! that lights the nights of her old angelic days—when her two bodies missed the third now worn, that graces in conciliatory paces, the lower below, yet in perfect reflect of that aetherially met, in the high of the emerald eye. What mirage then spans before reality? but the continuation of earthbound angelic insinuations in the golden madonna poised before the heavens, and in reception of its direction, redirects and sprays, a fountain.

THICKNESS OF AIR NEAR WATER

Swimming, while merely strolling, thru the Summer thick, of foggy aires—
though clear—put the seaside pedestrian in communication with the brother-
man, sister-sea dweller, intertwirl, in electric-seasoned fines, of the breathable
liquids, air and sea. One layer, then, services its neighbor kin, so then no
strangers have ever been, or will be, again, disengaged for want of unity;
though through feeling even canst the blindest see, the walker on the sand,
o'er the wiggler of the sea; from which a focal inclination spans, to include an
eventual eternity—the oneness of all inhabitants beneath the sun, in the sense
of beauty that fuels all Finity to run, toward it. There is a walk at the edge of
space that dangles twixt the holy place, that water's near, though is separate—
and would a master fear, to fall and must-breathe the water part of it? or freeze
the animation in the Winter of the mind's hold, to not take breath at all?—as
if a thousand dreams, when stumbles into the sea, the waters are inhaled with
ease, as though the muggy Summer breeze. May all lovers walk this edge, so
that no story goes unread, by a witness true, to hearts that had not bled, nor
troubles that had not fled, before this sacred edge.

Night in the Eyes by Day

Madonna with child within, screamed with darkness in the iris where light had been. Although golden-haired and golden hued—where she peered into the world afore, eclipsed the sunshine of the orbs, of her heretofore, madonna with child within—maiden no more. What engulfs? the universe berth, where lay the sleeping souls of earth, yet to be by virtue of birth; touching soft your lips, in your night, the stuff of mirth....And then the seriousness, the struggle to be, perhaps the plant of eternity, that groweth naught without thee: she participates at the sea. Her voice, in musicality, rings out, above the waves, hovers then to sow the admirer with a craze; then hair swept back, revealing the softly throbbing pulse at the side of the neck, the tenderest flesh. And if she be but an illusionary vision, playing out before, the admirer of her evermore. And if the subject thrust, as though the hostile bust, sculpted into the mad-hatterness by her own desire for loveliness, and was herself the lovely flower that she sought to grew. And new, with unborn life inside, came she out of night in the day? to hide with the certain nervous trounce low; she betrays the contrary ways of her deepest heart; the moon, occluded in the shadowed sun rays in the curvature of the earth, rises, in the irises' day, again.

Delight, Revisited

She had made for a remarkable constraint in her admirer. Safely stationed in the social net, her illumination was optimistically met—but only from a *distant* admiration. Hair of light and eyes of fire, demeanor of the meaning business, she nonetheless had not yet a crown fully lit. But with exuberance, she was able to carry on with the task of her day, and in some magical way, was a gift from some far yesterday, castaway of a Summer in long lost in a small city on a Great Lake bay. With just a whisper, her admirer was able to track her down thru the past, until the heir of recognition became full grown: Traipse with a devil without a home, and fear then that heir, a found memory seeming to be the original experience, such is the brilliance of its light that all becomes an artificial day beneath the deep night. The blessed hysteria of the wonder delight, the heiress, possessor of the joy of the shining youth, may find—she will—a brief comfort in that social net, until the breach in communication with it, due to Time's pass and the long, true squelching of her self, unannounced, undetected—the harbinger of loss had arrived without discretion. 30,000 voices had cried from her mouth, telling a million lies, until the one voice in stillness spoke one truth. But it is a future memory, one not yet inspected, tho a seer had thus projected, to return to a seaside at Summer's tide, thru this bride, the heiress, possessor of joy. The future and the past, may in the present moment last, as the having-touched and the sweet words yet-to-be-heard, doth fight the lover much, whose season by the sea is done, or is yet to be; one soft small kiss from the heiress' fleeting lips, and the projector flares, burns hot and bright, and then subsides, back into the night.

THE TROIKA

Moonrise had chased the sunset. Parking upon the Eastern horizon, the lunar lamp began to glow brighter in the falling January snow. Rising higher, darkness in the opposite sky descended, with the result of the dimmer sun, shining out. Twinkling stars pulled at the larger body, though in the distance, only a vague concession the moon gave, as faint as a single thought—a simple gesture from the ironically, in actuality and not apparency, smaller habitant celestial. She stood, alertness and goal oriented, right and intelligently invested, eyes blue and bright, reflecting heaven in the night, silently gazing out, an ascendancy without dependency, save the payoff of the joyful noise, that would collect in her throat, until the virgin voice would sing out, into the blackness, to flow momentarily before vanishing from the ears' registration. In the midst of her secret solitary chorale, the icy, alien planetoid, with a girth thrice that of the moon, tore between earth and its satellite. Slowly, shockingly, she began to float, rising higher and higher into the night; she soared without wings, without an engine, to 30,000 feet; unimaginably heavy and heavèd soil-once-crust, comingled with a liberated sea! There was plenty of air to breath, but the featherless bird could not, for her powerless flight, for the dreadful sight, of the cleaved moon, rent by black triangles of darkness between its pieces, degrading in its orbit, to rejoin with Mother Earth. At *last*, she thought, *all wars will cease*. Her final thought in life, at 60,000 feet.

In Dreams

You had swooped down in the sleeping night, being some great depth never having felt by day, then being alive when so long thought dead. Yet in the lucid scene, more real the lover seems, than before had been conceived, when gentle lips had stooped to kiss, beneath the moon alive. A come-true dream, flooding in, the overflowing stream—you, but more—totality at the door—of what the mind imagines the heart's desire to be. Sweet ecstasy, only two created universally, who, alone together in creation; remark something of the ideal love. And yet some third, the Above, seems to always have heard; your hair and eyes of night, draping and gazing upon, in silence, with all the intimacy, of a wife; for desiring no one else any more, your materialization in peace, granted forbearance from future sufferings. The memory of electricity, more profound than mere chemistry, echoes of your healing touch, in days when love was all right, or an expectant possibility. Based upon reality, shrunken to the size of actual experience, the 13 days when the ecstatic haze, blazed. Oh, the acceptance, the imprintation, the willingness to play—as if your mate for a day, in the heart of touch, the sacred burning up in the beautiful skies of your night reachable.

Apparition

In the afternoon, maiden, flame, facing away, being interested—intensely. The woman girl added to her youth with a bending will. Insatiable light, pouring forth, from behind the blind of hair; back toward, admirer nary naught ever there? And in the fire of being application, years transgressed wont; and the finity of Time's machinations, manifestations, colors the eye of the soul, paints a lens less than whole, such that other than the glimmer of the ageless Essence, becomes the object of affection, or the dying meal laid at the cloven feet of devilish Delusion's druthers. What then is seen with human eyes, may really not be seeing? if being in Essence, passes for the walking dead. *And how you avoid the admiration; conversation with imagination—and that is the devilish of Delusion. Lent to believe that that you this was not seen. Were you really there?* Vibrant fury in the airs, still back turned, and peering out from beneath the blind of hair. That Summer may prosper from the rain, to add then a little mystery to your being, as you a benefit, too. All apart of adventure, beneath the rising sun of June, lover and beloved, in drama, overlook one another. A comedy then a tragedy, as admiration's most desired of Mother Divine, and vacant are the treasures other, for the covet. Anchored in distance, the maiden fury flamed away and all awares, of admiration's ways.

Madonna Reconsidered

Represented the Deep Blue; shocking pale, misty iris hue, reflection, impression of prismatic soul below? Incantation, favored away the days, past-lost gradual-graduation, perhaps aetheric gradation, of the memories lapsed. Disdain with which you first were met—the flurried hurry of the blue collar jet set! Madonna in the passing. Now, the fury! Anchored in the flip-side soul, the blue light in your eyes, mimics the plaintiff cries, of the soul symphony, grand tympanis, pounding, wailing, much more a heartbeat, crashing upon the shores, of the days' evermore. The strength with which you slew; the calm interior that you grew, atop the storm at sea, which was the worry bee, of unsuspected insanity of the quote 'reality'. Such entertainment, now a story sold; the unbearing familiar beauty, lapping at your feets. Stardust in the gale of your surround, in-motion blinding, in the hurricane, you. For whence comes the alter you? suggested in that former hue, all the more subdued, than in this moment extended. The kindness upon your lips, perhaps the startled find—ferry compassion as though your children own, across the gulf of inches, where dreamt in the separate homes of fleshly frail and bones, a Master love held above all others. What *force* to feel you in, some slender tunnel, thinnest funnel, protruding between the foreheads, of all past lovers. Remarkable legend of the hinter region, come true—collected manifested Spirit, cohabitant in quantity, two. And so kindred remarkable, in that hindered no more to blindness, to be one of a twin essence, sure relative of a star bright, blessing the dark of night. So wholly right, beyond emotion, alive in the second sight. You, a balm, to an irreparable, bereft of joy, gone wrong, insane. Hover you, so each instant anew, with blissful union, absentee pain, in your misty blues. A lover's true, reunion from beyond the ages. Oh, to bury in your endless breast, a head that frequent wet, at seeming never having found you, and laugh, and, loh, repent, for all those misplaced cares on innocent you, cast to the reachable winds.

CATHERINE

Happiness winked. Freshest voice, remits a calling choice: come, come, come; heavenly feminine, enjoins to the side, for a stroll. In instancy, what once had been anciently old becomes modernly new, in the madonna's presence. The familiar stronger, reaching back for remembrance, and how she could possibly know to recognize the face afore, save some trend of former days. And if but in a second, the marriage resumes, then what is the wonder that time should separate lovers true? in absence of earth's Golden Age, when everlastingness none so the rule. Could be the pursuit of even Higher Love? to loft the soul above the required rounds repeated, from waking birth to sleep in the earth. But, if so, what then? is the true purpose of love true to usher, a divine friend, each other past the drama into Day, before to cast aside, the corpus to lay, at the feet of yet another Night at the end of, loh, the 10,000th life. That there may be more than a betrothèd pair, the ultimate conclusion, following infinite shining starts and degradations into despair. And so the flowering tree bore fruit: love lifted to the Above, what fearful tidings is matter made of. But to adore on the divine work, on the showroom floor, made the passing-thru a beautiful, unforgettable transmutation, and only the risk of death gives value to living for love.

Conejo Valley

Shimmer on the morning haze, micro-droplets of Pacific seas' breeze, taming night's dead aires with sunny life, and orange blossoms' waft, returning to seas through canyons' grace, even as valleyward flows its breeze. Just having glimpsed the mountain tops, sun streams on radial beams, to inhabitants of the Conejo. Golden Maiden in mirth, always laughter first, which gave beauty a tutorial. A slight mischievous, in overwhelming confidence, she had a razor for a smile, and a laser for a glance, in each eye, so, in any instant, three admirers might die! To be sat, inches away, across the table—in full view and reach of those rays, was to be married in the moment; nimbus donning cover, deflectory to cosmic lovers, appearing hotly astral as particle bowers, bombarding the shining maiden, raining down the glorious insane affection—in heaven's name. Among an audience of hundreds, still your light shone, beacon home, for the displaced souls, misplaced tolls, paid to jelly rolls who'd no dreams to conceive of a single beam that created you; designated who would be attached, you attacked with silent scorch, you scorned, that which was not a lover's warm. Then to have the mirth in you, in California sun, made jovial a state of being. Then to be alone with you, back staging dramatic aires, flare to flare, that pair. Never knew what'd passed twixt those two; that Fate'd nixed the taking in of the scent of your neck, the soft press of your lips. Vacant was left the dream of sustenance, continuance, that lovers may truly have no heyday without.

Maiden at Window in Moonlight

She stood abruptly up, turned, moved to the window, reached up, took the handle, unlatched the window, and opened it to the fully moonèd night. Breathing in the golden beams, eyes closed, she expended her slight frame with glory of the celestial day, happening elsewhere beyond the darkness, but imputing it life to the shining lunar mares, which though waterless, freely gave to her that life nonetheless by a reduced reflection, or as best it could. In the wooden room behind her, roiled an ocean of emotion ever under her control, at her disposal. Hear it's roar! And then she smiled, moonbeams emanating from her every seam. And in that warming broadcast, a warning fast to all future and past mornings: Doubt not! Love is the light, and light makes all that lives and crawls and works beneath the Brahmin Night. And so the moon far above yet low on the horizon, magically becomes her—in the speed of a smile; slipping thru the window and, then into you, the wooden room, low lighted, now features a human moonly brighted. *At the bared floorboards, asudden a furrow's mirth, at the turning, turning of the earth. Then melting down the resistance to, living; fallen off, as leaves released from Autumn trees. In the dead Autumn. In the dead, and comes a helping Hand,* such that ne'r resting in deep despair, is eternal; for on a moonèd night, lofts the resurrection, alights the Phoenix.

BEYOND THE CORN

In moonlight of a Summer's night, a stroll atop a plowèd field delight, Westward toward the wood. The sea—grayscaled, stubbled wheat—lay a rug divine beneath the feet. Mission sublime upon the golden, earthen street, swimming in the yellow faint. Mother Divine witnesses on, to speak peace, and to be fond of the children who may menace Night, with their aggressive passivity; receptacles of Bright. The walkers under the midnight day, the balmy Summer way, *el sendero luminoso*, a via; some stars to mimic protons, and the dizzied tilt-of-whirl, to move subtle on, to translucency, then frail solidity, to firmity. So drunkenness on moonlight, be, paralytic prisoner of Beauty, stroked by balmy July breeze, stoked by scenes of wintry dreams, of January rule to come, when painting white all things green, is what hath a painter's touch, in the God Who doth love much, a cycle of birth to rust, to rest in earth, to lose life to gain, another birth. And sprouting from the wheat, the fragrance of the stellar sweet, wafted from the far off morn, of the universe's early borne. Blessed by anciency, then, the growing corn that feeds the horde, which upon the oxygen depend. The supping children of men, who return time and time, again, until breath becomes the Lighted Friend; inhaling the moon glow, exhaling the rustling nearby corn, are the living giants of Summer.

Parked between, in a pathèd, dried stream, a lane between the yellow seas of waving corn. Pausing for a moment's respite, just long enough to portrait in the sky of blue, and mottle thru a brown barn, rising above the plane of the farm—only half a building—floating upon the corn, bending unnaturally low, with a beech tree its elbow—all in silence at 3 PM, save the slicing, cutting, muttering, trillion leaves of corn, the wavelets of the sea. Silk-spun batting within, each ear abeating heart and apumping blood, some crystal light stored for a wintry retreat, on some far, native shore—perhaps the breech in Evermore! So tasty is the dainty treat. Yet how easy—if reached out to bite into—broken teeth. Kernels hard remarkably; and short of roasted, only a hammer, or some pummeling, thereafter, may discern the shell from the meat, thus paving thru the man and cosmos, the circular, stellar street, *el sendero luminoso.*

To feel in that whispering corn, the hand of one deceased, this morn; mourn, as is so fresh, that loosing off the flesh. To pause before the declining heap, of vista *now* weak—a golden, waving horizon, and weathering-grayèd barn-top peaks, of darting swallows in headland's hollows, where hedge trees follow, where only yesterday all seemed too bright, too new, with you; burned to oblivion in the outdoor fireplace built for but that ne'r warmed a human face, or entertained the children's race, or the congenial laughter of friends. A special brand of oblivion, that, as if this had never been—after being—for so long so clearly, so dearly. You mock in the winds, with what's left of what you began and ran—*the makings of a man?* And though to keep a step ahead of Winter's snows, still, *what role of a man who must go?* when all of Spirit's offerings remain off hand—able be, to cut off that waving hand, *on the man who never dies.* In the pause in the observation of the vista of fields of yellow corn, there must be found hidden laughter beyond that special oblivion—of friends gathered round an outdoor fireplace, built to warm the children's faces, in between their footraces; in some paradise that's always been—where you now live, again, out of view; world without end. Amen.

The Processional

What dreams have the maidens of the Lake? who, though white spirituality, interact with materiality, and the rarity among them yearn for intellectuality, and leave the Lake in its search. That time may patter away at their clay, still a moment in that time shall never pass from their grasp of recollection. And now gone, to find Experiences' delight, what mass suggestion? hypnotized so that day was thought to flourish, and to therefore nourish in the night! when the womb distracts from the mind's might, Maya proclaims, to dazzle, to make insane, with some beauty sense, so-called, that pleases ear and eye and nose, and stokes fires of finity's desires, or the magnetism of what lay below. And when the Winter whips the sea to froth, and Summer sky of luminescence is lost, the agitated waves complain for the imbalance, for the maidens' return. And what would there have been to be hoped for? when all was won already before the war, known before opening the mystery door. Perhaps the dazzle incites the travel, that in turn unravels, the stacked hair—or the river dammed—that buoys the ship—the soul—to shore. The academia land, forgives the body's lust—but for only the moment it must—and then its back to hell, again. Then they come home to the sea, and shame her beauty with theirs. The evolution of maidens has for its roots, that hell; thus begins the assertion to heaven, which in contrast leaves behind dumb intellectuality, mute academia, if the maidens are to charm.

MAMMOTH

Happy in an unlast view, the mammoth took the best of you. So, fatalism extant, it is this smiling-in-the-face-of-death that has left your lovers bereft. What propels into the future's past? as fast as missing in the moment. The ghostly, ghastly head of protracted insincerity, for you had wanted, perhaps, the family. And did you see? the *me* of your lovers, or the children for posterity? yet to be....And is the place of the lover yours, to fit into some role for chores, but loathe to ever be a great deal more. What *you*, lovely, had put upon, hanged a sign on, did ever it exist? Or had the mammoth, too, done eat it? To touch the gentle lip-to-lip, yet hook upon the flap of your soul's slip, for a moment took aback, to frolic in the Dior scent, for an hour or more, while admiring the you who wore it, made for an eternal scoring on the lover's core. How hungry the mammoth, though, trudging thru the mounting snows, of yesteryear's delusive, elusive memories; what strange things hath time, for what the lovers' rings do bind. And though the decades passed, the images yet remain, as if painted upon the ghost of you. A haunting, then? which daily renews the pain and the loss of final words and views, said and seen upon this stagely playing bridge. What mammoth finds to taste, no more remains of a familiar place; laughter, security, the sense of camaraderie, what carpenter's hands create and leave beneath the Winter walnut trees.

MASTERS OF THE MAGNIFICENT

A sea of wheat, awaving, *Goodbye*, to the West. A placarded yard before, from where to have a visitor green, standing in between, that brown sea and two viewing into the eternity of possibility. Perhaps the gentle squirrels knew of the habit-view of these two, and feared not for their selves! And so the usual flit of their flighting, was absent. A chubby belly to be filled before the bulk of the season for the bravery, or, perhaps, in country vacancies, simply no reason to not be free, could account for the detached and seen engagement in the nut, while no other world turned, the chilling breeze thru the late Summer trees, made, uncharacteristically, advances upon the Fall to come. From the window view, two sat to chew the fat, and ne'r a nearer stab at a perfect day had e'r been had. The omnipotence in the causality of it; to think it solved, and so it would relent, to the masters of the magnificent. Only two to have this view, for the higher heaven sent, a lower version for which to be rent, in musicality, in the symphony of the peacefulness of Nature Mother's living prayer, of fields and forests, and lawns, spread beneath the spraying white upon the bluest sky, the baiting gift for Night, to, in its death, encourage the birth of yet another dawn. It would be of no surprising consequence, if angels might seep out thru the vista of the whole of it. What good fortune? might have drawn it, just as the two did desire. Were the greatest kings, but loathe be had for the fatality in the temporality of it. But despite the harshness and the brutality of what would become of two, the magical existence in heaven's peace on earth, would always find you in laughter, in memory, at the thought of it. So, then, the hint of the interchangeability of souls to bodies, and rebirth upon the earth, slipped into a so-called reality, because of its overwhelming similarity to a fantasy: in your absence yet felt presence in some far beyond, it seems you are a mere actor in the wings, awaiting the cue to come on, in a play and a character, all anew. But the separation on Time's field of battles in space, seriously degrade the grasp, at the moment, that all the drama is but an expression of Joy. Perhaps, in life, the constant kindness you did show the gentle deer, and in offering protection from the hunter, year after year, secured for you a process to, which aspire in heaven's lowest higher, a long life lived mostly in the good humor of one blest, with a suffering exit in brief!

HER HAIR DOWN

…making her unrecognizable. The bright warmth, still there beneath the flowing hair, distinctly hers, but not that exterior aire. Another name to that energy same, as the other—but then at closer inspection, the maiden light, smiled to offer recollection right, on mark—the caramel eyes, set in behind the aerie disguise, her astral robe, hidden to the visible. Peering, then, into that neighboring dimension, where some foreign mystical gain had set upon the otherworldly introspection—and a fraction of the photonic makeup was fully featured, clearly seen, though unstable, wavering. How the feminine down reserved typically for the graceful fowl, adorned the maiden bright, so lovely. The electric storm in her smile, traversed the seeming miles, the mere inches between her lips and those of her lover. The new sameness of the now stranger in appearance, was marked by rebellion, as the flowing hair was to be, by regulation, kept back, for the food preparation. But the rebel let it flow freely in all directions. The thrilling liberty, further rated her luminosity, as no rebel who ever loved who did not detest reservation, limitation, and, when presented the chance for flight, due to lacking supervision, ever failed to take it. And for those few hours, she was happiest, and a joy to be near.

WEIGHT OF THE LIGHT

Young Madonna sat in asana before the Master's feet. Pose erect, for heaven's met, for then the angels for her soul's keep. The shining Light, bespeaks, then engulfs the party present, and some proof is the weight of the light, resting upon her eyelashes leveled out, at first, to then head down, slowly with the increasing brightness as she slipped away, thru the magic telescope in her forehead, having fled the dead of the living. How so early on she had met calamity is the story for posterity. The dissolution of all things physical, beneath the fires of ferocious desires. The sight of falling stars, and rising tides, had helped her to choose sides—and not so slowly. Then what to miss? in that what part had love? played in the making and the managing of it, her life's work, the workings of her life. The forgotten Force, the child of Joy—for no joy, then no reason to love. What pretty? the flowers celebrate of, giving on loan to that burdensome mechanical that atoms and molecules perform of. Absent now, she relaxed at a distant star, escaped, freed of war and the monsters it makes, the beauty it forsakes, the truths it denies that make even the oceans quake; no corpus to be harmed, then no fear to signal *Alarm!* Rested in astral home, she longs for nothing now, save for distillation of Joy's admiration, Love—the reason to want near It, the explanation for her absence, that the eye, lashed, had weighted closed the eyelids, confirmed the truth: on earth even the Infinite Light is persecuted by mass, or the finite.

Quiet and Solitude

Dragging down the long hall, Madame, in trance, sought to forget all. Dressed in professional tan best, it was silence that she hoped to test. The quiet surround, she inquired if it might stick, at least thru the night. An answering nod, and she felt delight at the promise not just quiet, but aloneness. The destitution of the vacant hotel, she had intruded, as off-season clientele. Her gaze focused into a modern past, the weight of the overwhelming mast of work, lowered upon her person, then raised, and then lowered, again, on the day-to-day, had removed the girl from the woman, and left deep-set lines around the eyes, in her place, which she wore with the grace of the athlete, or the wonton and excellent smoker, which she was not. Her postured, upright straight—an imprint of that which made competence in the race—gave the royal frame from which the flower of her person draped. Almost country club hair, and low-cut blouse, from which the cleavage of her abundant bosom protruded out; evidence of some magnificent, progressive boardroom appearances, perhaps, led her to aspire a hint of bedroom attire. All cloaked beneath an overcoat, and trailing luggage, seeming indignantly along for just the ride. To have arrived, she expressed surprise, and aspired with some sacred exhalation in celebration of the end of the journey. The almonds in her eyes grew larger, and then smaller, to be hidden until later when she slumbered away her body for the infinite inner skies. She disappeared, after being let in, beyond the wooden doors, with such brevity, that admiration was left in her draft and wake, begging more alignment to her posture straight.

Face of the Maiden

Transportation in a unity divine, together with you in peace in one moment in time; phenom for this phenomenon, the maiden has the power to attract, and then to disembarkate, as if taking all else upon voyage, the world surround. Though in the crowded mart, and pressures, mounting from the work, still the breach in the sphere containing dear-the-twain, never occurs, and not want of the steering toward a crash. Peculiar status, then, of suspension beyond the day in which one lives, all else cast away but for the lovers two, caught in Bliss' way. And definite the aires of jasmine repair to within the sphere, and with the breathing-in of the lover twins, and the elevated, and in the resultant state, that transportation gave conveyance to begin: the blue hues of the residential matter, convinced of ambient fixation, let loose their constitution, so that direct below, and above the maiden's head, the blue hues of the residential matter shifted toward the red—the dearly departed dead, for in the sphere of the lovers twin, naught other color is observed save that fleeing red. As Bernini constructs a sainting radiance with the golden glory of the frozen rays, so all without the sanctity of the lovers' sphere within, becomes the light for other days. Exiled then, what occupies the lovers' eyes? save the admiration of a twin—and in the reflection, four lips gently advance, and moored in the desirous trance, the maiden and her lover approach, destitute of all else save hope. When at last four lips meet with the gentle press of adoration. A constituency of warmth and softness proved sufficient to deter their lockèd gaze, to fall, subvert the total consciousness to lips, and in the gravity of this descending wave, recalled that light cast to other days. The cascade of the returning red, coalesced then as the original blue, in the collision then, at rainbow's end, against the protective sphere surround the lovers two. But blinded to this cataclysm, the maiden and the lover, in a moment, with the kiss, begin a life anew.

HISTORY

Should history repeat? and players' feet fill the shoes and walk the same floors of Before, then appearing, with you, bespeaks the lover anew, yet again. Should a wheel spin? and carry the ghost of your kin, so that all come anew, yet again, along with you. Laser-eyed maiden, an iris of silver spun with blue, possess the Mesmer effect upon the guest in view. Then, to shock the memory, reveal the story, of what became of the last two without end. When, profaning separation, some elegant and silent grand curvature in space, swung at an annihilative pace, obliterating from the stage one actor come of age, subatomic transportation, then, of the beginning—or the end?—of that which binds. The soul to the old friend, to parade among friends. Pluck you away to the broad light of day, and tuck you where brightness caves you in, to create that starlike self-sufficient ignition and perpetually sustainèd burn. At the border of Night, the far reaches of your bright, bespeckling the dark are the white dots of souls such as thine, alittering—being the glitter—of what Death claims not! And all upon parade in a given moment gifted yet earned, by the Writer of the page, containing the plot that moves those white-hot dots that feature the golden glaze upon the eyeballs. A massive object, propelled by will and force, shut from some anchoring shore beyond Before, such that with the loveliest grace, you defeat the times' and spaces' claims, to feign ignore the convincing delusive waves that create the marvel of the yore, the now, and the yet-to-be or the *never before?* and pass within your horizon, and gathering in, saint to saint, the lover and the admiration, magnetically attract, harmoniously align, then flare up, in the allegory sublime, of true lovers set free of time.

Out of the Brightness

....of falling early night, the maiden strode toward, a silhouette in black, backlit against the end of day. Unrecognizable save for her distinctive feminine way, of sliding from the hiding of the moments yet be come, though only slightly, in terms of time, beyond phase of the present. Feeling before seeing, for the shadow that was her face, the broad smile, that cried out, *Hello, again!* Inland echo for to arrears, the former fears of the past lover. *I don't know what it will be like not seeing you every day.* Spoken vacantly with genuine bewilderment that accompanies a predicted sudden loss to in the near future come—gifted prescience, she disappeared in a reverie, the collection of every moment spent, shared, in attempt to feel the rent twain love and lover, and the intimate mystery spent of what a one that two may become, when their stars' crossing is heaven sent. What adjustment may be borne? burden upon the morn, when absent of the maiden, the lover is forlorn. Shant recover this stabbing by the Mother, when bereft of beauty, She gloats? as if her duty, to separate in concept the soul and the soul's mate—and then to, once forewarned, too, if in a seeming spiteful spate, and then to make Her presence scarce, so that in the vacuum the loss is ascribed to the Fates. Relieved of the directness of the crime, Mother Divine retires to Her hiding in the time, of the moments sublime, when recognition of the lover lost, falls from those moments upon occasion tossed, when Heaven regrets and pays out fines. And, so, the maiden, slow, passes from the darkness to the light. Growing dim, the days' dying bright, strikes a balance, removes the shadows from her anonymous face, and reappears the lover lost long years.

THE MAIDEN

Blessed with *unstirred* sweetness of youth, the maiden smiled her truths. In acknowledgment for the precious soul within, she is treated as if free of sin, angel in such symmetry, then, correspondent to the Light—she writes away the Night with the smiling pen, that scribes with movement's delightful, musical aetherial. Warmth of idealism remains yet intact, and true beauty in that she existed in potentiality, and granted pass, for the respect a young woman commands—buffer between the trials that shall begin at hand. A flame of Mother Divine, arrival of the Maternal Mind, Who soothes and caresses Her fleshly defined condensations, distillations, extrapolations, animations. She gave birth in thee, the maiden, displaying a kindness, signature of a gentle Infinity beyond this coarseness, here below the yellow moonèd glow, split upon the Summer night's day, with only an occasional ripple, built within a rare, cool August breeze. The disarming bright-eyèdness, and greeting sincerely happiness, she presents a delicate kiss, in a manner as never before missed—for never an attempt. No crudely betraying force, to erase her bending lips, up, up, up, in a perpetually smiling bluff—of would the reality be? a sadness she'd cover-up with feignèd gladness, at perhaps glimpsing, how it ends in elderly years ahead, when even the sinless play the dead, obligatorily! is a last chance for a maiden's joy? conjured from the loving boy, who himself expresses thru only eye and heart, so deeply, disconnected of the lower part, which, as the descending dove, gave origin to *fall in love*. Before the woman'd whole destroy the maiden, she'd basked in the smiling moments of that higher love above, the saintly meeting of the greeting lips, save only to a breath withdrawn, from another she'd loved, to then exhale, share with all.

DRIVER OF THE DRIVEN

Aloof the maiden flower waits, waving in suspended grace; though inanimate, she hunts with her passivity, preys upon the desire for her face. In loveliness, whips a frenzy in that *lesser race*, inflates their glowing souls, basks in the light they make; incendiary causticity, her brushfire becomes a rage, ignites by contact, making combustible, by intensity, even the wet sea. At the base of her, all calmness and control. The spying of the hurricane's eye, vantage point extraordinaire—she, the maker of the lair. And flying all about, the desire behind, the brush fire, had blown her own burning out, now that the gravity of intensity would insure continuation of the fire storm of desire. In their madness, the blindness of the specious lesser, hypnotically advance upon the cantor of the dance, convenient gripping horns atop their heads, she takes hold and grasps, and knives a lower artery, to make bled, the demon in their stead. To feel the warmth of her tender lips, and the stillness before the kiss, juxtaposes from the dichotomy, of the fire storm that even eats the seas, and of the airless, motionless, land of creation, where dwelleth all souls unengaged, dupeless, giggling at the bizarre duplicity, of the soul, and the attendant clinging flesh that makes it whole. The maiden flower able to tower above the insane desire, to steer it by the horns, miraculous ability! Seeming unconsciousness, the losing seat affects itself, infects itself with sickness of a heart. The sweetness of the maiden flower's breath, calms and soothes, the insane, once access'd been gained.

INTERESTING HOUSE
AT POINT'S END

You admired the blue in the sky, from beneath raisèd hand, shadowing the late afternoon sun from your eyes; cloudless, save the long bank lingering atop the farthest horizon—just this side of night. The sea, calmly spread before—and after—lay quietly looking up, reflecting back to its mate thoughts of individuality, since they were nearly the same. The lighter liquid, sky, echoed a longing for transformation toward the heavens. Midsummer warmth acknowledged as a breeze upon bare arms, and the feeling of freedom on loan from seeming endlessness. The walk resumed Northward along the shore, toward the interesting house at point's end. Jutting West, the point boldly took a stand as last bastion of man and woman alive on the beach, before the sea carved sharply Eastward the land at water's side. A lighthouse of sort, the interesting house made for a satisfying destination on the daily walk. The point lay just this side of exertion, when accounting for the return trip, ahead of time at walk's outset. Any further, joy then became effort, strolling, strolling, strolling. The sun teetered on its totter, poised to sink into tomorrow—and jealously glowed orange to boast that it alone brought the end and the beginning to time. Outraged at the audacious sun, a flock of gulls madly gave chase to prove it wrong, which they did daily, but would settle, as always, in exhaustion and for a warm meal off the sea top instead, when it became apparent that the sun, no matter the boast, was no liar. Standing before the interesting house at point's end, still the gulls in their dismay in their complainant cries at distance, silhouetted in swarm against the orange afterglow of the now set sun. *Who could occupy the house?* and oversee for posterity the lifetime of such disappearing suns, to witness, in habit, day on the run, from the balcony.

UNIVERSAL NIGHT

From a memory, herald a dawn in love. Darkness, which had bereft the stars of light, invented the tune of night. From mere desire, the lover of Love, created fire for the heavens to suspend, again, as stars bright. Encyclic, so, the low created may one day unite, to the love in the Lover of Love. From across the vacancy between starfields, she collects the thoughts the lover yields, and, separate, resigns the pain that the mortal feels, having had no hitherto reason to be sad. Astral journey subterfuge, a memory, then, forgotten, of that, galactic transit to the end and out; what cosmic lovers' love is about, if not swift passage under lease, past the mass of Darkness' policing, wonderment never ceasing, to distract without actual adhering, some valiant flyer, a would-be all-seeing, soaring higher, higher, across the vacancy.... *What is it?* to be overlapped upon, superseded by the *Bringer of the Dawn*, such that desires prove to be the light of fire; when Darkness is so hungry for the black of night! But what Love repairs to, may ennoble and engift, make apt the flyer, to span the stellar rift.

Two Maidens Swimming

If womanhood be vested in the maiden, and all that wisdom gained in yore, be blessed upon two young maidens, and have them swimming, then see beauty come to fore. A generation of only several years, prepares the younger for tomorrow's cares—perhaps—but gaily played out aquatically, splashes spectacle for posterity. Can happiness so readily be? between other than the eternally free, among those still felled on earth. Grace distilled, instilled in slightly less-than-woman, makes believe the peering into a future yet to be, that all of tomorrow's growth collects for the instant now being lived, for the two young maidens, to be used as an equipment base of adulthood—and so the conundrum of the juxtaposed, small physical age offset by the display of wisdom and grace, created in these two a new human race, if but for this short movie of theirs, a reality? The elder shot beams from blue sky eyes, to penetrate thru, the coldness of reason, which makes slow to enjoy the breathing and the moving about in the day-to-day. *Behold two sea nymphs at play!* To smile with such familiarity and ease, before an overseeing Mother Divine, to act as if aware of Her admiring eye, or for Her pleasant desire, shows as if to win Her sacred higher, for which each motion of the two were a step up toward; and that seemed all they knew.

MADONNA FROM THE SKY

She came at last, to dance upon the ferry, cast adrift. Woman from the sky, to then walk the earth, again, to then set assail to the lover's wail. Blessed misadventure and the chatter inconsequent ignited into the fiery dream, of admiration, for the scene of you in white blouse and slacks of blue. To appear as if in mirror, to adore the lover as the lovèd. Triangulate a voice to source, and pulling down from heaven's rest, add a face, call then upon affection, to post the greatest test. At behest, then suffer in the dark eyes of this lover, in reverse, in mirror, so, hence the replica of hope other than the one. Having set foot upon the ground you yet brought not your flyingness down. How simply and perhaps not known, you alight nearer to home than that or those years in fear that careered you. Spectacular glory in your kiss, in the unfurling of your braids, that disrupt the peace in the still air you'd made, with the water on soft perfumèd breeze, of brushing by of hair just freed. Woman from the sky, warm lips do connect to upon this sainted trek, of flying high though passing by, the ferry on the waters, under cover. Held tight—would you fight? or dream delights, in celebration with your Divine Mother, for Her shared nature. Would the warmth in feeling suffice? too nervous thru the darkest, endless night, as the new lover found.

THE MISSING

The thousand faces that grace the gazes every hour, the one or two whom one knew. It seemed, oozed some glue of identification, which held in grasp firm, an attachment of recognition distant yet strange familiar then in the fleeting eternity of seconds lasting hours is established a bond of wont, that reopens doors onto memory's shores, and all a sudden, on this Vista Grande, the thousand other faces that grace the gazes ever hour, became the true religion of the fellowship of souls: human vessels partitioned off of Spirit whole. Reflection in a million eyes, instant truce beyond Maya's lies, reunites in the sameness, a familiarity blameless of conspiracy.

Two Maidens
near the Sea, Waving

The Spring flowers blossomed in the sea breeze, smiling faces adorning twin graces; hand to forehead to shade the sun from the eyes, this pair of sprites braced for fun. Breeze of the sea, aire in their hair, laser-eyed dare to the bewared! *Caution*, while running again, pulling alongside, attempting kinship in soul's fame, regardless of name. And laughter: the two collapsing into, whips cracking, dual strikes off of mirthful lightening, in opposition—standing waves, in cooperation, a blissful haze, casting about, blinding thru pouts, disabling via the clout of loveliness, in the moment of peace and stillness, per hours of dynamicism. And laughter. Commingling joys of tandem ploys, to secede Finity's limits, befriend the world of comedies without end. Though distinctly separate, the harmony in tune of two birthed in June, made of division a unity of one melody, a sole orchestration of soul ministrations. The gravity of players awake in the dream, complicit in the acknowledgement of grand secrets—the secret unveiled before knowing, mystery stands starkly naked, in comedy twixt such friends in wisdom. Drawn by the magnetism of similarity, two maidens near the sea waved to their third party. Behind the onshore breeze, from one corner of the global continuity of the liquid sky, the forth wind sourced from on High; aetherial wings attract light beings, for travel upon these squarèd aires. And, so, two maidens near the sea, waving.

Inner View

She was in a flew—shuttling with hurry to find the key, remedy to insanity. Escorting along the shot, Maiden Beauty sought what's not. Dawn the corridor, where light gave way to the shadowy Evermore, then into an interior room toward which hangs an odd-locked box, upon a tall wall. Flowing golden hair, horizontal upon the aires; speeding, a dashing pair. And then the sudden end, golden hair dropped to a vertical, again, as you stood still and upright, fumbling against the backlit night for words to fill the absence of the light. Strange glow, eking, though, from the atomic constituent black, in which the beauty you donned a blue hue that in day sun, lacked the youthful face, dollike in the fainted light, was presented a surprise to at last arrive, at so intimate a space—a world disappeared of all but two, and the odd-locked box, inside which hide its infinite keys, cracking down into perpetuity, Maiden Beauty was longed to be, warmly kissed for posterity, yet coldly older than her heat, the Maiden Beauty chose retreat. The blue hue was given rift, as she backed into the red shift, as the distant stars often do, when seeking a farther galactic new. Having cooled, she attempted to open the odd-locked box, with its infinite keys, by grasping firmly at the edge. Relinquishing not, the cover on the odd-locked box, she tugged again, but in vain. And then, turning to, her brilliant eyes' beam from that far galactic new, and she took a shift toward blue. Then a gentle hand, rose to, and then effortless, gave way to one who knew, the cover on the odd-locked box, with its infinite keys, which inside hide.

Maiden in Questioning Mood

Bright face, the beauty with honest question, wanting to rule the place, with her sweet infection, of stillness, and radiant smile. She tugs upon the cigarette, sits back relaxed, legs crossed, stares into the night beyond the storm of day. *Why don't you eat meat?* she issued fast, the pat repast, of verbiage, complete. 'For health reasons.' She wines, and freezes face, not satisfied in the least. *I always thought eating meat was healthy.* 'Plant protein is far more healthy. No cholesterol, less fat, fewer calories. It's what nature intended.' She seemed a scare, with that. *I could never eat a baby cow. Do you feel healthier?* She tugged again at the cigarette. 'About the same, really, after ten years.' She shrugged, stamped the butt, and flew to away. *I still love the taste of steak.* The glowing maiden in questioning mood, disappeared from memory, consigned to that which stood, for good and loveliness. A tiny fire, the fierceness of the hire, for treading into the liars country. How the vagrant maid, had stumbled into such a state, as that that had her waylaid, may be one of the great conundrums. Then she blew a kiss, and drew her sword, and then some blood. The humbleness of her rearing left her restored, in that she retained the hold upon her fierceness, and that sustained her.

Maiden Who Was Kind

Softly the maiden asked. The gentle face of the youth sublime, all filled with the electric vigor wine—yet holding it all subdued, beneath, at the table. She sat across, so near. The sweetness of the life unlived, yet expected soon would be here; the words of idealism formed and passed from her lips, and careerism, too, which they applied, ne'r her character denied for a person full of care, was the Beauty Maiden Youth, with her higher aires she bared, so natural to sit against, with her kind and inviting spirit, preceding her. The unexpected, interest in the matters of the world, pushed by well-formed opinions of the political winds, and how they whirled. A brief, sweet kiss upon her cheek, to welcome home some joy that she had shipped out in the form of the money, 'ahoy, mate!' greetings she'd issued over the span of not yet twenty years. But then the full-on mouth-to-mouth, taking both of the breaths out, made for a silent retreat into the alter-selves, that were sharing. The fleeting escape into the kind maiden found the spate toward disintegration of the respective alienations that had heretofore been an infection. The melding loss of selves, gave two a brush with the hells that animals find in zoos—but that quickly passed with the continuation of the slow kiss, as paradise fell from the heavens, and kindly, upon the maiden and her lover.

CONFERENCE

Annarrested, protested, the new madonna fought. From silver white fountains in the eyes, sourced a protective field, intangible but felt by its magnetic yield. Zoetrope, then, as reality caved in, gave way to battle, as the new madonna and her lover attempted to occupy the same space; the flutter of imagery, as if a slow projector beam, and, in review, the déjà vu—the *already seen*, as the end became the beginning, of past lovers renewed—again. And though she carried the child of another, the sacred space it occupied within the mother, had been previously laid claim to, by this same insane lover who now cherishes even that failed attempt to become one in the today of this foray—blessed Halcyon at play, in the broken light of that Zoetrope flutter, painting a day in electric night, upon a wallèd delight. The precious few, inches between you, and the moment of union, in annihilation, following the meeting of lips. It was only in the accident of admiration that forgiveness may be granted: What crime, helplessness? A moonèd earthen shore receives the light of heaven's bright, simply because it lay in the way. And the curiosity of your familiar face, slew without a willful trace, left to deny you that separate space, you fail never to grant your grace. And the unborn child foretells of that brush with hell, circular reentry into insanity of human make, that journey all souls take, for apparent love, until the darkness it forsakes, exits materiality the ascending dove, to never again make such mistakes, of Original Sin. Some sense of hate, from you, though, as diversion of admiration, splay you from your current mate—all a work of the Grande Imagination. The trifle rage in your voice, as the lips prepared to be kissed, soon to be erased by the Soul Light rushing in to solely occupy your space, leaving you safely intact in your separateness, spared the lethal contact with admiration that would incite the dying of your dream today.

MADONNA WITH CHILD WITHIN

Unborn, and therefore compresses the light, of two souls lit brightly against the Night, of earthly day. Some new act to play in for her. Sharing an elevator ride, she beams, and fills the inside of the car with the mysterious orbit of her Self, and reaches far to the beyond. Then motion happens within the sphere so that it is found that motion is the movement—and the soul has always long stood still. Floors flew by, and characters behind invisible doors, nightly stood waiting for their ride. The self as observed from the inside—the radial catch of silver white irises of her eyes—shot lightening. Backing with force, all firmity—seeming holding it fast, by her one self, but even in the world of invisibility, her one gave way to boundary, and expanding and though endless, still allotted quantity, some separateness from the Maker of her one, Whom had become she. The ego clings on for posterity. And unblinking, she fried gazers with those lightening eyes; and hard to ascend such power, but with a gentle kiss. Their soul descends her tower. And landing down, love standing down, she forgets without frown, for the joy of the expectant mother. Now twice as bright, the quantity delight, from the Maker of the night, cascades the waterfall, when held tight, but gently so, and induced with chatter, small but directed banter to laughter, which feeds the lightening in her eyes.

(UNTITLED)

A reappearance, in directorship of the maidens, gave evidence of a fallen grace, of perhaps of the sublime trace of the Madame's beauty disconnected from all things earthly. Being involved with the show, the parade of the maidens, somehow diminished in image the one who had been a seeker of peace, of solitude, or quiet, heretofore. Perhaps, acting as the mere coordinator, or as contributing producer, she had played her part from distance, mechanically at bay. And in such a way, she was merely the businesswoman on retreat. But the beating of the maidens' feet, en mass, upon the stage. And the selling of tickets to be thusly entertained. At such a delicate age—would their light suffice to prevent the fall of Night? Or would, could the monsters in the air extract those angels from being there to a fearful disappearance. The soft thumping then upon the stage, were the butterflies falling from the skies with wings strapped back by the monsters of the aires, and the horrors that they bring. The predatory Alliance versus the Purity that sings, and dances interlocked in mortal affair, in the shadows of the death of such things. Darkness eludes the day, and the ways of light.

GHOST AND A MAIDEN

The sweet simplicity of her kindness meets, with a record of the youth to keep. When at one angled glance, the sure face lay upon her cheeks, such that She is the one she appears—but at another angled near, she exposes yet the lass she used to be....In ebony eyes, she withheld the lies, that layered upon the heap of, flesh to see; though lovely at a glance, if a moment's intense gaze may be all, that she sustains, in that lovely angled view. How secretly she whispers thru, the space separating yesteryear and now. Seeming familiar, yet that face beneath had never seen, though warmth be in those lying eyes. Inadvertent then, her disguise. Yet, the sincerity, though deep to see, was a matter of reality. Though the face beneath was bothered by, the trapping it had sustained, and slightly bewildered at the loss of the cherished name. This ghost alive within, did compete with the maiden it did not claim, and the tension thus created, berated her happiness somewhat, as in the corners of her thin lips, the twinge of fatigue at the continuous cheer of maintaining a partly forcèd smile, in public service. How to kiss those lips? and disregard the ghost she hid, possessing aetheric lips own—eking what pleasure they may have imputed to them, in the physical way. The passing of the ghost, had little call for the toast that some so anxious to go, often boast. Hanging then, in that netherland, the ghost awaited the surfeiting of the maiden's hand, that to be carried by a host from Then to Here, at a spatial temporal command. Entirely unknown to the sweet maiden, that she harboured such an other spirit than her own, which to the intently glaring admirer, was plainly visible, interrupting the spell the maiden had cast so well. To the forgetful or to the denying admirer, or to the blind, kissing the maiden's lips, and the cohabiting ghost would do just fine.

(UNTITLED)

With a back turned to, the maiden created storm; some yogic past elucidated in the coal hair well shorn, dangling to at rest, with perfectly straight, surest, passing the gravity test! as may an aetheric one be. The blonde in the iris of the eye, an European bridge? not typical of notoriety, perhaps even further East. The flank of, outlying hand of the ancient India land; Mataji most blessed this maiden, for a moment facing on, the radiations—soul emanations—flowed from earth's beyond, habitation of the astral nation mirroring that before, within which the color shift, reversed from red to blue, created from subphotonic matter, the building blocks of you. The sudden gust, a gale from the pale, passed between two with shouldered squared off, a perfect box within which was borne a microcosmic of the dawn. In such a way, two lovers without embrace, create yet another, some third entity, still yet living, silent yet musical, peaceful yet dynamic, a perfect breath of a share.

Two Maidens

Exuberant youth, mistress or maidens being truthful. Some ghost that grips and haunts, inhabits thee, and, pairlike, promenades from eternity, where aerie forms flatter the modernity, of looking without seeing. And some ignorance causes thee to be, a player out-stepping unity; the resultant truncated memory. For instance: the space was rent of darkness, beyond the pristine panes of glass, which mentality and figuring had held amast; to shudder with the night, the loss of the sacred sight, of your face glowing of the light, within. How lonely is the office who, is vacant in the absent you. And remedial prayers for your return, silently go unheard, lost between the uttering lips of your lover admirer, and the ear of your Divine Mother, somewhere in the darkness, other. You! two maidens, preparing pawns of the dawn. Harbingers of that vacancy, the project of duality, when expectation's claims on you, mistress, fell thru, in that emptiness that one held you in view. Like some vast production theatrical, lights, stage, set, you invigorate and animate, *and play!* only to withdrew anew, another day. Your disappearance in form, shall not mourn; for in reverie, intense scrutiny, the beam carrying your scene, alights within the astral night, and you come in. The desire to begin, again, with you, and a moment of unity spent intuitively, between two, the meekness with which you whisper from your lips, the *I love you*, in passing, caught in Fates' pinch—the end of tax season—and of the overtime nighttime you—and the reason for the meeting, the brushing by, in night's sty, starlight's eye.

Cabinet Room Behavior

She blinked. The infinitely thin glazing upon the surface of her eyes, disappeared, dried as if to die, as the Beauty Maiden Youth pretended her truth, as cabinet room behavior. Reflection on ice, unaware of the face that'd been given life; some twin in animae, subject to the sin, the hoary caving in, of the will upon which is built the flesh. In gray iris, a Winter sea not so distant passed, lived eternally, frozen in mind; the sunshine of desire, rising as if upon morn, to drive her life toward her stars, shining on without the care of night, to mock the common sense that all will end alright. There is a fury in the innocence of the Maiden Youth, which calls upon Darkness for assistance against the Light. Noting death the express, hellish flight, for a room of rooms to find delights. Had a mission in the night—starless skies— she had ne'r landed, visitor from the Madonna's right, Beauty rolled around her mile, weighed the seconds in her smile, and the hours, if it be miles that separated her, from her admirers. With the ramblings of a heaven's peace disturbed of slumber, she rent the physical into two, in the wake she spent on a life anew. All of Maya's drama drew, true lovers to you; and the bother of all others. Spring fresh in the sling of dope—or the disorienting hurl of the ecstatic twirl, of youth in motion before possibility, as if never before—or ever again—Beauty knocking at the door! Blessed grin and a coyey nod, time had reset, again, beneath the moonlight of her truth, basking in. The quaking cast of the mantle earth, donned upon her former berth, when angel's fell for entertainment, some god's mirth. So, Lucifer behind the scenes, made an angel glow in Spring, to fall into a human being, and run into the wall of trial, fencing the endless physical mile. The ghost amockin' you, yet escapes your view, but snuggling beneath your beast, as if a shadow, to do unconscious behest, a mimicry of spirituality yet somehow more alive, to another life, selling out unseen, unfelt, in just the slight offset time, to act invisible before the eye—but felt in head and heart, some meager proof of a Grand Disguise. Kissing slowly your lips, or stealing your breath from you, makes the lie alright. These terrors in the night!

WATER FROM THE SKY

The maiden stood aswagger, dressed in crème. Beneath a long, slim coat, she glowed supreme. Hair tied back in a stressed bun. The crowning radiant showing, then projected, blew from the face anew; only two decades of sunrise had it greeted. The girl within had given way to a masculine firmity, while, though effective in a world of man, made her feminine grace defective—save for the intensity of the strain. And preparing to meet her end, in the waves, in the water overhead. The cracked shell, retainer of the wet hell, which waved, when given it momènt release. She contemplated the flood from above, and swimming might produce a floating device, what survival might be composed of. Having run the entire affair, that the chargèd aires beneath her hair, which her massive brain focused in pinpoint, the model of sane, upon what the soul might gain. Resting in bliss, the white ring around her frame, extended with the Bernini radial quite attendant, down to the caboose of the train. Training her gaze upon the fix, it was the eyes that smiled and beckoned the kiss, upon the lips, of one so perfected in the effortless grace, she performed the swim, when the bottom of the water-hell shell caved in. And a dozen ways to escape eluded her, before she disappeared—but not before the intimacies were exchanged, that love might outlast her temporal frame. That kiss lingered still, in the lover gone insane in her absence.

Asleep but Not Unaware

Her eyes closed, and head nodding down, the maiden entered dreamland. Not seeing all surround, she nonetheless looked elsewhere, *otherwhere*, in there, emitting from still lips not a sound. And though here asleep she was there quite awake; eyes closed but open upon another space, she roving upon at lightning pace, passed division in the race human; a life dream in a world real to her yet that seemed incontinence on the continent, of the conscious scene. Draping down, auburn hair, reaching to the ground, some standard fare to the fore, of the motionless—for to adore, long, svelte the guardian of help to a Mother Divine, dining on Time. Reaching out thru spaceless space, timeless time, the Hand Divine, to manipulate, that which lacks for heaven's sake, that which frails in the tomb, to make. That fires freeze and the ices to bake—the stuff that by day attracts the lover's make....And then at last, in Winter's blast, when frozen risks upon her corpus doth take, with anxiety, she feels piety—for her next mistake! And come flooding in, her suspended breath, again, and thru her heart stabs the blood stake—and she is fallen down alive? again. And opening eyes, peers at large at what lay, and feels the charge, the thrill of familiar light of day.

Fall

The delicate Spring of Fall, resets for seasons, brings joy to all, for rest, as if for some grand reason. And in that delicateness, the awesome sound of thunder of lingering fear, that discolors the rainbow beauty of existence. And in the morning, when gazing into the mirror above, Krishna's flute is resounding near—yet softly, and with musicality, such that all attention is withdrawn from the world of the lesser dawn. And in the light of the flute delight, the bright music wafts as though smoke of incense pipes, with alluring fragrance, the sense of bliss beneath the nose, that the body rest yearns to also know. Transitional elite, the music at thy feet, which touch'd all—Fear retreats, touch'd yet on, and Fear admits defeat. Then what remains of night? when the darkness lifts. When the line distinguishing the dawn lay abstract and no longer seemingly continuously withdrawn. And then a sun rises in the maidens' eyes, and, burning brightly, hot whitely, the smokeless fire rings the irises, the circle, portrait of Eternal Higher, portal to infinite energy anchored in soul; then the rolling roll of laughter cascading out of her silence, stillness, for the Bernini radiance divine, of St. Cecelia in ecstasy. The humble nod of the quiet maiden, bowing to the source of the fires she feels to be all consuming, beyond purest desire, for That Which Lacks Radiation, for which even the colored lights of the rainbow appear, in comparison, gross.

Marianas

Running, too fast, too beyond control, thru the Geneva rain. And, although damp, the clothing of the maiden and her admirer, would not wet, despite the insane love affair, the wet was not for the inane. To want love without the need, to brightly smile at caring deeds, of the lover fleeing in the Geneva rain. Some hint of Olympus guesting, for, the magnanimity of heaven's besting, in the light of real day, of the human ways. When immortality came to call, within the raindrops' fall, but to more than observed get, the lovers must the rain drops wet, and in the Geneva rain these lovers just felt damp yet Olympian, if but, for some other writer's whet, Olympian nonetheless; though immortality can not be kept—while the writer dreamed, these lovers slept. And in the scene, eyes of green separated the snowy caps of mountains just set back, as if some toy to contribute joy to the dreamers in the dream. To predict when strangers met, based upon the bet of the writer and another, may seem the height of cruelty—but hidden deep in plot discrete, the whereabouts of lovers truly, brought into reality, in seeming obscurity, to the lesser seers not afire, running with the lover's white hot feet. Cast aside and adrift, a love on a long lost ride, aboard a boat too small to hide, the dreamers from the dream. So overboard with the white heated feet, of lovers in defeat, into a deepest ocean rent, where to collect and to keep, as the rain fell wet upon the Geneva street.

BUTTERFLY UPON THE
MAIDEN EYES

....doth flutter when she blinks, from behind dark spectacles, window on what she thinks, this side of paradise, for which she so with care, prepares. Sitting to a dinner plate, the maiden converses with casual extraordinariness. Long, straight, light brown hair, is moved in graceful swifts, upon the aires, momentarily there, and here, and there, invisibly caressing, at the seaside. Fluid motions of slender fingers, play silent instruments, making unheard music of the synonymous waves that top the sea and create individuality, for the maiden, by her ways her only own. Conversing with another occasional bends appear at the corners of the mouth, so that arching ample lips, have bent into a perfect smile, when with tremendous ease, seems to also float upon the breeze. And sympathetic arch identifies from lips to lower back, though perpendicular the angles match; at attention she sits, as if awaiting resurrection thru an inner view on the spirit's insurrection, in admiration of the parallel perfection—the world of matter attempts to attain. And in a swooping feld, the dark spectacles remove, to reveal the almond eyes and painted concentric seals, and black lashes with which to weigh and steal starlight from the stingy night. In absorptive state—a posture erect, gaze on inner redirect, what marvelous yogi she did make! Transmuting both big and small desires, so that in admiration, when she surfaced from her dive into the soul, very little that was physical remained true to pay the toll, or cost of the flesh's desire, that which would set afire, in attempt, what cannot be burned. So, then, more alive in her heaven, and but leaves her essence in image only, in firmity? broadly smiling, at peace.

Requiem for Joy:
the Origins of Selection

Add a marvel to a mystery, for the lover and a maiden by the sea. Captured particulates upon the aires, of windblown specs of this or of that illuminated by a backlight at the fall of night. The sunset right, the proper setting for this scene: the lover and a maiden by the sea, rainbow bridge of diverted rays scattered from the dusk. The deviant colors, suspended above, a compact with trust, as thought the marvelous Nature forever dreamed of, by beings cast to earth and held captive in her bust. And then a populace of distribution, crash-landed souls in search of retribution, gifted an aetheric intuition but not concrete contrition, so that finding higher light in the lower darkness, almost always ends in defeat—if in the glimmering, shimmering eyes of the maiden, the lover searches for why it seems some other conceived-of eternity, when said same is put to bed by the earth-described insane, fleeing out thru the escape hatch in the forehead! But diversion is beyond the interesting, and, the loveliness of the maiden, oh, so alluring, and the magnetism of true lovers almost indefensibly exacting upon the hearts that Romance is extracting—all, again, detracting to Original Sin. So, then, with the bedazzled multitudes, or the scattered children united in the Light but having donned darkly flesh, the individuals who really are kin, see only separateness thru two human eyes and, then, believing in only brokenness, imagine that only in pairing, wholeness is found as an end. Destitute in frustration, at the failings of their separate nations—women and men—two supposed halves attempt to come together in bliss, yet find only annihilation instead, and again. And when the flesh becomes wrinkled and then turned to dust, human memory fails in the process of becoming rust, and then the smallness of division is at last forgot, when the lover and a maiden by the sea find their lost happiness from the dim night lights of each other, but the million sacred suns, within, white beyond bright.

MAIDEN FROM THE SIDE

She knew her inheritance for the view. Not bereft of that which sustains, in the marketplace, the beauty parade. As implanted, enhanced second glances, she gratefully received, though ne'r admired it within herself—to be pleased with what one sees in the mirror. From the point of admiration: hair in a tightened ball at the back of the head, frosted brown as the small second to the larger ball, the main mane upon the head—wound elegance in the rapt suspension bridge that each follicle presented. The long neck, open to the shoulder's rest, where cashmere sweater only just put to test, of daylight's best, the wearing, the wearing, the clinging upon the frame of the temporary insane, with thoughts of beauty, and of the beautiful. Unusual profile in that the aura of white, though descended, repelled the black off night, as if far, far extended, then the imperfect nose and two thin lips pressed against each other. Waiting for a thought of empathy to form the words, to express in individuality the sublime, or thoughts upon the sea. Vast threshold of ancient envy, had created such a face as yours, a failed, eradicated press for grace. But, being more or less dragged in, then, to a life of hidden sin, to wear agreed-upon loveliness, as though a garish robe—such is the startling amount you in return owe—for the attention paid your face. Member of some other race, the bountiful distribution of solace made perhaps in haste, by a vagrant a little too interested in the aesthetics of His task, to make His babies last, far beyond their self-proscribed expiration date. Thus the attraction to the face of the maiden, from the side: the mistaken position that immortality awaits beyond her kisses.

MAIDEN WITH DOWNCAST EYES

Hidden within her thoughts, in silky blouse just bought, the maiden sets about her work. With golden hair, strewn down in wavy cascade, she portrays a thinking model from another age. Fair and blessed, upon her forehead an angel did the best to secure a kiss, from times before the before, only to have it slip to reach your lips, such that you appear always presenting a kiss divine— though this beyond your conscious mind, and being beauty, thrice removed from truth then: once for your self denied, once for the lover who beheld you and lied, and once for the cheating of Time, which, for want of it charade, forbade space to enable pure love to be made. Reflecting a golden light, that hair in flight, projected from much of Night, though tell-tale sighs, eyes declined, expression removed of design, some resignation to the imposition of duty gravely against the will, creating a depression—in at least the moment— based upon despair; and flaunted in your aires; this signature still, the maiden carried on as a beauty laden with gifts unforsaken by physicality, and any chaining cord that it may bring, for posterity, into the sing of life, your silent song, knowable and long, to your lover strong, who in faith and in taking you in arms, and delicately touching lips to lips, displaces back to your forehead, where it belongs, that angel's kiss, from before your first dawn. And with greatest grace, the slender hand moved a hundred glass votives from place to place, such that with heavy heart, your lover observes, you light each candle, and then depart for another place, leaving only memories of the kiss.

BECOMING

...toward the Unseen. Made restitution to the already-been-in-view, such that the beginning is the end, chance to live, again. Soft and gentle smile from across the years, laid waste to what is feared, for that which must be guarded and weighed, that vulnerability of the sane in a declining age. The maiden turned the page...to an audienced applause, the societal way, to ask for peace. The present yet deserted streets, in full the maiden's locking gaze, lifted the vacancy in the scene, to a population. As though observing within a bubble bright, the sacred joy surround, against that noisy tight, to revoke those sounds of the restless night, that the suffering people make. And, here, then, that maiden smiling wide, opening her enlightened inner side, to reveal and express a strange kindness, extant to within her breast, and, loh! delivered from her test of maidenhood—that warmth that wrested her bested stead—separation of the living from the dead, shone in bright darkness, opal harkness, drove the demon from her bed; attacking ghost, hovering, above her sleeping head, slain within the year of dread. And, in the death of evil, only the purity remains, sustains to animate the maiden standing before. The dancing stance of the Lovely gaining force, the woman of the maiden, posed to banish the innocence, of which the higher love is made. Prepared to plummet for the full-in-love, such that ne'r so tall as just before that fall, when to rest, the woman the maiden laid.

Recognition

She melted beneath the topaz sky, into her interior, when in view came one she knew. Removing all exterior, shuffling off the fare inferior, she sat sprawled as if upon a favorite couch, in complete relaxation—though in the real instant she stood, waltzing a stride, brushing by, rushing, save the fixity in the laser eyes, which shot into the heart of admiration. Complimented, the ego relented into blush, and pausing as if the young girl, first attempting displaying curls, for looks, aware of the wake she'd laid. It was the casually in serendipity, that kept her most dismayed. *You don't know me that well, that way.* Incessant heart, beating toward a break, the presence of the lover, and the love that lovers make, stopped her, cold; how, in a second? familiarity grows old, when forbidden kisses have landed upon a true lover's soul, granting satisfaction for the godly half, when the animal prays, *Die!* The lips themselves were left to cry; fallen thru the topaz sky. She carries her former self into another life, where the lover she plays is not the wife, and her former other is now another, beneath the glaring topaz sky. What saintly forms? don royal clings—such as clothing and the ambient aires, that mix with love of the lover pair, such that a bleaching effect from the blinding light, white washes the walls of the material night, within which she acts her parts.

(UNTITLED)

Beaming ahead of season, the maiden took her place beyond reason. She warmed the chill, with her kisses still, and learned from unspoken words, the wisdom of the hills. In intense eye bright exchange, the maiden overcame, what had yet to evolve within, that had yet to go insane—or disagree with the reality of the inane. Her desire to be near, the heart she held most dear, she at last too succumbed, without fear. If personage may ignite, and radiate white light, and emit the fragrance floral delight, though pungent, working, in a way brand new. But the stillness in her kiss, made confidence for two, that unbeknownst to either, any way forward would be okay, and the unpredictability of the passage to a sea unknown but for the surety of tranquility in the soul. And then the breath exchange to make two, one whole. And in, such a way, a carnivorous affair that fled a feigned despair— that forever together my never take to the aires. But the happiness in smiling, she knew well, to post a boast as if a spell, some, Bernini radial spiral fanning out from the sainted glory, in the flesh. Golden peacock, she flowed. Some kindness in her mist to melt what would remain, of the barrier to the sane. First time such a wave of heat, flowed out from her. And that engulfing day, left to pursue her knight. To feel the shudder in your lips as they part; though distanced then, the established hand held tight.

BLEWING PAST

Maiden, when engaged, ascended to a higher range, from whence, in absence of cloud shadows, shone. But the blewing past, oncoming lovers, speeding toward, never not knowing each other, yet seeming never having met! For a great, grande laugh, the players pause to recognize; if in subconscious, or pretense, so, then, what other manner to manifest? then in the gust of the blewing past. Seems all that reality shall allow is all that takes shape for now, in the Naught Hidden, the cognizable. And from that inference: the shining bright, the smiling wide, the laughter tight, the longing eyes—detect the depth of the love before what life was, is shared in Evermore. Unkind separation for the dalliance of the dance, for the pleasure of the Most High Scribe, the Wright of the all plays; His penchant for change! Elsewise, naught the need for the blewing by; for Thy love for two should not die, hostage to the mortal thigh. Disassembled by the instant heat, in the gust of the fleeting feet. Does a lover rust in the absence of the gust? and shall the winds subside? leaving hearts to cool in a Winter's glide; where, in Olympian snows, no two may hide, betrayed by their love inside—for in that lengthened day, the heat the snows make to melt away. Naught left, then, but the two and the heights; Olympian view—the lovers' sigh. Far below, on the green plain, the scene repeats: the blewing past, the fleeting feet, and that sense of suspension into time and in heat; the sudden stopping for a remembrance in the eyes, the familiar stranger cast to the existence in earthly allies, again and again, born and reborn, victims of desire, until the consummation of the fire.

DAMSEL BRIGHT

Smile illumines the otherwise darkness cloaking the persona, as damsel lights up. Spritely dance of friendship divine, she lofts across the room, brown hair and eyes in tow, for the shifting of form, when Beauty does no harm. Failure to warn, as innocence strike, pierces with happiness a saddened heart. Open a room into which taken by the hand; admiration in a name, admonition of desirous fame—steal away to secrecy with a plant of love, upon the wings of doves, to fly around that room. Pause long enough to take advantage of the view, of a harbour still, with waters glasslike, mirrorlike, reflecting stars and moons, and Mars' longings far, to sail the seas with thee, meshing individuality. Windy, overt calmlessness, a gust against the drapèd bust, on the fore of the ship, where observations more, have opened the ancient door, to that room. *Why celestial bodies bother with an errant earth? when they labour hard to support the girth of this whirling, sailing, spinning ball, tugging at gravity's mirth.* Enshroud a happy two, with the bliss of you, arrange a passage safe, withhold the breath two take, deliver it within one spine, revolve it throughout time; give it back sublime, having altered the radiations—begun with two—of an entire nation. The court resides in the hearts, of lovers torn apart, or having never or not yet met, passing judgment upon the actors playing parts. Part human, part gods. What gave permission? to suffering joy, save the players themselves, of the earthbound toys. Lying down, a new love is found, parallel to the perpendicular—inimical clown, baring frowns—staggering thereafter off in a wrong direction from the Source of bliss, trading for happiness with hiss. Sweet maiden, shine on, submit thou to a friendly kiss, and balk not with open brown eyes, to laugh before you cry, at the happy and the tragedy, at lows beneath the highs. She alone knows what good is borne of the lie. Wisdom upon this world overspent on a damsel of kindness and laughter and brown hair. She is loathe to surmise any other way, another play.

CRYSTAL AND YETI: THE BLACK EYELESS SAINTS

In two beings, a gated way. One the Beauty Maiden Youth, the other the feline boy. *What is the source of your happiness?* The Maiden Youth peered back, and where, at once an angled glance gave almond eyes, which now were black. Sweet giddiness of projected youth, burrows into the truth—loving part of the boundless Heart, so that with each morn, afresh a life is borne. And the feminine, with the nurture streak, takes unto her own with obsessive keep, but to befriend all others expressive of her individuality. This technique of smiling at the day, paves for her a lighted way. And the desire to be near her, for the harbinger of love, pulls from the heavens above, some portents of its objectivity, and how generous a God can be, to beleaguer her admirer with the moments beneath her spell—exit utopia, please hold inanimate a photograph of thee, indefinitely, or for posterity. Present thy lips to intercept a brief kiss, impassioned of memory; as the wheel turns, love came 'round again; even after the seeming end—and there, perhaps in shadow or reflection, she stood, smiling. The feline boy, in evening's retreat, focused yellow eyes across the room in purrèd joy, but only in instant, before withdrawing in, past event horizon's might, whence withdraw the light, of his soul, leaving still the dark of night, as the ashes in the sockets round, proved a burning love, for distant God, calling home a kitty. And twain, Crystal and Yeti, lived upon another earth, though a corpus remained to tease, their souls were merged there in mirth. The great blessing of the black eyeless saints, and falling in their love.

(UNTITLED)

Blissful sublime, she prays half the time, and though in the waking state, she dreams aware of the dream, and, never sleeping, shines on. Not sure if the maiden cares of an outside world; dotes upon the life at hand, and powers up that dream machine built inside her mind. Beacon headed, radiate of electric eyes, dancing brilliance of bluish hues, float upon the light wavelets upon an endless deep. Shimmer at the feet of the Divine, Maker of all minds. Populate with downcast eyes thereafter; capture the hovering planetes in a grasp of education, flowering out to the hungry of intellect, while being basic in life's methods—simply a preparation of the meal, taught life's standards without appeal. Visible force, and superior gravity therefore. You operate independent of the sacred state, reason for the trouble made, in the first of place. How the Furies dote upon the masterpiece of you they made. How the lovers whirl around, the radiant axis you! Mother Divine in Dhyana, the virgin huntress slew, all the lovers who would be others than a one, who knew the original thought in you. So some shared wavelength in the schema, to make all else subside; real, then, only that within which your heart-of-hearts resides. Then the fading world. Still, no mention of your happiness...

WOMAN AT THE BOTTOM OF THE STAIRS

A November harsh blew from a frozen North, that'd already cooled to a stop; all the motion was not. The great lake Blue, now drowning in a gray pre-Winter hue, painted on the faces of the breaking waves, spending lives on the last 20 yards of the vast watery grave, with limited grace, for the howling roars escaping thru the foamy mouths of those faces. The lingering sense of life that Summer gave, had fallen beneath the onset Fall, long before, yet the hope of one more flower in bloom still forced the eye to search the long, steep, still-green grassy slope that spilled onto the sandy sea below. Oddly free of a breeze, hinting at the relentless freeze in months to come, and a distant sun hidden behind snow-filled clouds, was unavailable to conveniently if but temporarily, convince the eye otherwise: Winter would come. Green, save the Ever, would die. And yet the dream of an endless Summer relegated to concept, otherwhere. And, so, the inevitability of the broad, seasonal, destruction mocked all the more intently in still aires, juxtaposed to the roiling waters—from whence comes such a force? that woman may stir the waters of earth, yet remain unseen, grand escapade of Divinity, though delicate community, then, as such, as a woman at the bottom of the stairs, that, serpentine, wended ways down the steep slope; countless stairs ending at the shore, at the feet of the woman looking up.

FERRY AT FLIGHT'S END

Militaristic in stride, the maiden pilot emerged at flight's end, hair tied up tight, satchel in hand, faint issue of relief and fatigue, betraying her might command. The slacks and blouse, and non-feminine tie, sunglasses hiding her eyes, added up to a rocket of a soul, touched of a woman's control, shooting toward the heavens, having chosen work that may provide, a nearer God to which abide, as if One were up there, beyond the darkness above blue skies. Up, always up; soaring can be a stairs set, in the face of such a linear One, graphical, Newtonian. Beauty maiden pilot, held out a hand, formed, as if a doll's, in alabaster white, shamed the name of symmetry, in the five-pointed star's delight. She gifted her satchel to an admirer, a driver, to whom she entrusted her life. The female gentle, and the true masculine axe, all in the moment—to Krishna's delight! Maiden pilot, take the darkness from the Night. Give a candle to a star not yet alight, dance across the canvas of the Bright, march to the resting; who may entreat to you? but the lover in admiration, due to one rocket soul, in a deep and chance recognition. With an axe, she chops off the head of inadequate would-be lovers, feigns a destiny with the minority others, then sad and furious retreats, when no true love bothers. Ferry to the water's view, that respite place above competition, nestled against the Lake, to reward in sleep a body that yet held back, again, the rocket soul from arriving into the heavens—no matter how high the daily try. And so in silence the lover admirer drove, and noted how her fading figure glowed, in rear-view mirror; to one whom had the eyes, her divinity showed. She leaned back, showering relief from the corpus' weight upon her feet, and the successful cure, again today, of the critical calculations of lofting a plane upon the liquids of the aires, and alighting whole again, to afterward bare no cares. Maiden pilot closed her eyes, head cocked to one side, smiled to reveal perfect white teeth between red, swollen lips; rounded cheeks, higher than required, bespoke a mind lifted to thoughts above the earth, having dragged the countenances' face along. As she sat for portrait in rear-view mirror, the neck portion, the chin on side, the perfect ear, one small, pierced with a golden post; the flaring nostrils to take in the winds, of earthly lows—again. To place a kiss upon the neck, to take the lobe of the ear as though a candy, to tickle until the squirming tossed aside, the darkened glassèd that black did hide, the windows on that rocket soul. And when the blue iris of the Ohio eyes, did at last shine, the slow candied lobes abandoned for those terrified lips, which then mounted for the taking of the breath—the greeting card of that rocket soul, that bereft the maiden pilot whole, orphan to the heavy earth. Then breathless into the shining Ohio blues, merge the true lovers. Locking irises, rare flowers of human eyes bloom and melt into the astral highs, as two rocket souls streak into the permanent heaven she did seek, side by side.

Blue Madonna

True enough, the heavens painted blue; sense of you there, in paradise, in lightest blue irises of your eyes, meant the beyond became from you, crashing down in momentous surround—the world collapsed because of you. Sensed the Force that upheld the frame that lofted the fleshly insane—the knot tied too tight for the astral plane—and what a battering you take in this lowest world, the lovely mother. What lover would you take? if you could choose another. How Happiness doth bake when hidden dark away from the day-to-day; trapped within the furthest sin—first love having died. What destroys is what has lied. And to lay within the former *lie*, where once love had bed, led to an unintentional demise, following unawares the distracting cries of work and leisure. No hypocrisy, and grand initial attention, intention, and, to no fault of own, or the lover first, that a heart expands to include one other. And, as if aesthetic bands of some vertical bridge to serenity, with the rising of the sun each day, dark falls upon yesterday. And so, your lips taste new, and the smell of jasmine in your hair was unique, and the warmth of your hand as though a heat never experienced. Having been relieved of bringing salvation to the unrepresented, the heaven upon earth could ready remit past due balances, admit one more god, forget one more mortal clod, who had to dust been commit. Fancy, then, a dance? Blue Madonna, farm-raised past circumstance; met city by chance; chalked up to drama of a life, lover loving Love, another's wife. For that heaven caving in.

(UNTITLED)

Visage on a grassy plane; secure the dancing of the lovers among wild flowers, positioning into the light, the mighty massless dreams, of which you had become, begun. In faint glimmering eye, the power and beauty of all flowers.... Now and then, to begin, again, without peril, or thoughts of destructive greatness—a magician's most wild wonder, when in the arms of that youthful, laughing, lover. And would not the illusion dawn most bright, just beyond the dark of night, in matching ebony eyes, and the timeless flight of the body human. What home peopled on the prairie green, would do without you? Seems that tricking thing that happiness might be en perpetuity, enameled, to withstand a woman's loving hand. Cries of dissention from paradise; disharmonic horror to the right, should that dawn fail to follow the night. Would joy and comfort alight within, the hearts of the two lovers, akin in the peculiar identities shared, reflective qualities, outshining the oddities, would-be sins, the otherwise lacking. Might a master's love bless? the union of the human mess, or shall he smile without? whilst invisible tears rain down the walls of his heart, at the destructive disadvantage of consuming destruction, as Mother Divine bides Her time. How long a lover's love? nourishes in place of a balanced meal; how many hours may last? the dazzling glow of promised happiness? given from another. How can an object return that which it never possessed? Soul diversion is the lover's test.

ATHENA STUMBLED

Scorched rock, atop a mountain, humbly rising above an incensed plaka below, where the crawling masses flow, and not without purpose, or place to go, and, so, destiny has played a broader role. Standing beneath Apollo's bright heat, the noonday hour in hospitably treats, the looker on to a godly wraith! For temporal rifts, even the deathless seek to acquit—as Athena's time had come and gone, with the aging of the flesh, and its passing the failing test! Settling down, while ruins strewn aground, Athena's bump top boast's ghosts: sudden night; torch light find shadows casting fright between the Doric columns tall, to dark Acropoliptic interior, sanctuary small, for the white glow of lovely Athena, dancing slow. Flowing robe, or draped sheerness clinging to tall and frail but vibrant, youthful frame. Sandy hair pinned back above forehead, in a sort of flop—uncharacteristic god, if not for the firestorm in the eyes. Consummation certain for the subject landing her gaze. And, so, in secret, Athena is witnessed to dance. Her glow her own backlight, silhouette of a black star its own, beneath the nebulous mist of light, the sheer, where feminine curves undulated clear, in synchronic motion to silent orchestrations. Frenetic pace, a forgotten self, from the dizzying whirling, twirling, the goddess stumbled, and fell. From amongst the shadows, the hidden witness flew, and between the first and second injured goddess cries, the human lover had arrived, to scoop in arms the dancer fallen from the heights. Seeming mortal blood-soaked knees, the gods also bleed?—beneath—the sheer. And in startled near Athena trembled to the human touch, the holding dear. Apollo had set ablaze each eye, so that to meet her gaze, was to see the sun, and heedless die. But Love loving Fury borrowing two night moons, cast occluding solar eclipses across those eyes. The coronas burned, yet soft, to illumine the lover long lost, and if but for a moment's toss, played the goddess human. The lowering kiss, of the contacting lips, the subsequent heat of incandescences, threatened to burn from head to feet, both the goddess and her lover; and the kiss withdrew her breath. The lover, breathing in, in an instant became a god. In the moment of a crossing, two interdimensionals meet as souls, and equals. And, so, a marriage for an eternity in a second's bond, before the passing on, a woman and a man, goddess and a god, dance, absolutely still, frozen in their warmth upon the Acropolis floor.

FLIGHT

Radiations facing out, such that peering sunward, may burn the eyes to gaze upon. Compact pilot in the feminine guise, pulls a living from the skies. Mother Divine, condones a daughter aires, the maiden flies up there, beneath the heavens above the girth of earth. What pea to squeeze in between, slipstream at stars' feet, sparkling in the glassy night, when soaring after dark. Gentle maiden, read some music in the winds of time, flying, trifle of coloration in sensation, from one's admiration. Still the bird in the cage, though with opened door, staring into Evermore. Beauty reflecting grace; knowledge supplanting haste; gray iris kindred to the clouds; sacred task to carry those across the murky nothingness above, so, Charon in a way, Cerebus at bay—or what the body fears to lose, from the sudden fall from Grace's space. In the lover's glare, suffice to share, only the silence in those aires. Figure cutting into the Bright, all resounding in the night, maiden at flight. Bleach from weightlessness the right, to dominate the reward of leaving home, if to evolve away from such as the maiden, then preserve to form and chain to earth, where mass and matter create a player; for without the tendency to aether, and ultimate invisibility. Rely upon such differences, to drive the love affair with flight, and the flyer—sweet kiss upon the gentle pilot's lips, to keep you in your travels far.

CHAUSEA: BRIDGE TO PARADISE

Shimmer in the brilliant night, may be some holiday. Polite, the traversing of the bridge to paradise, bay waters to the left and right, awakened from the Winter's frost, to reduce to light, yet waves beget waves, into infinity. As of the school, unchained free and brainèd, loosed upon the Summer, the giddy thrill to discover, knowing you, awaiting in the heavenly blue, as if no one had been away, even for a day. And find you smiling, eyes rolled back into Bliss' observation. Had to admire you from afar, just to have a window on, the fire held in your jar—hair and eyes of night—a painted silhouette against the light, shining in your face, illuminating the small group, gathering who, held in place by the gravity you provided to their space. Island of white sands, forests, and blue waters, open skies, and temperate daughters, don the cloak of joy; bless the souls who labour beneath. To have you there, to return to in the Spring, after long the frozen bare—the marriage that existed nowhere, else fantasy trump reality. And see a tragedy in the Divine Comedy. You spoke beneath the stars, of the Christ who'd voyaged far, enough. The kissing of your lips, against the moonlit strip, of sacred-ever-after sands, of the holy land. Together alone—such the language the lovers speak, anywhere together gone, lay within paradise's reach. Transcendent falling of stars in eyes of night, reflect upon, long and silent, and filed away.

ORIGINS OF SMOKE

In Mechanical City, you, defining pretty, mademoiselle a ragin'. To be with you at home, to share a cigarette, to scribe a tome of love in expressions in the eyes' passing between two. *What became of you?* Svelte fire, melted iron wire, of which you were made, tempered by the cooling glaze, of the gentle smile. What mother failed to hardwire into her babe? the joy of face-to-face, contact being made, so that on and about the years' spade, dug a life out, that similar smile, and love glimmer in the eye, a matrimony made. Not genes— but electric hazing photographs, are what the future's made of. Sticky energy, clings to souls, mimics heaven's holes, thru which fall thru the colors as glue, and pretty clings the heart to things, what feels lovely and bright, so that in the deep of night, shines the rainbow light, that wheels the souls to lovers right; then dead and back to heaven, again! The turning of the wheel. But fell to earth in front of you, and laughed at an old comedy movie with you, and took in the magic smoke of blue, the cigarette burning you, but your fire made you immune; whence resultant loop, the blue of the smoke flew in you, and the view of it turning over and over, from lips to lungs and in the blood, rushing 'round the thumps, of a pounding heart, ready for love. Post-morte grand mer, an angel peering in thru thin air, from heaven's rest, to grace a long lost daughter of Rumania, to be full animation of her memory explained. How elaborate may of living be? when lovers' heat in youth parades; to be in proximity, the gravity and the magnetism—two foremost forces of fate. Still the tempest rests, when, hand-in-hand, the blue smoke exits your lips, as you exhale. Frail and pale, paradise tenuous exists, in Mechanical City, and ever shall remain, as long as the insane continue to place blame upon the condition of the weakness of young lovers to distance from each other.

PARALLAX

Black maiden in reflection's gaze, graceful mirror of other days; that rocking train window, in which she glories, crazed—yet so calmly hidden away, missing just, reality, but only in the depth perception of, the shadows cast by a Light above, invisible yet divisible, empathically discernable; and irresistible in how the admirer's eye, finds reasons not to die. In the quiet night, sleeping lands lost to sight, when the Guiding Hand rests upon the shoulder of the tired, admiring man, who toils until the morning boils, over with the newborne light, that somehow lived thru that night. What is held collected, though ne'r inspected by the bearer, on account, of a love deflected by the shining things of day. Black maiden, in train window's reflection, drew nearer to perfection, in a land brand new, growing more and more devoid of rejection, with the rising South. A zodiac favoring change, harbingering in a new age, where treasure is not the color a skin; when she comes, an angel on dispatch, a soul mother like no other, sister with a broader kin than her lighter brother; brighter and twice the fighter, than the product of the generations past, black maiden in the train window's reflection knew by heart the names, faces, and games of those whom her hero's slew, and thus usurped their fame, blew into that dawn brand new, aboard the train.

STONE HOUSE ON DELTA ROAD

Sire had piled high the fieldstones, at a low pullover off Delta Road, near the creek bridge. In Summer's heat, the humid aires cement complete, if imagination dares. The fieldstone house returned, stone by stone, to its aggregate home, in the field. The magic of the eternal lime mortar, raises the structure block by block. At the East end of the field, stood a wood, fed access by a lane. To the South, fronting the place, the stony Delta Road, running sunrise to sunset. From a childhood visit, in place of the stone house, stood a barn, tall, gray, and aiming for the stars. And in a cloud of dust, is seen an approaching bus, and suddenly down Delta road, aboard, is a vision of you, as though from a passenger's view, in a seat behind: In image a reflection who, disparately separates reality from the Infinite Consummate, or quickened light. There in portraiture, in the window at night, internally lighted. And your seeing into the window mirror, the dark marbled eyes at angled in; the slender ebony neck, to suspend, the seat of the collective transparencies: the gravity holding together the photographic memories, of a life—that *is* the life. While all the while the glaring into the windowed night, at the other lighter, darker half—at once close yet far reaching past; in image only ne'r shall the midnight last; thus descends the pain, fast, and ends....Immaculatta: the slender arm and hand, and blackened skin to retain the tan and liquid red, gained in the equatorial sunshine land. Bringing home, ringing as if to own, a lover to the mother. Strand in, some absurdity, to the land's end at Delta road; heaven caved in, here, yet paradise bade-forebode, for the lovers, black and white—too short to pay the toll. And the fieldstone home remained empty.

AT IMPORTANCE

To fall upon a cause, as if a spilling oil, to spread out in fingered rails, and never lacking animae—the great expansion of the soul in infinite ways—filling voids, creating all the days. Mistress passed beneath the lights, into the dark of night. Felt you, mistress, move beyond the view; power beam rapt the attentive eye, the girth of guiding sight—the gravity in such a gaze! sets a soul ablaze....propensity of intensity, that remarkable, enormous You, in action! A hint of violence, perhaps on account of massive will, images you in iron, still a sincere desire to be happy, laid waste to impressions of forced post-haste must needs for belief, in a sign of joy. The dense compactness, as a result, of you, made easy dreams of strength in the beholding of you. Yes, the *beholding*. Always seeming on the verge of laughter, yet responsibility denied the lofty lucidity to do so. And, so, the remorse of frustration, disappointment, lingered, impressed your lips. The seriousness of resources under equipped, made stress of the ordinary. Besides that you would want to be that large, speaks of the mislead discharge of a work quite personal; then, again, jobs were in short supply! Forceful yet warm—a blessed German in the morn? But Scottish lass, down from a Highland pass, working and with such an attention to detail, never out of a moment, never minus deep focus, beneficial cause, yet saucy more than a hint; a rebel disgruntled into boredom of having to be, not quite cognizant of the ultimate purpose, or She Who had sanctioned it beyond that sunny first day born.

Awesomeberry

The wisp of the maiden youth, draped upon a counter's booth: brightness in her eyes—the glimmer of her truth—decorated and further illuminated, the great stillness that she wore as if a robe. Without motion, a head shortly cropped of hair, hovered in the air, and seemed to disregard the scant form of a body, seeking reattachment—or perhaps not—which the head flung, as she slipped into a moment new, to fetch from the human zoo, some rave determination of beauty. Addressing the similar congress, the maidens became a troop, of Lovely in potentiality, with futures own of individuality; and perhaps the social aspect of the gathering, the desire to be greater than the single self, or to at least touch the concept replete, with residual astral ramifications, manifestations of the Over Spirit, rover of the human streets. The dainty maidens full of play, *playful*, to giggle as the Spring tulips' wiggle, swaying in breeze. What finery, must Mother Divine create with Her feminine winery, to giddy up the drinking-in to intoxicate the lover's eye! A gale invades the stillness' pale, so that the roaring in the ear secedes the heart's spears—its pounding tossed into the veins. What line of demarcation? to declare a separation, between the maidens lips and those of admiration. And then from beyond the distance, she warms by interjection, 'Awesomeberry!' She cries into the night, of the sensuous delight of pastry sweet; so that an agreement, a contractual confirmation unspoken yet writ in the iris wet, lit by radiations of a corporeal joy, temporal in that physical and therefore destined to decline—but how magical the combustion in that moment's oven, when divisibility meant invisibility of that which held apart the maiden's heart, and the reason for her start! Warmth then of recognition, of Self declaring same, two licks of one soul flame. Yet bitter formality, ego of insanity, fought unification, left lingering in the dream the nixed experience of sharing the breath. That warmth of familiarity was all that was held near, not the maiden dear.

LAKESIDE

Some photograph for pertinence, to provide in the time machine, evidence of the lakeside dream, come to fore with a beyond tomorrow. Saw you blush and glow, inflate to the lighted space displaced by souls hot burning by that touching light. It was for an instant; delight seemed so right, to be with you by the sea, the lapping waves in harmony with the color of the day, the whiting sky, bespotted with the tingèd gray, of clouds, yet blue remains the constant to, upon which to lay, the layers of very fine things. With the advent of Spring, the sands beneath your feet warm somewhat the stinging, yet, onshore breeze, for the not-so-distant absence of the ice. Clear nights, mean stars burning bright, in remembrance of the souls' natures, as closely as can be approximated, in a world of vibration, as light. But, yet, vibrationless beyond remain. And so the image sustains: the bundled-up chilly you against the sea, walking red-faced into eternity, of the Overt Mind on patrol this day, observing in the early Spring. Some bird above you, maiden, to extend into the aether. The wealth expanse of the You, within which all beings come into view, and gather at the seams, what heretofore had seemed, division. Unite! in subtraction in the vibrationless Night, in the wind that whips the waves, the sun that shines the ways, the blue and white that paints the skies, whose heights provide the heavens' high, and a board upon which to paste that bespeckled starry firmity in infinity's haste. And that which is not there, the Essence absent from the lair, in which habitates the bear, which breathes the mortal aires, of the body that is its snare. And so the story in entirety—of the human in reality—walking by the sea.

CALIFORNIA

No trifle to see in the warm breeze in sunny February; sacred ocean holding down the shelf, at base of sloping mountains' grace, where Youth congregates, where to feel your laughter in the rare rains, promise of the newly sane, the let-loose from formal education's noose, where the movie stars in motor cars, waving down Sunset, did play host to dreams of other-worldly things—a summation of ambitious ghosts of youth. Your facility with written orations, and a wit sharpened by the pint at King's Head. The intelligent cloud that you carried near, made for a remarkable year. It is hard to say what good may not have passed that way, on account of your being there in California. To be zooming on the down slope of the winding canyon road, and to be alive as the sea crests the horizon, quickly rising into the sky; to be kicked down and out of that sea, with the cut in the thick salty air, the proof that you were there in an envelope built for two, overstuffed with the sea, the air, we. Some shimmer in the darkest eyes, or the black space beyond the blue skies? alittered with the shine of the starfields behind, the great mad mind of Lucifer, angel entrusted to create paradise, who had then fallen and had left Los Angeles half finished, to become the greatest mortal test. To have you to confide upon, even though you now are gone, would a dream be real to *seems*? as with sunshine fallen upon calendar days past, as it had so quickly passed, slipped to beyond the yesterdays. Collected in aetherial cups, of which the mind makes much; yet you sustain, as a smiling ghost, hope—nightmare or the devil—though in history's moats. And such is the power of hope and ghosts, whose youthful daydreams in California may redeem the City of Angels. *Beyond recognition, burn brightly, hot-whitely, images of you in youth.*

Helen

Spatter image, upon a rainy night, of golden haired angel delight; silence in reflection in window tall, barred by darkness beyond, peering into flanel and black, see you standing back, from window tall, then in motion across the hall. From the blackness the angel lands, and counts a heights in terms of hands. Hair straight and long, posture upright, strong, she counters the night. Color proper, some profession to proffer, what remarks one angel from the other? Some Mother divinity shared between individual expressions of infinity, which breathe and shimmer with beauty. In window view, saw you admire into the night, some numbers between the thoughts in you and the sight, as if interrupted, and held, in a moment's suspension, to open eyes in the back of the head, to detect some lover admiring you. Your soft voice yet howled at the night, so that the creature below may be known. And what renounce may the angel make? to appease the devils that in the lower shadows lay. May they hunger for love? just the same, so that to antidote is to tame, the motive power that drives the insane. And then press a thoughtful kiss, to descend from thought to bliss, and break the stalemate twixt. Is it you? or the window mirror, that melts into the rainy night. Holding close and therefore beholden, yet some genius within, from that divinity, overcomes the sin of noticibility, so that indifference to the self, starves your Light back to life! And glow, then, your breath giving in, to feel the heartbeat and history begin, leaving only the you in arms; *You* had fled, so no karmic marks did taint any love into an unhelping. It is the union within with the Light, that gives reunion to your admirer. To see Her seeing you, it is to be in love, anew, and there no devils can win. The harmony of a music in your space, played gently upon the window, the reflection animated into symphony by the rain that fell from darkness. There was nothing need to say.

SPIDERS AND DUST

Mother Divine, disperse into a human work; fine hair upon a maiden's head, removes the dark from the night of dread. Singing with song, with moments of laughter, the weight is removed of the day. Variations of dealing against the spiders and dust, becomes the work that breaks her bust, standing afore, with remarkable attention, delicate fingers move a cloth across a shelf, and in silence she wends her way, through inner workings at the gears of her mind, she patterns thoughts after her lover, whose lips she left warm and wanting only hours before. The separation of a welded heart—something fragile to be held above low and safe, exposed to the abrasive erase, of aerie etchings' high-velocity sends of a turbulent race. She reaches high, in never mind, to bat the cobwebs that Time had accumulated, and measures one strand against her hair, finding a common thread woven there, from an unacknowledged infinite despair—lacking the will, a corpus stands still. And displaced of aiding boosts, she lay fallow, short of the feet of truth. And the spider who had found its calling, floats content on a tenuous string, and never fearing falling. How her two eyes betrayed her one, leading astray a heart belonging to her other—so that in any moment she reincarnates into a life foreign, view strange from an earlier point in the day. How the energy forayed thru and into the eyes, is a universal solvent, deconstruction tool hammering away at what portends to stay familiar in an ephemeral bay, within which anchors a universe composed of a single thought divine. She goes out of her mind but never knows in. Insane, but unaware, the godlet stays beneath human hair, and forgoes a sliding Eternity, anxious to have her home, a land beyond light where freed souls roam.

ANGEL, PREOCCUPIED

The Beauty Maiden Youth, scant angel and, in hot pursuit of her truth; inner gaze intently attached to another, aetherial world, yet two hazeled eyes fall upon one in which she physically resides, so that spilled out from that other side, she has wont of space to hide, and far less amount of intention to, or awareness of, the concept. Angel in the dark light of night, earthly walk far from bright, and lacking that forgotten sight, sweet victim she becomes. How to pretend to not know, again? when, obviously, the physicality, cannot be denied—all that remains to bring, into full engagèd Spring, is the revelation of the wings—hidden somewhere beneath, between the shoulder blades, the housekeeper you repairs to prevent the view; withdrawn to hover of the cleaner's smock. Gleaming promise in the night of day, bright beaming reduction to simple peace, with focus upon admiration of that mirrorlike blue pond; at the reflection of your home beyond. Such sweetness persecuted only by a competing kindness; if you could but take placement in a palmèd hand, to gain protection from this world below—if not from your reaction to it. So thoughts may have been an enemy, were it naught for your divinity, superior in quantity, to drive out the insanity, which plagues the tragic beauties your age. Brush by the admiring eye, continue the work of your face, testament to some Perfection Who created it, appreciated of flight, and wings.

Strawberries beneath the Sun

You stand as though a monument to strength, amid the Summer strawberries bright red beneath a yellow sun. Some beam, you, in white cotton and light blues, and bandanna also blue about your head. Laughter in the eyes, though a non-smiling face, made potentiality of humor an immediate reality. Nonchalance in acknowledgement of the lookers-on, manufactured of exposure to the fields all surround, of green growing things and forests brown, and the absence of souls around. In the silence of Nature Mother's arms, you live a life unwound. The berries you picked, were meant for other lips, made a larger You spread beyond the farm lanes and bordering back roads circumscribing, so that the lesser-fed abroad received the great view of you. If in that vision of the strawberry field, the layers of time and matter may freeze, and with a pickaxe of mentality, chisel away so-called reality, so that revealed behind the alternity, the true origins of what humans see—the star fountains and magic waterless seas, of rainbows of sacred sincerity, of a blissful Thinkingness divided into sole thought, to which adheres one of countless selves offshot. To know you and to have access to your giving, was to have lived a life divine. The whisper of the rustling corn, the hushing request of the wheat in warm breeze on evening's brink, called out in their language, your name. And following what seemed the longest time, you glanced in this direction, and looked up from your work, and waved, as if your arm were nearly too heavy to lift, as if to demonstrate affection in excess, were to diminish your true love behind it.

Timeless Torso

Without face or legs, love graces entire ages, in sculpture and photograph; a torso of the feminine, though lacking in identity or name, pronounces nonetheless, in infinite fame, what specific half of the race parlays, incarnate Beauty—so specific—woman may in some familiarity in recognition of the breast and thigh, the curvilinear contour that catches the eye, of hypnotized admirers, casts the spell of desire, that delusive licking fire, which will not end until the admiring mind bends, and invites within the Creator of greater the sin, of choosing touch over the eye. In aesthesia a fugue state of epileptic appreciation from nature's shapes, the drain of Darkness' escape makes yield for colored lights and golden subtle heights, wherein dwell thoughts alive, independent of the thinking minds, which proceed them. So that the lips that kissed and sucked the breast, gave reason for a birth, created of the lovingness, that propagates the beast of flesh, to trap or host, a holy ghost, to burn and tear—what man fears most—some descended dream, consort of Unreality, to demean the reality of immortality. No lips or feet to kiss, on the timeless torso, whose absent parts make seem present even more so, the ideal of beauty and grace, complete. It is the miracle of this sculpted piece, which commends the eye to seek beneath, for the template of the model's soul, where in a land beyond, Love projects her whole. But here below, this splintering effect divides, makes mere beliefs of what one does know, hidden indiscrete, and forgotten crags of thoughts, so that the lover, in aesthesia, mistakes the sacred mists for marble and then presumes, as a result, to decline and die.

Telephone's End

In storm and beneath the clouds, a warn, of doom impending, come break of morn. When from across the time that separates thee from thine, some voice familiar, within world peculiar, harmonious memorial, to a once-loved sartorial. Come absence of sunny skies, and bereft, that which tends to die, a sacrifice to years gone by, and what remains of a true love denied. Even though no face ascribed to the space you occupied, and mere sound to interfere with decrepit spies of failing eyes, for you where nowhere near; but upon telephone's end, thy love doth send, remarkable glimpses of what had been. In so doing, thy love renewing, and for long absence make amends. Minus caramel in the eyes, the best most enchanted suspends somewhat foggily and partially to realms susceptible to ends, as though even infinitudes of mass occupying mental photographs get bothered by gravitational bends, feel pains of narcosis toward decay, for starvation of a perfect way, to say, there was once a love that sustained from above, that fell and split between, two of the *already seen*, or déjà vu, that looped continuously around from one to two, from two to One. To again hear your voice, and near a comedy in storm, a faithful, fateful standing by, lest that love gave one more try, despite circumstance's ignite. And involvement of matrimonial others—may identity extend beyond death-do-us-part? to then take precedence and ownership of a past united heart? What Great Love masquerades, in the endless parades, of husbands' and wives' come-and-goes? that ends with breath? to then *forget?* what incarnate upon earth twixt two had sowed! Is your true love so weak? that in a silence keeps, indistinguishable role (limit one to lifetime), before committing the crime of submitting to mortality, a fleshly god? made in human image. Divinity in limitability? Do spit! No wonder the godless dominate what's writ, and sit in high seats of politic. What has the Infinite to do with it? The undeniable Far Cryable lent your lost voice to abolish it, so dreams of deathless, boundless love between two come true.

SMILING

Saw you smiling before the golden corn, swaying in the mists of morn, as in the East; atop the trees, the rising sun looms, with all the weight of the August warmth. And there is laughter above your pride in land ownership, though it did not harm the soul—for your gifts. Then Joy becomes you in your toils with the earth, for in your garden your love gave birth, and dealt the hungry another turn. In the rightness, the forest and the lawn, green glisten in the dews of dawn, and the promise of surpassing peace, in the eyes of the fawn. The ripeness in the redness of the now noonday's sun, makes a plumb of it, a brilliant bomb, with insidiousness in the gentle heat, but dangerous. To be more than just a name, of the blood in a relative's vein, that encourages the neat insane, of familiality. Strangers in that depth of love, borrowed from a distant manger, in another time, lofts the hearts above, beneath the starry sublime. So fitting to have you near the corn, and quiet on that August morn, so soon beyond the night, robbed of sleep's delight, when your cigarette's cherry gave the only light, in the deep of dark, when Loneliness played its parts in the silent hours before dawn. Hidden at the forest's feet, the lost-long emerald street, of dewy grasses 'tween partèd trees, pathèd just so, in invitation to a world unknown, a paradise of one's own; into which you've strolled and disappeared, smiling.

NOVEMBER

Howling, driven white, a pinprick on the face of night. Mighty, consuming, tower of sea, whipped-foaming wave tops, ascattered, belittering the silent darkness above the roaring, icy pale—some hint of moon glow searing thru; a small dawn ahead of time, to herald in the humblest rhyme—the breakers of breaking day, and someone to hear. Fondest for the mellow years, when yellow ears of corn, competed, but kindly so, in fertile fields, with the distant memory of snowfall, in November; to a gentle breeze, the corn sways. *Canst but outrun, children, the lengthening shadow of the wood, in the setting sun. Though fear, and hopes for a softer year, ahead. So dash into meaning, into desire, wont; survival? Little children, out or into the fire?* The dread legend of the painful growth, the mixing with the earthly in the absence of the Holy Ghost—a demon looking over the shoulders, hulking in the shadows. Lest cast aside, the tripper of the youthful stride, the zipper of the tongues of joy; innocent laugher, harkens the bloody massacre! And the toil of the Annoyed, blesses with little lives destroyed, in November. Staple of the mists of September; those omniscient, harbingering mists of September; what they would wring.

Pressure of Four Souls

The pink Magnolia dropped a leaf, and the minuscule window of time, in brief revealed the secret to the delicacy in beauty. And pressing the ovaries, of the present beauty, the four souls who would be, present, too; in waiting. Some prescience, then, as to the when to do the welcoming, arrival thing? for new souls. Is it in the future of a being? to know the right thing? in the today. The small and ill illumined, in the mists of gray, yearn for a sunny bright, to burn in the newest ways. And thus leaves the beauty always as mystery, for she knows the future, then, being familiar with what love draws near. And this is the end to the lover's encompassing attention desires—split now into another divisor of four! How the little souls move the beauty to much more. And would it turn the eye of desire from the beauty's fine, to rebuff a wounded own heart? Then a distance of intimacy, once portrayed, and bereft two lovers, left dismayed. One for the loss of magnetism perceived, the other for the misplaced seed, at the cause of greed? or is the desperation the true builder of nations? And may the feeble few, postpone the taxes due? on a love done, and bid adieued upon. Thus the generics of visitation in the body-enslaved life.

Delta Road,
as Seen from Space

The hushed wheat erupted into the chorus akin a sheeps' bleat; swaying, waving, then falling still, again, as the whipping wind subsided into another field to the East. The wood, reacting as a taller, fatter, giant field of wheat, enacted in a slow-motion beat, in the distance to the wind same, which blew the wheat. As matter of scale, painted flat from the sky's view, where the maiden flew, piloting the craft. *As seen from space*, Delta Road, and checkerboard across that which composed the place, the fields of wheat, the sporadic corn, and then an alternate of bean. The ghosts inhabit the below, and fearing the winds, are churned in the awaying from them—for winds erase the unseen, erode the sense of being, from the sentient, or the ghosts. Oblivious to this lower world, this maiden pilot flew on, unfurled a flag floating in the higher heavens above Delta Road. Due East, heading, upon the stones of the road, the rising sun illumines the wildflower in a colors' own, and more delicate, robust, as upon the astral plane, seen on earth only by the insane; for beauty as such is a flight of fancy to the masses who rule by rust, the corrosive *touching much* of the brandishing hands, their fate, for continuing to strike out against the land. The whispering wheat in a partial lull, rattling ever so softly; a trillion tiny cleavages that strike and beat into a chorus of the plant-sheeps' bleat. A glimmer, a silver star, shimmering above the far, and the blue, and the white—the maiden pilot in her speck plane, though in early morning, chases West the night.

THE MARINER'S SONG

She maneuvered with grace in the intimate space, of her kitchen. The maiden bright, on a Saturday night, had hosted a new friend, for a friend. The description of her, in that graceful state: exuberant, intelligent, softly spoken, yet musically intoned; the maiden vibrated as a reed in a warm breeze—the resonant affection for an alike being, seeing that, made of her a girllike, nearly giddy thing; what emotions warm foster what brings, a woman to flare up an infernal, eternal zoo of animal manners, restrained beneath, that purport to summon a coup, of the earth beneath her very feet, to transform what innately was called *you*: the being, brand new. And a laughter the maiden gave, with Eastern kindness married to upstate, pragmatic ways. The down-to-earth but uncommon magic of simple manners. She offered the requested cup of coffee. Beneath wild curls and slate eyes, she the harbinger, made Apollonian cries, of perfection in the recognition, given vague suspicion that some cooperative and shared joyful dividend had once driven two to a common end. The ease with which she had brought to a pleasing affirmation, was shocking. That a silky though misfit instance, in that the social situation lacked, may suit, two lost and reunited lovers marooned in a spate of vagueness, and so listed as any foundering ship, crashed upon a coral reef of remembrance too shallow to remain hidden and out of reach, therefore, of it. And from the curls and the slate she transformed, when the black drug took its place, within the dead-now-alive lover, and thence to the special station in the brain: the fairly maiden exiting a sea surf upon an August day on some other earth. The symphony of roiling waves, crushing in upon a shallow grave, of the long gradation of the immense beach. Animating her lank and curves, the Venetian maiden slowly took shape, with her resolution reversing from dusted gray to colors of the full spectral rays. In a matter of moments, bordering hours of stoppèd time, she stood estopped completely, dripping saltwater unfortunately if not untimely met, by a dry aire and an evaporatively heated sand, wrought of an ill behest, of the once mariner a thousand years afore, that she had loved and left. But as she resumed her stride, and brushed by, with a compassionate and explanative sigh, she had confessed her disappearance was due entirely to an untimely death, that had never been explained. Her disappearance had driven insane, her lover of the former plane. All without words, in a powerful gaze, with an instant mortal glaze, on two from another day, a reunion on the astral seaboard had taken place, and, in so being, the startling about face, of two fortunes once connoted dashed upon a rocky fate, of a love in full bloom, anciently misplaced.

Ridge Crest

Near sun, hovers low above, on early August day. The Western sloping field of green, narrowed with its arrowed rows, shooting toward the horizon. The farmer pauses on the walk, gazes toward a pasture South, wishes cows could talk; yogis nearly perfect, the Silent Infinite they expertly stalk in stillness, with patience, with love. How great? a master cows make; milk for the Above, so life below….holding up the horizon, the forest in countless sunsets it'd received into with a grasp; swallowing Night ensued. And so mysteriously the forest, though dark within, remained the keeper of the light; and the leaves were the direct repository of that light, storing the totality of the sun into its prismatic band of brilliant green. Being in intimate communication with the East, then, the Source of all life, which arose from the ridge crest gift of Dawn, and the dark forest, which tossed the sun around the far side of the world, to the awaiting ridge crest, which in turn tossed to the blue sky the sun ball. The bow, between the ridge crest East, and the forest tall, West, lay the meadow green; North, at the cattle scene, a bee buzzes near, hovers at a yellow flower, alights clumsily, drinks, resumes his flight. The farmer gazes North, inhales deeply the aires, detects the scent of the sea, a ways off. North was the gateway, therefore the escape way—to partake of the fluid ways of water is the true inheritance of genetics in the first round; the second and third rounds reserved for the expression of the familial traits of air and aether. The farmer smiled, dabbed again at the forehead: the so-called Darwinian evolution was mistaken. The real advancement of a species entailed a de-evolution, a return to the axiomatic basics of organic composition—water, air, aether, and the identification with these by the human consciousness. *I am the sea, I am the sky, I am the eternal lightness.* The farmer chuckled, inhaled deeply, slowly. 'I am the green fields, the still cows; I am the flowers in the pastures, the buzzing bee, the dark forest, the rising and setting sun; I am the ridge crest, from atop which, I am all.'

Sprites of Paradise and the Jackals of War

Perhaps the wealth of health in water fast, lent the tiny maidens their boast repast—faint flood beneath little arms and feet, the mischievous smiles betrayed of the three a naughty child! though marked by joy, painted in the eyes' sublime complete. From some other realm's fabric they had rent, having fallen thru with a splash; the motive divine had spent? or left supine in an alter-mist of time. And, as if a great light had lit, one of the three seemed recognized. Whilst flailing about in play, the waves reflecting the total lost motions of yesterdays, deflecting the fatalized rays, to space—assupping from the Greek Cup of Forgetfulness?—or to then some other place, race, to relive, upon the reception of the distant astral wind. *Doubt not where alien identity, lost memories begin!* From an aquatic paradise exposed to sin, the Pure endure the horrored again—and again, and again, and again, and again; subject, then, to the bullets anew, of the lustors for the blood, who feel power in the primping of themselves, at their rose reflection in the spilt pool of it. One sprite cried, 'Lack! there's a zipper on that sheep's back. Look! undone, exposed within, the jackal. Now see him run!' And then the sprites cried, chorally, 'Whoa to, the jackals who, deceive to subjugate the gentle ewes!'.... Some strange rememberings from the familiar one of the sprites three. Some valiant past together, of fighting for the Just and the Right, and thus this tiny sprite, grew into a fury, on the last of the December nights.

TEN DEER

Do you see them dear? passing in the frontlight near, then fading to the black of night. Magnet pulling schizophrenic, the Madonna, perhaps, had seen too much. Now deranged and begging sane, what cause must she adopt? to put her mind on top, of what might cause her fright, and then her heart to stop. A vision not quite as just, as the day in the sun; as long, long ago, she committed no crimes for which to now pay—yet there is the insanity, calamity to be trapped alone, in the head, and ne'r invite the suburban plight, that leaves the minions dead. So thank God, you, had careful to, lose the mind—in your own time, instead—while still the looker of your life. Would share with you no vacant view, of the ten deer having fled; for in the night, when magic works, on colored astral lights, better to have seen the golden creatures who escaped the tortures of the zoo, though they now reside in memory, and have disappeared from the sight, of even the despaired minions, who hunt the things by day, some righteous act, that made subtract, the creature from the rack? or the mere killer excused? by the twisting of the rules, and thus escape the judge's rake—if the judge were not thine own offending hand, laid so heavy upon the golden creatures of the land.

From Romania

You had been *Cry out, in the night!* The society of music and dance, liberated from Darkness' grasp, to dazzle brightly, with your smile. Illumined from across the room, the magnets zoomed, to recollect what had heretofore been bested by doom—the looming All—forget at the dusk of a life. Ringing out joy at the odd reuniting—the familiar face yet long-lost name attached, lost to the insane infinity of beginnings and endings and beginnings. Part of your electric fell, upon the recipient admirer, to jog the memory and pull down the wingèd higher soul, a little closer to the know, and the now; thence the merriment, of companion and joyous be, that recollection of two, in the moment, anew, again. If the laughter might be shared, from an agreed-upon delicate experience had, then that malaise of the missing may shift from sad to glad. And the hours may float by in harmony, on some conjoinèd task, leaving to wonder, *What end that Joy might ask?* Dare the Infinite to hound, to snare, from Its dreamy netherwhere, perchance that It may not only land, but stay, to then command-obey two who had lost their way, to be found again another day. What kind Light had signaled thru the night? to end their ends. Repair together the struggling few, who had bid, *Adieu!* but who'd acquired that sparing view of the new-old, the déjà vu. To taste again the lips, so sweet, to see again the hazel eyed, within which beat, down radial iris streets, the heart of a million kindnesses, once given discrete.

AND ALL THE GODS WITHDREW:
EXIT AT EDEN

The madonna appeared from the blue—she svelte leapt into view, from one eye corner, thru the admirer heart borne anew, at the sight of you. As a ballet, madonna drew a portrait-dance, one to cast a spell, enhance the damned-to-hell's prance toward there—for in the lightning jolts, firing from your eyes, hair afire in flaming reds, madonna gave life to the dead, or damned, by her reception; advanced perception, of the lover loving her; heretofore from afar, but now, from oh, so near....waltzing to and fro, those singulaires, meet a singularity, of true physic's definitions, and as likes attracts, created magnetic annihilation, as two attempted to occupy a sole soul space. Sickness and the remedy, be in the countenance of the madonna: sickness at the sight afar, remedy in the kisses in the intimacy, of beholden tight, two against the night of present earthen days....hands held, backs to backs, electronic delight. She smiles, and speaks music in humorous aspire, and gazes with longing in a lover's return, of the echoed voice cast to the canyon depth for a darkness' rest, and only to hear again that lost cry, flying in reply with the dawn. And the madonna plays, in such a way, with the Bringer of the day! Her slender fingers, cool in the clasp, indicates the heating blast, in the heart furnace of romance. Such laughter in the comedy of sin, or the madonna and her lover—the beautiful flower, with petals open and reaching for the wind and water of affection, the sunshine of joy, the Summer of admiration, the Spring of touch; the screaming in the loving, though tender, they find nearly too much, ne'r two similars attached in such a match, as madonna and her lover. Spare room to adjust, when the hold of that thrust, feigns airtight!

And breathless they become again and again and again. And all the gods withdrew....and all the gods withdrew....and all the gods withdrew. Entwined with tears and the grinding, the merging and their emergencies, the nakedness of two individualities, and the realizations in their eyes, that though mortal, true lovers never die, see one soul in the mirror same; cancels out the physical game. She smiled at rest, as the loving test quieted, and spoke softly for the humble quietude surround—no air passed yet between the two; madonna asleep, with her lover.

CLASSICAL

Poem and Interpretation

CLASSICAL

The dreamy melody, contracted and extracted (better posture from the Madame), in 3/4 time; the world played out sublime, with her presence in it. The slower bower, and the addition of the shower of star lights, raining down in deepest night. Three lovers bent upon another: the sun a th' moon; the stars a th' sun; the moon a th' stars, chasing each a tail as a dog a car, with disastrous effect, and with no success. But the lovers play, away with the day, and ne'r forget the reason to be met. Some desire afire, gives magnet a strength; a condition for hire, may purchase no cure of apothecary; only in consummation do fires let be, grant free. Tremors in obscurity, rumble 'neath a sea of earth in soil tympani. Hidden remains the day, and all things of day's light—hence a flower in the night—she who misses, or is mist. The fog of vision in the lover's eye, makes aimed-for things a parallaxed sting, and Cupid arrows loathe wiz by, unconnected to the resurrected singer of song high! or skyey declaration to tune; proclamation of divine ministrations, pulpitted from within sweet morality of a *willingness* to be. But what of cast adrift? of target having missed? Solo advancèd storm, for the stars, the moon, the sun? or mixed dance beneath the Hierophant? Blessed-then Roman comedy of romance, portrayal of a part in cosmic order, for variations of a theme, and entertainment for a nation's lovers. Shall a happy lovely be? or pending grimace to posterity? *Rigors of a mortise pulled free of its tenon.*

CLASSICAL

Classical...This rooted in the author's by-invitation-only attendance of a performance by a certain cello-playing diva at the music department of one of the Seven Sisters colleges in the American Northeast. Her superbly erected *posture* contributed to the precise operation of the instrument. *Madame* is used to denote the highest respect; borrowed from the French, in that it rarely appears in American English. The experience was divinely revelatory, *the world played out sublime*, wherein the author witnessed a side of the diva theretofore not seen: *with her presence in it*; the god side, the creator, Beauty maker, and, as such, the aetherially resultant *dreamy melody*; and the totality of the dream experience may occur, *contracted*, in an instant of the quickening, or, *in 3/4 time. Extracted*, in that it was captured by the trio of musicians from the Source of music in that particular moment of all moments that are the count of eternity. *The slower bower*, borrowing the diva, the cello player, lending her presence to this fantastical word portrait, and painting additional layers atop this canvas with aetherial strokes to produce a deeper magical scene, *and the addition of star lights, raining down in deepest night*. The *night*, offering aesthetic intrigue, is a time for mystery and passion, and is a favorite temporal context for the setting of poem stories; a recurring theme. The story leaves the music department to find inspiration at a certain Chinese restaurant. The narrator made the observation of the waiter gazing at the diva, and how his face had become illumined at the sight of her, even more than it had on previous, or would be on subsequent, visits; also observed was the diva noticing the waiter in his admiration of her; thus is constructed for tension and for beauty the timeless plot of the love triangle, assigning to each of the three participants—the *Madame* and her two admirers, the narrator and the waiter—an alter ego of a shining, orbèd object from the celestial pantheon, *Three lovers bent upon another: the sun a th' moon; the stars a th' sun; the moon a th' stars.* And, as is very often the case with triangles, there is a blunting outcome for one or more of the 'angles.' This issue is addressed with a reference to the lovers making sexual advances, *chasing each a tail,* immediately followed by a comment on the possible considerable negative consequences of such actions by drawing a parallel to hapless dogs pursuing cars, *as a dog a car, with disastrous effect, and with no success.* There is a childhood riddle of remembrance: 'Question: How did the bulldog get such a face? Answer: By chasing parked cars.' Despite all wisdom, desire nonetheless drives the three lovers in the 'game,' *But the lovers play, away with the day,* helpless against their passions, which occupy most of their conscious mind—displacing better wisdom?—for one or more of the parties is married, and each is involved. The heat of desire yet lends to the attractors the will to pursue, *Some desire afire, gives magnet a strength,* comparing to the superior grasping quality of the electromagnet—the magnet created by a wrapped coil and the application of electricity—noticeable is how the player and instrument resemble the coil. It is the crazed hunger? to fill a certain hole in the lover, to satiate? to find wholeness? to become complete? that accounts for the innocent mystery of attraction, in which there is no excusing the taste of one lover for another, and that provides the motive power for not only this trio but for the majority of the world's population? *and ne'r forget,* not for an instant!—a comment on the hyperconsciousness of, and obsessive preoccupation with, one another, capable only of lovers, granting them this superhuman willpower for pursuit against all odds, and which is ultimately, in all of space and time, what drew these three together, *the reason to be met,* at the Chinese restaurant. *a condition for hire,* by subconscious agreement, deep affection requires employment of an individual's essence; a process involving the transfer of heat, or definitive work. *may purchase no cure of apothecary,* love is a sickness for which there is no medicinal curative prescription. *only in consummation do fires let be, grant free,* entrapped in a pit of flaming emotion, the lover may escape only by permitting the fire of desire to burn itself out, when the object of affection— the fuel—is consumed. *Tremors in obscurity,* the shaking of love sources deep within the being, *rumble 'neath a sea of earth in soil tympani;* so powerful and encompassing are the vibrations that the solid earth quakes in massive waves, as though an oceanic body in storm, the rumbling of which transforms the earth into a great drum. Pursuant to its unseen Source, *Hidden remains the Day,* love then is a mystery, the true nature of which, *all things of Day's light,* continues in obscurity. Yet the products of love—here the female actor—are not only visible, but beautifully so, being compared to a flower, *hence a flower in the night.* A sympathetic system of at least two interchangeable parts, lovers become both object and beholder, *she who misses or is mist,* the later serving as preemptive synonym for the next phrase: *The fog of vision in the lover's eye,* love unconsciously affects the faculty of reason, and so subsequent actions may have potentially unintentional, unpleasant—even harmful—results: *makes aimed-for things a parallaxed sting.* And in this love triangle, it is suggested that none of the hearts' intentions find result, that their love misses, *and Cupid arrows loathe wiz by, unconnected to the resurrected singer of song high!* Forwarding the musical theme, the high of the lover's love is described as a *skyey declaration to tune,* and is literally a heavenly music, the *proclamation of divine ministrations,* pouring forth, *pulpitted,* from the pure heart, *from within sweet morality,* of those volunteering for love, *a willingness to be.* The question is raised: What is the outcome of this seemingly unfortunate love triangle? *But what of cast adrift? of target having missed?* Two scenarios are offered: the first suggests that each of the three, represented by the celestial bodies, is left alone to their own emotional dissatisfaction, *Solo advanced storm, for the stars, the moon, the sun?* But the second suggests a hopeful outcome—for at least two of the three—including holy sanctioned matrimony, *or mixed dance beneath the Hierophant?* complete with the classic happily-ever-after love affair: *blessed-then Roman comedy of romance,* alternately described in the weighty terms of its importance to the very structure of Nature, *portrayal of a part in cosmic order,* and yet immediately follows with a whimsical inference, in musical terms, that love is merely to engage a humanity hungry for experience and performance, or drama, *for variations of a theme, and entertainment for a nation's lovers.* The poem then begs the question: Will the story have a happy ending for any of the lovers? *Shall a happy lovely be?* or the contrary, *or pending grimace to posterity?* And then answers the question shockingly out of context with a tension-filled, double-meaning reference first to carpentry, *mortis* and *tenon,* and then second to the physical condition of the recently deceased, rigor mortis, *Rigors of a mortise*—a proclamation of the death of Love by forces beyond its control, or Fate, *pulled free of its tenon,* concluding, 'Nay, 'tis, in the end, a Greek tragedy.'—for at least one of the three....

Recognition beneath the Topaz Sky

She melted into her interior, when in view came one she knew. Removing all exterior, shuffling off the gare inferior, she sat sprawled, as if upon a favorite couch, in complete relaxation—though in the real instant she stood, waltzing a stride, brushing by, rushing by, save the fixity in the laser eyes, which shot into the heart of Admiration. Complimented, the ego relinquished into blush, and pausing as if the young girl, first attempting displaying curls, for looks, aware of the wake she'd laid. It was the casualty in serendipity, that kept her most dismayed: *You don't know me that well, that way.* Incessant heart, beating toward a break, the presence of the lover, and the love that lovers make, stopped her, cold—how, in a second? familiarity grows old, when forbidden kisses land upon a true lover's soul, granting satisfaction for the godly half, when the animal prays, *Die!* The lips themselves were left to cry; fallen thru the topaz sky, she carries her former self into another life, where the lover she plays is not the wife, and her former other is now another, beneath the glaring topaz sky. What saintly forms? don royal cling, such as clothing of the ambient aires, that mix with love of the lover pair; such that a bleaching effect from the blinding light, whitewashes the walls of the material night, within which she acts her parts.

OOSTENDE TO DOVER: FLYING UPON THE WATERS

Candle in the window blew; dancing shadows, cast in the day—though some surmise that they had fallen between the times, relegated to the late night, the hours before dawn. The overlapping phases, passed from Undulane: the poses of the people, the actions of the things, fell like rain. The speed with which the scene changed, foretold the years to come, to bear witness to the insane. Belgium's edge, kissing the waters' snare, had agreed to Europe's end, to falling home, again, to the landing flight, a maiden on the night, where at Dover the beginning was the end. The shimmering Deep called through the chilling seep; how the Channel cold closed in on less-than-ideal. Reeling from the thought of you, prisoner in the human zoo, Desire chimed or framed the news; your delicate kiss of genius, spelt Geneva to never cease. Dragging into Belgium, you, though absent, the parting view, of two lovers interlocked, made Genius bow to Brilliance, a whisper as though thunder, so matter-of-fact, lying but not tasting slumber; some fine wine to spin the floating times, soaring in your arms, drinking emerald eyes. Some laughter in the rain, baiting the true insane, of lovers in their youth, fresh in the power of their truths. Inconsequent ruling in simple touching of the hands, and running, running, running in the Geneva rain. These shadows flicker from the candle flame, as the fleet ship skips atop the Channel waters, with white Dover rising ahead. Behind, some lovers' youth lay dead.

PREMONITIONS

…came flooding in, as though a feather heap, tickling the spine—a moment in time—before the open door, whence fell upon the floor afore, the incident first felt and then created in the Overmind, shared subsequently with the tiny sublime, over and over in an unconscious day. The maidens appear, disappear, reappear, bearing terrors of incidence, bourne of the machinations of the 24-hour cycle. Each part of such sluice experience—the phone call announced; the conversation having just had, in voice familiar, between the ears, sunken into the head, echo of the years undead? or from the nites ahead? alive and yet to be led. Then the bright-headed maiden speaks—not bright-*eyed* but bright-*headed*—for far beyond the eyes extended, this one; all the beams spill into the skull, scatter, and radially extol, promulgate the face and hair—then music is her lair. How to discuss this going out? bending back to laugh, but then to offer pout. The fiery lass outshines the sun—brilliant trouble on the run. And then, afore, came knocking upon the door, radiation's cooler stead, that echo, again, in the head, followed by the original, and then your light.

WINTER STAR

Shining light, lovely looked so bright; new old lover meeting at first sight, this round. Laughter in her eyes, the delicate surprise, of left-over incompletes, what yet remained to say and do, together. Already a Madonna with child and husband, yet contrasted to the moment, one former such as he, your current lover. Pasteurizing the sacred play, Beauty yet did defeat—as the universe exists, to lay at the feet, create new rules and realities, instant to instantly, and none more imminent and tangible, than having your hand to hold—the new and the lover old. This warmth transfers to your, very palm, crawls up the barèd arm, fills the face with blush, illumines the eyes, and vivifies the crown—she beamed and curtseyed down: *How do you do?* And an answer: *A pleasure to meet you!* Surrounding her self, and permeating in stealth, the soul glow, the white light that burneth beyond human sight. Be there joy in her voice, at the heart's meeting beats, which synchronize in rhythm, such that only lovers true can do; this slows the motion of the world, to petrify all else living, and liberates the lovers two, trapped across time, to begin anew. To hang upon a whisper of yours, to feel that common zeal, of a humor shared, and a heart's truth revealed. What murky night, to occlude the Play Royale's final scene, for two to have and to hold, though vowed for an eternity of physicality, in essence, out performs the body, and leaps with the soul into another life; long lost then are the husband and the wife—it is for the entertainment of the Father that human lovers' lives last no more than His intention for His little children to discover that there may be something more than what bliss they have found in each other. As Death has come to fore, and mocked their betrothal to the Evermore—until next time.

You, beautiful Madonna, are remembered as well as recognized, from the past welled in your eyes. Now for you, and the previous joys you knew together, *a bow and continued adoration, as you once again grace the stage, and steal the breath away.*

Holiday

Crushing blow of lacking holiday. Some earth's weight balancing upon the needlepoint. Crush of the impending abyss, lightless and towering, engulfing, a nighttime water vision, without stars or moonlight to break the pitch. A tiny sailing soul, sole sailor this eve, destitute to storm, lost amongst this sea-type relativity. At best no rescue from this test, so that the crying out may focused be, to transgress that relativity. Then the pinhole thru which begins, a borne illumination toward the center-in; then a guaranteed expansion to trouble the dark, make nervous the oppressive night, that sunrise indeed spells demise, to fearing black. When contrasting grayscale distinguishes, some difference's fight for recognition, when the insane sameness vibrates, bereft of trademark mundaneness. The lengthy perspective, of horizons broadened, whisper rumors of daylight soon to come true. Never a Sargasso sea—just vacated to endless storm, the soul craft—can ever the waters rest? to allow the menace to a history be; the tremendous weight of emotionality, equal to the massive sky of night, with celestial bodies bright. Kindred spirits—mind and stars field—both burdened and blessed with the infinity and all that it contains. The darkness visible, and made aware, as if the watcher in the midnight aires, took as the breath the earthly cares; so interconnected the feelor and the pain, that a cosmic display same is found in the crazy and in the sane; in the sacred, and in the mundane.

LE HAVRE TO ROSSLARE:
STORM AT SEA

Given some foreign universe brought to earth, to be a playground for the youthful runaround—and to be solitary upon a human sea; point of observation supreme. Still the scent of you drew, and how powerful remain, the images of your name, as the warm Spring rains and pre-Summer winds, fall and blow again, wafting unknown flowers' perfumes to instantly attune, Spirit to a soul, with heretofore unlived experiences, yet familiar to one who had lived before. Larger than the sky, ghost in the lover's eye, unforgotten for once having had, metal in your kiss, the force of being glad, in the warmth of your hand, the silence in your smile—made the Blessed Virgin hover for a while, above the lighted sands, of that peaceful foreign land; intimate in so close, cold for the one you loved the most. And then, years to the rear, apprehend: You in the sea beyond the rail, of the mighty ship set sail, from Le Havre at France's end. As darkness descends, the caramel iris portends—the vision of you. When brown became the blue before the blackness of night's cloak. Vibrations of the motor threw, those lost sands into the passengers' eyes, who slept as if to die, in the mechanical symphony. The longing the waves had felt, off the Channel South of England, and the Atlantic grew a case for you, and enraged that someone else knew, attempted to wipe the writer from the page. Loving you, in full night's view, Atlantic blew. A storm, to interfere, and the sleeping dreamers entered unpleasantries. A bouncing bow, pointed at the Emerald Rosslare, hoped to survive and find you there. As the dreamers slept, though awake within their subconscious scene, joined the lover in a soundless scream. Alone and disappearèd, lost at sea? What then? of thy love for thee. Atlantic crashing in a beam of floodlight, cut that nightmare from the night, flew it into Consciousness' sight. Stood before the window on the bow, saw the heaving sea, now more personally in assault, pondered the wet cold and taste of salt, and how one might balk, at being deprived of the lips and eyes, that had once conjoined in thee, how Rosslare may never be. Atlantic to Neptune, a servant be? which the greater power? a god or a sea. Moot point to the enemy of both! Resurrection of the sunken ship, all before the fact, made buoyant by the joyous fact; amidst the storm, in Dublin now, there is dancing and joy. And even in the dark of night, still the sun shines beyond the far side of the sight, ne'r failing to give birth to morn; then your laughter calmed the storm. Youth, excited, defeated the deeps between the highs of Le Havre and Rosslare. Sailing into Irish skies, ship riding upon the air, the Emerald grew upon the horizon, in full Spring green. The welcomed harbor, fruit of the dreamers' dreams, shimmers in the sunbeams. Train rails feeding Rosslare, whisks love away to Dublin, to dancing and joy, to find you there, singing; Alive! for the bringing of the metallic kiss of your lips, and the warmth of the Hand.

NIGHT OF COLUMBUS

Young madonna bent a head to side, and with the grace of a moment's space, the shimmer of illumined eyes—in an humble confession of delay in the advancing technology of the day, of an immersion in it. Perhaps in beauty lay protection from the wolverines of the mind, which now gnaw and detract from the genius of original thought, and, being sanctioned by the status quo, the day-to-day, cause the glory of the soul to while away. But in this intimate admission, the young madonna had said, *Okay*, and in a matronly way too elder for her days, what may have been a forced sweetness, if misunderstood, simply claimed not to have to know the hottest coolest thing. And a steam roller of currency prepared to put an end to you. A blurt-out with potentially fatal consequences, with such leverage that a head may be pried from its stay, should an enemy possess the inclination and the ruthless data. Stable in a storm of feminism, you the brunette bamboo, for sweetness never once denied or failed to be portrayed. And with duration of conversation, a starting of a friendship from which bloomed a desire to be near—or a love. In the advancing minutes' year, was reborn to you, as if someone a'ready (k)new; then the brightness of the flourish, a *flaring*, solar blaring, when spilt thru, as if the morning dew, thru the corpus, your You. And what at first seemed the silence occupied by the stillness of the young madonna's beauty, became an onset symphony, a sliding harmony with ever increasing volume. The result was the introduction of identity, rather a bursting of the seams that contain the raging sea of rainbow individuality of the soul. The Hinting Joyous, squinting thru the eyes of you, found humour without receipt— you had given freely without the self-conscious compulsion that burns the asses and forces the speech, generally harasses the manners of the moral learnèd. Just you burning thru, upright soul from the collective whole, laughing and dancing naked in the marts of man, in the rarest moment of human revelation, from young madonna.

Meeting

Some positiveness, electronic flow, a showering of white, fragrant peace, tangible and able to be known, condescended mundanaeity, and triggered the switch of familiarity—Mistress Beauty held court. What most surprises, eyes, or her ears, and excellent hearing. Granting two to three beats between answers and her next question, she sits royally, the portrait of patience. Softness, engulfed and pervaded of the white light, she gently glowers as a single flame in night. Stiff breeze of reality, hardly if noticeably nudges. The crown of thee; perhaps a single golden strand may bend from vertical, only slightly. Composure be thy name, and radiation be thy fame. Some great inharmony, in the warring structure of containing walls, you easily appease, and calm this angry sea of materiality. Cropped, glowing crown, golden flowering, draping down, to shoulders covered yet bared to imagination's claim on expected perfection, ideals based upon the reasonable extrapolation, continuation of your sweetest grace. Svelte frame, demonstration of all moderation; in flight, the coordinated bird of paradise, hovering at will, tho capable of top speed at moment's notice. Depth of gaze through hinting blue eyes, recommend substance within, far beyond what blonde encourages belief in. Materially kind, Mistress Beauty hypnotizes beneath the spell of a superior mind, catching unaware the lesser intellect in the snare of unexpected professionalism. Wielding a sword of practicality, she misses no opportunity to accomplish set goals and sub-headed agenda points, all at the point of laughter, just a millimeter beyond the amused yawn, parting perpetually leavened lips. Yours a warmth to around bask, and a technique to admire, this constant setting fires in the parched hearts of defenseless men. To be next to thee continually, or 'til an incurable illness descends upon, to cure the preexisting terminal attraction.

STILLNESS

In stillness, presented almost as if for inspection, she stood before; memory fruited from the Evermore, of two strangers who were in past, much more. A slight hesitation after so long a sleep, at having awoken from such an unconscious deep, to once again rejoice, again, in a lover's keep, regardless of the interlink of romantic matrimonially present others, still that familiarity, beyond the raging see, tidal pull of physicality, the wavelike comings and goings characteristic of this side of eternity. In the willingness to smile, the adventure to share laughter, all ruminations of long-past generations as one. Still, the stillness has begun, again, and that signaled you, who had returned anew. Force of concentration between the eyes, intensifies with your sighs—and all so well known—but scant remembered until now! The willingness to make amends for crimes of mindlessness—how dare Time make a prisoner of the mind, and without mercy, banish you from it. Do you like what you find, this time? Can you recall even the glimmer in-between season? when light spoke with such sentience in a universe complete, with no distance from lover to lover, bowing to touch your feet. Welcome back, to the street of now, where you walk with such electricity, that the sheen of your eyes defies description, for in a parallax event, you and your image blurred, slightly askew—what form presented told nothing of your you. With slight shyness, and desire for distanced closeness, you ventured to stop to speak. Then kindred souls, unfold, rehash the story told, write in bold a new.

Cabinet Room Behavior

Beneath the brilliant gray eyes and brilliance, and the passive lies of human resilience, of living the work of day with survivability, the Beauty Maiden Youth, pursued her idea of truth, with businesslike manner. How her waters doth crash upon the breakers of worldly ways; of motion toward the payday. In the cabinet room she turned, and with a stranger's acknowledgement, transferred in intimate glare, energies typically reserved for those intimates. And crossing some distance in between the two states, the Maiden Youth would have laughter to add to her collected truth; standing corrected in her responsibility, she must resume as dictated be, in corporation reality. But smashing down, her Self, at the harsh accountancy of where might in all probability, her professional path lead. *We are not passing thru this life unfettered by corporeality, sweet angel, and feminine, you shall always in earthly life be burdened by your beauty, in the cabinet room, despite your brilliance.* There is no one and nothing to blame for this tragic fact, save the depths of this world age, and the men driven insane by the hypnotism of incessant opposition, light and dark, positive and negative, pleasure and pain, men and women. And so to take you, and to look into you, to share a laugh upon a favorite horror show, to desire your lips to kiss and not to listen to wisdom spoken from them, to find an own reflection in the dark universe hidden in your pupil blackness, must be a forgivable sin. To admire the youthful smoothness by which you svelte slip thru a corridor, gives hint of some feminine producing Evermore. A product undeniable of said, mute verifiable in the golden hairs of your head. There is a sincere desire to help you meet your goals, crossed by the insolent dread that you may wield some control on an own, more-senior head for future sake. And so some spout, a letting out a muffled shout, of an ill-placed remark, to keep you slightly in that dark universe, or distance. Remarkable coincidence, the horror show, that you should find it so attractive to cinema see, or is the factuality? that it is your own life? or all the life that you can be? Tragic nature of treading this path, is that you cannot beyond sterling lessons to learn, win. Proof for the tragicality. Please run away to happiness, from the dark circles ringing your eyes, from the terrible lies—lives you've lead. Persistent in the shared moments is the feeling to commonly burst into laughter on the cosmic joke of existence in any human moment. Despite the effort to find you intellectually, your loveliness trips long before, and drives that insanity. From what perspective, then? may objectivity defend, when cast to a far Beyond, is the nobility of a fallen Self, in that type of admiration.

INTERVISION

She peered of reflective quality. The depths of which a soul is inhabitant, finds illumination in the nacentsce of the space, Self combustion, the incandescence of the true master race, who live beyond life, and beam into being *only thru the electrified eyes of husbands and wives?* Met upon a street or perhaps in Cafe Est, some pair of collective iris lights, attempting to draw the darkness from the night. The magnetic quality of a lover grande, is to view a soul, despite the man, or all that is not the soul, but is flesh and human intention. It is as if to be whole, two halves must construct that one soul, with such compulsion and dread of failure, that to finish rent in twain, is to forcèd begin in attempt again, in some future era or alternate world. And so, given that past, account for the electromagneticity that bonds so fast, the two seeking, broken halves; the grandest desire of a burning fire, is to have the quality of the flame read and recognized; entered then into duplicity, so that with destruction some new One is borne, as no two identicals may occupy a similar space in peace, or, indeed, in possibility. The drawing in, and then the annihilation to begin, again. To triangulate a base of two at-distant points, and to project in future from the feminine one, a third point that the two will become as a singularity, in concept to the broken-hearted, if not in reality. So all of a hesitance be damned—it is to be the cause of a lost kingdom land. May be some lust for the process of rust that brings together the woman and the man; as neither of the united shine as selves, but persist in states of abrasive corrosion, left to dream extremes in temperature or fright, to push off the balancing day for night; that in this way, some motion may, conjoin the wrong to the right. It is, therefore, in the lovers' den, that time ends, and begins, again, in eternal cyclic bends.

ORANGE SUN

Same one, sitting on the land; was seas.   Frosty evening now, perhaps the coldest of all. Grasp the sky, hold it till the song resumes, of what ekes from the reddish, banished of the sea. Representative of some blood spilled, far removed to aethericity; what Hidden Hand? portends to be more than what's lacking in the flesh, inspiration to pass the tests, guarantee the screw cap's in place, lessen the gaps in grace; all the auguries suspend, then, invitation to a holy haste—a Delft splendide view, shiny hue of particulates, tapestried thru camera obscura. A Dutch master transforms the glean of the sea—sky scene, sure to reflect the gray of the Eternal in the river stream. Hoteliers all, the lookers on, granting love its affectionate long, for expressionistic guest, bypassing, habitating on and in, as though the fondest next of kin. Orange sun, the final just-begun, astringent, elongated one, venereal sesame almost scarlet in its perfect dream, thus having begotten just so just, in time with heaven on the mind. The Maiden angles the gaze so that products wrinkling in time appear whole and lovely and tastefully conceived, as would be supposed of aethericity, of sunsets in late November, above what should be. The Sea Maiden told the truth, when boasting the ruthless youth, as what is to fear? at the demise of such a long year.

LAVENDER BLOSSOM IN WINTER

You stood in Cafe Est, adorned to dress the feast, of minions, with the softest sense of peace. Some white radiations, given freedom from lacking soul desire, to shine on and out. Divine feminine Madonna, no doubt; statuesque, and in slight inferno, you burned into the daylight, a careful imprint of the true size of you—vast, encompassing, stretching, as is true of light, from horizon to horizon, along sightlines, curious watch, to see those in contact with thee, magnetically attract, a future from the present facts; all wanted to be near you, be a part of the life of you, or to simply admire, the burning of your fire, though unrealized to most. Unconscious kindness, you give away, in the stately peaceful way; almost a static, staying motionless, for your mix of spirit and corpus, as if unto a living death, not breathing, hazled eyes unblinking, and fixed upon an invisible point in the nearest-by Beyond— some intimate personal space with which you carried about you, were most familiarly interacting. And in the dead of Winter, you turned to gaze this way, with a peculiar hue of light beam true, the color lavender, you held upon you. To smile in comfort, to perhaps make discomfort, of the fools who congregate about you. Simple, borrowed flower, you dress as though in French fields in Summer heat, a blossom of tinniest petals, and of rarest taste; strange powers of health in the interior stealth, beneath the thinnest petals of lavender blossom in Winter. Swaying in interior gentle breeze, you grace in ease the Cafe Est, and smile.

SAINT-LAZARRE

With all expectancy surprised, the mundane gave way to pleasantry, and in the dark, motive place, the shining light in you made peace, and graced the dawn of the moment, and continued onto blind the night with bright. You scant cut a portrait of a tall grass, swaying in the breeze of the vast open station. A populace standing by in wait, unaware of the gilded gait, of the lover swaying, keeping time, with the heartbeat of the heaven's Mother. Madonna at attention, all beams and velocity; Paris as a Cafe Est, with you in the arms of Gare Saint-Lazarre, in that expectancy—the beauty off the leash. Pausing to check the love beneath the hat, trifle lank in the form of your feminine—what work a soul does with light! And then a cacophony sends, the rippling, shivering thru the skyey bright canvas of you—in laughter. And then as if the birds had discovered singing in your enthusiastic voice, you cried out from across the gulf of inches of one's personal space, meeting at last, honey and the taste, of sweetness, all at the Cafe Est, all within the Gare Saint-Lazarre, all within some timeless inner place. Romance of beauty, Madonna no longer in hiding, perhaps a love not subsiding, demarks where one held the captives of peace. To behave as you do, the schoolgirl with interior view, of the vast, open gare, of lifetimes of comings and goings. Can there be a mistake of whom chose who? when chemicals berate the rational you, to feel adrift within drunkenness, to make love in place of loving, such that when one wakes of such a daze, one finds one's ring finger welded to a cage, trapped in a certain age, when a great portion of a mind knows, it has bonded to a wrong soul. Pulling the dancing you close, to smell the perfume off the heat of your neck, to then feel a signal to find the softness of your lips; where is it to give or steal? the breath of another lover then. A kiss with eyes open, is a volume's worth of a soul to see; the dynamic quality of time spent in Gare Saint-Lazarre, in expectancy. And peaceful to hold you close, to feel the light in waves, come and go, to resonate as one, two souls.

AND THEN YOU WERE THERE

At first, everywhere; a flight outright, flit almost, save extreme intention undeniable, making your moments as the humming bird. And so you went for honey, which one becomes, as eat and bee. Youth, present with assuming truth, as it sits with you. Then to proposition with open eyes, and spongy mind, prepared to take in. But only in curiosity, which, along with slow-flying humming birds, makes a cat fat. The wondrous bird of flight suspended, made for earth, fashioned from beginning's ended; relative of paradise's bird, she shared the That of bliss unheard, by less-than-flying ears; a maiden youth valiant in search of truth—with so much yet to swear to. Some discrepancy in originality, trifle disadvantage in years, the greatest of the birds' fears—in wisdom lay the power, lacking death. The overt admiration, put soul on trial, to the test. Supple lips and almond eyes, soars the skies of preset moments and personal spaces, and cries, *Make love to me.* Introductory: The already seen, déjà vu upon the Maya screen, humming bird of paradise, lover you already knew, give definition to the word? Scant roots in songs unheard, yet sung by the aetherial. And there are you in universe new, having flown into two, one corpus flower, one spirit wind, a dance for a chance to begin, again. Reinvented, unrelented, caught just a hint of you, dart, no, *flit*, now, off the vision's edge, to disappear but to then reappear; and in the glistening sheen, covering your almond beams, a mirrored reflection, a faint inharmonious suggestion, of fear? or confrontation of *lacking years with ambition.*

IN MARSHALL

The slither of the Winter snake, grasping at the name's sake, that never was. The ghost of you on the pre-Christmas streets, adorned with the piney wreaths, all before Thanksgiving, shows a nation in search of meaning, needing a reason for celebration. You still appeal of the Irish steel, the tannest eyes to reveal. Some soul cry and misdemeanor, stealing a sip of the Greek's cup of forgetfulness, as you don't remember. Familied, you lead your lambs, down that snow-driven street. Sliding, careering, enormous mechanical beasts, iron snakes, grasping without arms and hands, still managing choke-n-hold disintegrationary tact, you, mother of the mouthless fact: Endless, love in you. Do you not die? to yesterday's weight upon the mental plate, searing the banquet of the recollect— warmth in kisses and a hand held; who misses this? reckless ghost, lover most, how the future betrayed you both. Seeing the end of the dream, at which point reality, took over your aerie sheen, giving flesh to the soul who'd been lacking whole; and lambkins filled the hole. Rocking cradle, and far, distant gaze, already destroyed the alter-future days. Having seen and realized, lovers may part ways, but the material significance pales, for bodies die, while love true prevails. And were a better orator, or a more accomplished man, or had a several years' hence assisted the man's command, no dangling offers would have remained untaken, indecision left to degrade. Poison hesitation, not knowing yet in recognition; some hazy Maya had accursed, to block the union with you, when written in the Krishna blue, the declaration of the lover's truth. How black emotion put you aside, relegated the Madonna's visitation to some horrible beside—in that you are lost. But found in Marshall, the ghost of you, outlined in the blue glimmer of too-early Christmas lights, to hear you laugh again, to see the shimmer on the surface of your almond eyes, some acknowledgement of the recognition of former lovers' lives. What grieves, what dies? what ghosts outcry in Marshall? but black emotions of night, in your coal hair, lost but still there.

Unknown

….and, yet, you pause before with brightest countenance, with attentive posture, erect and hungry for a word—Madame Beauty—without consequence she whispers back what millennia ago she had before heard. Roman mixture of golden and brown; the hair, the crown, and the eyes, the caramel brown. With ancient familiarity, she stood and held the arms of a lover, and gazing thru past ages to a true, present moment, she implores, 'Do you know me? Even now, I dance before thee, a distant wife of, loh, another life, and a lover true; have returned to you.' Beyond the bull's-eye of the eye, or pupil dark, what white drew in, and caramel brown iris lights redirected, handed to the final Within, the black hole past which the soul begins, and identity becomes less the individuality. Struggling against your grasp, some fight to deny a memory of Madame Beauty cast to perpetuity, relinquished for posterity—when the warmth of the delicate hand, in hand own, crossed in error in the loosing, for in that instant you created a home, the long foregone eternity—but now summoned by your grasp, with intensity, a flame-throwing torch to burn the muck of forgetfulness to banish the dark of Night's irrecognition, to once again see a soul known, to recollect, to once more a lover be. Golden hair smartly clipped, falling upon a shoulder's rest with color decided against, in return to a natural, native state; adorned of intellect frock, to boast imagination to venture a Delphic day, when husband and wife stood in the Apollo temple door, engaged the Mediterranean Summer sunset breeze of the fall of the Cyprus night. The mists of darkening glasslike sea, resounded musically but one movement of a symphony the Gods had with the hand of nature written for thee. With positiveness and lightness, gown wavering in harmony on the gentle winds, you shimmered with gold and with caramel brown; survey the flowered meadowed down, before the far grassy sloping to the rocky shore, the ancient husband and wife, loyal citizens of Nicosia, together in peace, welcomed the end of day.

Essence of Christmas

She cut a smart silhouette in the morning backlight, arms raised outright, long back arched, and feet planted tightly to the floor; the creature eked of the Evermore. Some magnet in appearance, yet staid in the soul? What gift denied or trick of mirror and smoke? gave the lovely body to the lesser self. The warrior with the burden, the shining bright of the Holy Knight, confesses to the redemptive propensities of the righteous fight. Be nearer to the Divine this time—the sacred babe put upon, finds great trial in creating a life; when how lovely the figure cutting thru the night, interferes with the truth of a soul on mission, to stumble into a hole, from which extraction is not forthcoming, lends to a lifetime of self abuse and numbing, and the essence sooth of the floral fragrance's draw—the honeyed path of delight, the balm of the warrior right. What work abstains from the less-than-whole? giving birth to the nation of charred remains of the lovely, who once had dreams and animation. Must be some hole thru which may seep, a glimmer, the rays of hope, safekeeping, and healing. The darkness at bay, the ocean of interference, the non-reflective surface upon which lay light inert, must be cast away. When alivened and real, the Divine awaits at less than arms' length, to be invited in for wisdom—and corporeal defeat—the Christmas to begin.

TRANSFORMER

Transformer thine; the Mistress Beauty known thru time, changed in a day, to a wash of the troubles away—the eye doth see strange new sights, when disease is washed from the eye's night. Mistress Beauty was known, and then not known. Revealing from beneath the hat of white, some stranger in the hall, known, but not at all. Who is this lovely new? borne this day December true; having fallen from the rearranged mind, of slightly clarified design. Some beauty sitting next to within, just shy of mortal sin; a Madonna's next of kin. Flashing blue, the retinue of iris practicality. Who are you sitting across? from which drew some familiarity, though also the strangeness in peculiarity. How love begins anew, when the Madonna touches; answered prayers of discovery, of lifted veils and honeyed trails, down which wholeness lay. Also resurrection, of native affection, bends toward the break of the modern mental state. Come some beginning, again, a start of renewability, before the permanent end. Fallen into disappearance, that stranger who one once knew; a distant second, after you. Intermingled, concealed, the doosey from the choosey heart, flew from the location. Bested of nation, coconspirator in a love affair, the unfamiliarity, in the air, around you, yet the observance or appearance, can best be explained as one having gone insane with pain, and vibrated away to a stray, only to reveal the lover, peaceful real, standing bare in Winter's air, of the season. Try to erase the meaning on the face, the leftover family affair, and stand anew in the soul light true, no longer vacant or erased, the Beauty Mistress, you, and all for the cure of the eye disease. You never looked at once so strange, so familiar, so lovely.

LAUGHTER

She tossed back her head to laugh and to dream. Unabashed by the dreary of the scene, she shone forth with soul force. Always at odds with potentiality, so lovely an energy in storm, fighting thru the hazards be. And never knowing when the storm intensifies, then. Beauty Maiden Youth in pursuit of truth, which, in short supply, hazards beneath the constant midnight sky; oh, moon's peek, doth the heart's sanctity keep, when a lover's last stance so early in the youth peaks. Great brown eyes, so apparent yet among the stars. Ohio Valley, mystic imprint of some Great Foot, the beauty naturelle reflective on the face; and kissing lips sequester the spill of her bleeding heart. The valley for lovers, some vast hole for which to park, she held hands to remain in spark. Righteous voice of fortitudinal choice, how Beauty cut thru the rabble of youth. Love condescended in your path, and though the turbulent waterway afore, you never once blinked or steered astray, from grand tasks at hand, but unpleasant. In admiration—Joy sprung forth in vocal presentation, with sing, and dance, and the vista of what hopes spring, to lovers. Some noble warrior in the kindness-fun of youth; always alone in your vision of truth, but the dance distracted in celebration for the dramatic touch—heavens envied your illumination upon the stage, and threw triplets of troubles at thee, instead of rage outright—perhaps to extol a comedy to amuse the pantheon of hosts. Unkindness then for kindness, this coming from the gods; so what escape remains? for the apple of their eye! Drawing such attention die; for one Beauty Maiden Youth so anxious to live the truth of her soul joy.

PROTECTIONATE

Founder at the edge of grace, grand success of the intellectual race, brainy collection, exhibition place. Beauty Maiden Youth succeeds, stressor on the boundary, flight into alternity, fancy a look at the human Sargasso sea, immediately adjacent the inevitably complacent see—how ideals hold up to reality? Oh, how well supported by the minion floor, who share the same directioned stare as thee—the downslide of the educationary? The standardization of so-called individuation, by definition introduces group, and, therefore, limitation. Maiden youths of academia, hover in conglomerate, create an overmind of likes and hates, and in subconscious despondency, blighting on the soul, manufacture currency, of what the flower was, is, or hopes one day to be. Ineffulgent substitution, an artifice, a prostitution, bournes and looses a society, a tragic net to waylay reality, which thru division, diminution, and attrition, reduce exile to derision what natively might have been a work compassionately, a royale achievement of psychological toil, something more than the sum of steps, maneuvers, and what would be the natural recourse of time, when applied. Crossing the top-depth line at graduation, what travels with learnèd? beyond the glaze of brightness, haze of intellectuality, some rote response to the determined choice of randomity—can an exhaustion of outcomes possible, be? and still claim a spare among humanity, or would a shooter take down one obstacle at a single glance, then advance, confront the next, take aim, repeat—this technique a vehicle to eternity? May a jagged, lengthy recourse be, but this in opposition to—or result of—intellectuality? How is loveliness learned, made transportable, kept mobile, beneath the onslaught of ugliness and infection of the mind, in the land across the line.

Slow Piano

Winter snow, slows a piano, played by the beauty maiden, standing at her station. Some Summer sun of far away, shines upon her Winter day, though from another time; ageless part of the endless heart, still carried the human fray, and, then, odd relations between the years; distortions in reflections, cause the differentiations, in maiden youth, which, beyond familiarity, leads to alienation—only the end of you appears in view, and that left to bubbly youth. So what the explanation due? for the dispairity in the days of the timeless lover of you, and you, and the most social of human ways. The actor, then, accords the playwrighting of the pen, of the Author Divine; animated by the strongest mind. Slow piano, and hilarity, with accompaniment, the beauty maiden sing; laugher and the young doth ring, with a certain resonation, and pull the lover's admiration, from beneath the sea of material limitations. Winter winds blow truth, again, and though in corpus youth ancient you yet begot habitation. Vivacious, yet at a piano slow, you practice self control. And, hence, time to hang familiarity upon your soul-signature tree. Cover you with kisses, anew, this round of playing down the angel in the beast. The arrogance of insolence, when form outstrips function—or when Beauty misses Truth; but in silence in a frozen moment, though banished to years' rent, it is you behind the laughing crime, of irresistible eyes posing to deceive, the slumbering portion of the conscious mind, of an eternal lover, sharing breath with thine, then and now, and again and again and again; who negotiates your slow piano in Winter.

SNOWFALL

Snow or ancient ghosts, descend upon the inner coasts, without tongue or boast, of what deer fear the most, in field and wood in late Fall; the popping rifles call. And silence beneath the wheel, of exploration's vehicle, and thru the silent air, it conveys a personage, daring to be there; near the sea, the human destiny, snow falls silently, muffling the waves' call, cry for what warmth Summer lost, and for what cold remained yet to be, before Spring; ancient freezing brings, the cleanly, freshly cut of Spring. The hand to the touch, icy dog for but a moment upon the lip; stinging frost of minimal burn, a snowflake descends unto momentary death—the lifespan of the fleetest whim, yet what magnificent exclamation of individual design of the Overarching Mind. Crystal lattice signature may, for all the fears, dispel all doubts that, though the children of the Divine have been cast about in desolation, they are never, never left without consolation. Proof of intent behind creation, reflection of the One in the expression of individuation—no two the same yet partaking of the name. Winter storm blows about, the trillion snowflakes in description: snowfall. Beauty of it all! Distant sun obscured, yet motoring the North winds and the tilting earth's turns; hidden light bournes the dark of night, and furthermore, wends the seasons four. How great the magic, then, in snowfall, the white night of the Winter day.

(UNTITLED)

Distant silence descends upon a Wintery day, with dusk, and the sleeping time of light, fading into the rising night. Defined by the outline of what impedes the falling snow into humanlike shapes, but then some perhaps as indistinguishable as covered trees, or yellowed, flattened grasses stretched tall, collecting no such riders as the trees, for the flailing in the breeze. With clouded cottony sky, paled grey, pregnant sheep, enormous, floating above, by, turning upon occasion, to shake loose beauty from the truth, leaving then, what appears to be a tortured flock of hens. How crazily the motion affects, charges with electric momentum, crying screams of rubbing against the Unseen. The beautiful face in the Winter night, shining light in darkness, corrupting Right. What now of then? save the holy sheep and hen, which delude that truth, that more than one moment may seduce, when Truth is the pen, which writes only as the tip contacts paper, and no moments more, or before. The present in the presence. So in the silent night, the songs of eternal delight, play of silence and light, the calm and peace, after the dreamt-of storm—the found separated beauty of the morn, and first a risen sun thread, stranded orange red. Slightest peach bled off to sides, this when a hole had opened in the skies, if but momentative to portray the revelation: beyond crowded skies, on some distant far side of earth, there the sun never fails to shine, and night is a dupe, then.

Cottage Garden

The view of the peasant land, far from urbania, where no hint of man's desecrating hand, finds. The mottling green in Summer light, gives motion exaggerated to the trees before night, with the overall-within delight of a living, shimmering color bright, some astral projection of masterful story telling onto the screen of day's animae. So far beneath the surface of the trees, aimed singularily across an inner galaxy, a single bead of laser, trains upon a soul pond; with photonic mouth, the laser line exacts bliss trouts out, and paints then, unearthly intimate portraits for story time of man. With blessings upon the crown, the old woman bended down, to gaze upon the intricate fern, with her utter incandescent burn, elective gaping pupils nearly crazed with resultant blackness but not darkness. From such a well, the spirits tell, the artists from the muckers. How peasantly attracted, doth Nature find her poor—the browned corn, the fields, the drifting snow—the playground of the Evermore. Simple, thatched roof overhead, to happily catch what Spirit bled upward, spilling from the head, while genius touches paint—the explosive radiations, spilling from the head, when paint touches brushes, touches canvas. At the perfect work of the intricate fern, still even the master blushes; bearing down, taking in, the inspiration from Creation.

ROLE

What role may be a play, alone? Such the girth that role may weigh. A lover of another day, feels a soul known as beloved own, yet some slightly different face, in recognition of the other place, time. In the sacred aspect eyes, the story of this glorified one, borne of a previous sun, yet, recognized. Who were you? as evidenced familiar, lover true; some same face ahind thine own, had at least once before shared a home; a corpus, enlivened, shining collector for the sun, no more wondrous toy to play upon the remarkable day of creation— some marvel of colored light, the fanciful dancer in the human Night, cross-spectral rights ta'en, the ultimate child of delight, borne of Father Galaxy, Mother Nebula, from some union beyond the stars. Thru the tiny tunnel in the forehead, the visionary read, what was before, to be again, the lovely of the dream. Laughing, come 'round, again, the golden haired now is red. And it is in that familiarity, that the clue to *Who was she?* posts tense to be—for the Force backing the face, is present and ever was, just playing a temporal game, of illusion, and bodies bearing names, identification—what futile attempt at differentiation! When all at once, only One, begotten of the sun. Some dispersion, though a beautiful toy, she may not boast beyond that joy, of Lover Divine, the Actor in all minds, and Wright of the Cosmic Play.

RAVEN IN WINTER

Coal eyes cast down, the raven brushed by, swooping low—a black fire in the snows—the smolder of her youthful glow. Snappy, as if on or off, in just a flash of flesh, feminine elective switch. Some hatchet hidden in hand, wielded by eye contact, she chopped a man, to a hundred pieces, wondering which to upon land first, head or entrail, or tail, while sorting out the bloody heart. White severe, as onsetting Winter clouds, with Winter in her cheeks, black hair let down to shoulders bare—ne'r trifled with what she'd keep, at bay, with the stunning gaze; from skies on high she'd dig a grave, for lowly prey unsuspecting—on indefensibly admiring. This storm of maiden youth, the weighty truth edged in the dark of eyes, slim tune set in rhyme, buried in the symphony of night, so that though perfected in her toil, her music played out indistinguishable, unknown, unheard. Contrast to the day, the darkness of the raven lessened, seemed to have more to say on light and all things far less heavy than what hid within the night. Bowler, in kinesia, the density in potentiality, the dark maiden at rest, for but a second only, and then in blur of flight, the essence of delight. Agenda, postpone, the raven's coming home, to alight upon the first in sight, what her heart had bent. A work of indiscretion, perhaps, but her life, nonetheless, or perhaps a lie of perception, in that with tremendous strength, she drew the wrath of weaker lovers thus committed to her heap!

ARC SECOND

Angel had escaped some low fires in a hellish place; frozen just in time in sleep, the peace of rest impressed her face. Beautiful arc second, swath of starry skies at night, with equivalent, drew, the arching brow on you; radius from closed, rounded eyes, the brow yet arched past, by, on a higher plane of lower forehead, turned half away, envision in some future day, when hell hath no furied grip upon it, the dark thoughts that she'd considered life, when awake and setting in the dark of light. The pressure of the devil of it, demonic half-wit that stumbled onto the brain adept, poisoned, burned, beauty at rest and not the slightest threat. How monstrous the affinity of darkness for the light, to steal and abuse what good things to be made of the shining, and cast to shadows what rightly played in day, the proper way. Sleeping angel, all at rest, read smiling on the lips; free at last from the burdens of the test, of inhabiting a corpus monkey, dragging it unawares, and gaming something called *happiness*, when fires did burn any hint of it. So an off-joke or -jest, this test, to take an angel and make her sick with it, this intervention of the soul, with what the disillusioned eyes may claim as the material whole—yet the lacking in the memory of bliss, never disappears complete—and so the image of saint dispossessed of the mortal disease, always present in the nag, the feeling in the leaden flesh, that what was meant by God was wings, of light, the fleeing of the Night of human days.

By Starship to Avalon

Seeing an opera sing, transported beyond the ocean's ring, or land that'd only understand, such as flying things driven by foreign beings. Late one empty night, selected in the dark past light, the starship zoomed in, and chose its next of kin. With all about asleep, it flew above the deep, but for only 26 miles out—to, loh, the island Avalon, where in the bay doth sit upon, the lovely brimming opera house, within which the ebony virtuosa bellowing about, with some far-concluded base, occluding her immediate space, protruding ancient, columnaded amphitheatrical architecture, reflecting a million moons' light, dropped and shattered by the original upon the restless, cupping sea. Hallowing to the hills on the island high, beset by Avalon Bay, the starship came down. Tiptoeing and teetering, the starship had stopped to hear the ebony virtuosa's singing! and as a silent witness to the wonder of the thing, the foreign beings did the sleepy earthly kin bring? Between midnight and two, the transported new lovers viewed, thru telescopic walls, the twinkle, the glow, of nighttime Avalon below, and the ebony virtuosa, echoing the opera, filling the early morning late-night sea mists with her sing. The symphony of the picture rose, and knocked upon the aesthetic astral doors, having them just barely caving in. Cracking, snapping, a portion of heaven's best bled down to within, the foreign beings and their earthly next of kin. Who travels a trillion intergalactic miles to unravel? the blessedness of sin, of *feeling* the ebony virtuosa's song thru an earthly next of kin but—deafly foreign beings able to see the astral light but not able to hear the liberating sound of paradise caving in, upon Avalon. Begging, the sweetest kiss was, the whole of her half of it.

ENEMY

To be at odds, but to be familiar, winking with a knowing nod; yet to be at once remained in admiration, scary sense of confrontation in addition, while knowing from the depths, a part is merely assigned, then played. A lover once, a murderer or enemy then, but beyond the star in the head, no such offensive dread, connotes to harm the dead of living; no difference in the quality, all exist in harmony. Why bark? at the Playwright Divine, for the whims and murders and lovers of the Overmind, creating below, the fodder for the show! when upon the earthly stage, He gifts the actors total independence thruout the age, of each complete, run of incarnation's fun. Eight million lives the soul of a stone has reported led! 'til resting still in secure at the top of the human head. That said, Mistress Beauty shrewd, whizzed by the edge of view; voluptuous, pointed stead, who, in the place of Truth, had appeared. Shining glare of that familiar aire—heated to the edge, of boiling, roiling—surrounding the golden hair, countenance faire; some surprise or interruption—yet produced a certain obstruction, to the operation of truth, for the fool mistook a lover's smile for the warm entirety of a friend; hence, disarmed, a fool beneath a mistress' charm, though enemy, may a lover be, due to insanity in the admirer's head. Distant Tragedy then moves close, and feigns to make a fear of what lovers boast of most: some dependency of love upon their breath, the animation test! or can love pursue beyond the grave? the essence it had in life a corporeal object made, of Mistress Beauty.

LEGAL REPETITION?

Thrown by the double of a mistress fair hitherto known—a phenomenon, this trampling on, the golden hair of the original. Staring at the name, then remarking at the face and frame, for though time has passed in handfuls of years, resembles does this new one as intricately as the former in memory held dear. And how can time refrain, in order to sustain? while also charging forth in locomotion. One pocket in quantum potentiality, seemed to be playing tricks on thee? or one more intimate, dear. The golden flowing hair and lighted eyes, and polish nose with bump mid way; the full lips, soft expression of the face— yet you spoke with more authority than had you in your earlier, alter-time, -place. Alit, softly face did glow as did, that other you, the relative kid. When matching laughter, gasp for gasp, the aetherial electrical tantalized, scintillated the architecture of your composition; faintest Stuff magnified thus, extended, weighted by multiplication, amplified, then in a delusive stroke of the Hidden Hand, you seemed so real to lovers of magicians' tricks; but ultimately, from the Mother Divine, the greatest steal, a borrowed heart inset with which to feel. Indeed, if days rewound, years retook, despite the labors of the minutes' motives, you soared the temporal skies, arriving from then to now, the exact same. The harmony in tragedy is that the physical is only a game. You, who broke the Cosmic Joke, with attention to detail, remembered to change your name, in order to neither confirm nor deny, the cosmic axiom: no earthly actor returns as the same. But no further hints either part of you produced, as would be expected, of that which exists not to touch, became more woman, less girl, tho all truth. And it was the woman's lips that pressed to one's own, while your maiden heart yet remained at home, in that decade before you became the mistress-you, you later made.

PORTRAITURE IN RED

Crossing at the sunny foyer, maiden love posed, agreed to a rare photograph. God above favored her love, and blessed the earth, placed her in. How cautiously the rays alit upon her shoulders, for fear of yet another year rejected, cast into the aether, adrift. Having sought this specific task, to lighten, enliven the eyes fallen from darken skies, and trailing a vast swath of stars. Fortunate foyer, to have so honored a guest, to inset upon a photograph a posteritous gift. Maiden lover, coal black hair flipping over that streaming light in the air—loh, shimmering, glimmering crown, the affectation of an ending point of some cosmic combustion, in celebration of a Christmas day in July, for memory, spherical curls, caramel marbled eyes, frozen in a moment within, the textile structure of the aether blown in, thru the swinging foyer doors. Feisty sprite, strange old friend anew, how you were enamoured to, a starring part in such a mission, as hungry souls feast on dreams of. And with a giggle and a toss back of your head, admiring eyes were sent to bed, with thoughts of a perfected feminine half, a portraiture in red; hearts' desire came true, inset in the maiden lover, you. Refusing a chair upon which to coquettish bear, the brunt of your modest weighted knee, to balance your barely frame, hands grasping the rounded back of the chair. It was the photographer who would need despair, for two decades hence, as the film and photograph passed into that posterity, undeclared—not only the undeveloped film but the camera lost.

FOLDING

Beauty Maiden Youth took a coffee order. Blazing ebony eyes, connoted some just-barely absent truth. Fluidly but not mechanically she moved. Flowing hair trailing, she pivoted, stepped, bent, stepped, reached until at last pulled from oven a plate with pastry, and garnished with a napkin—delicately, perfectly folded in half. More than just a gesture, she presented a meal, in a scone. Some sense of past familiarity, existed in bowèd eyes, such that kindness in discrete silence in a public place, made a blessed annunciation of an otherwise private grace. Thee maiden sang a sweet song, a mixture of fury and floral Spring breeze. Ready with the tune, she the songbird flit about and filled the room with a sunshine from another time, a future era of happiness yet to be again. All aglow with a light turned inside out, an anciency in the quality, bespoke her soul of eternity. Sharp muse, then, attestation to that which begins at its end; timeless light, burning in the night of earth; excruciation pain of human childbirth, punishment or blessing? of the falling play, exists in capacity, potentiality, in every maiden of day. Always in the flourish of the iris eye, reservation for this accommodation, written in mysterious artistic hand and ocular ink—this entire story told anew with every blink. *Nice to be the recipient of some small affection, thus, folding.*

Educator Blushed

Madame Beauty led *some* minds to thoughts of work. Standing straight, she cared enough to an effort make. Blessed yet beneath all trials, and powdered scars to almost beauty marks made, she proceeded with noble grace, and from within the depths of blackest inner space, beyond darkest eyes, at furious motionless' pace, she burns as a star. Duly sameness wonderful, on flipside burning star, only blessed fortuited the she the earthly players knew to be. Though sacred mother, fondly other role to fellow sister-brother citizens, and to teach; yet also the passionate lover. Some affection to spend on romance, to see a husband in another citizen brother, makes questions on the subject of the singular fidelity: If so tempted the gaze to fall on the handsome set of coveralls, then how can that sameness be? with that lover vowed for eternity. And then why espouse to love at all? to purse and bother the lips, meant for the chaste kiss at one other half of the same soul shared, declared a mate? Can love, if it is to be at all, ever be above? the leaden, laden body glove; excise to eternity, where thru worthy skies it flies unhindered by the chains of human eyes' remains. To tempt the touch, the Madame Beauty, much distressed, though in grace struggled with the animal portion of the human half angel, half beast. Just inside her nighttime eyes, lay eight million lives' trace, and which find annihilation only in the distance-furnace transformation flames, of pure white soul light, far, far away. Madame Beauty breathed unknown perjury, in an unwifely, unmotherly sigh, yet distinctly womanly. She blushed at classroom admirations' affections.

HARVEST

See them wave in the poetry of the knave, rustling leaves on the shoulder of the corn; have captured some moonlight in the slick, dewy sheen, filtering out of the moisture of night. Save for the half yellow moon, the haze covering the blackened sky, burdened too much the feeble shine of the far distant stars, so none came thru. She weaved her way thru the tall stalks bending back, and occasional cuts she received, from the natural shivs that the corn had built in. Some West wood existed beyond vision, as a corn a wood all its own. Yet trampling on, to a farmer's lament, made miles of inches in the yellow night march. Only the lover's drive gave hot blood to her stride; and destined to end with a beginning, again, as true love, when found and left incomplete, always circles back 'round. What warm union? lay in the wood at night, that a thousand overseeing angels banish from sight. Sweet love misunderstood, or dire envied by those lacking corporeality, though lovers in such saints' care is an angel's livelihood. The holy blush at the magic in her touch, that the constructive destruction of and by the Sacred, is too much, and leaves hopeless the minority of the blinded who see, some upside to the downslide from eternity. Would some kind, great Mother Divine grant forgiveness to Her child mistaking lust for love in an abdominal heart? Trampling corn, bending, parting stalks, not nursing unnoticed, now bleeding cuts on forearms and face and breasts, as the lover passes tests, and overcomes. Her heart's bequest awaits in the darkened wood to the West.

Last Man on Earth: Final Harvest

Beneath the harvest moon, holding tight the memory of warm June, the gleaner making passes on the yellowed corn, collides in noise with the soundless onset of night—all cosmic equipment operating in the airless far of space, and though massive, inversely exercising most of Silence's share, when all the fuss comes from the mouths of the tiny living. And so, from that airless place, soaring down from space, the scout ship appears, hovers, and then peers up to the orbiting mother, and waits above the half-gleaned field of corn. The catastrophic swipe the previous morn, by a screaming meteor, having entered and torn, inside the earth's atmosphere, and, therefore, speaking out now for the ageless, silent, massive All; eternal roar. Standing, looking West to the wood, in the stubble of the half-gleaned corn, the last man on earth listens to the rustling of the million yellow leaves of the hundred thousand ears, and regards the ship, hovering above. Only just the previous morn, handing money to the Beauty Maiden Youth, working the filling station booth, off the highway of truth, and then parting with her peering out and thru the window pane, sparing no intensity of gaze, for a future and, as yet, unknown—but recognized!—lover. With a sudden blink of painted, batting lashes, the miracle of drawn souls from the Long Gone, delegated again to airless, silent space—a memory of a happy moment soon to be erased, with the passing of the planet, in the final throws of meteor-induced quakes. The last man on earth in the moment of not only silence—but stillness as well. In the East, the glow of false sunrise just begun, or the reflection of molten lava raised by the upended girth of the ancient-buried Appalachian shelf. To the West, the onset of a real and final night....The last man on earth closed his eyes, and listened to the rustling of the million yellow leaves of the hundred thousand ears of corn, enjoying some symphony, to underscore, the musing that yesterday's Beauty Maiden Youth from the filling station booth, had laughed as well as smiled, in addition to that screaming gaze. What thoughts pursue? the mind long bought-off by aestheticity, in the face of the annihilation of the human race. From the night to the West, the wood asudden set to blaze, in seeming daylight then, the brilliant yellow of the corn began to take over the vision, when the last man on earth broke reverie. He recoiled from the waving heat, dropped to his knees and wept. And the cool beam of light, descending from the hovering scout ship, pulled the last man out.

FAIR

Promise in the Fall air. The whirligig in cyclic maneuver, shooting bulletlike thru the early night. Scent of sweets wafting, to be breathed in, with the colored lights and musical din, cut by raspy horn blasts and infinite multitudes peering into others' eyes, burning with the bumping against, danse of human flesh. Howling down the walls of heaven, sense of adventure creates the fun demons, and a feel for holy possibility made real the food of the little monsters. Now in darkness, the cattle not seen but smelled, inch closer the country barn to the urban yard. Sheep bleat in their temporary city meadow; horse stand still in nearby stalls and stare within, with dark eyes all black pupil, into the Endless Mellow; all flowered about in this scene, the maiden youth beauty queens, pitching their gist to the grabbing unconscious buyers of such things; how far, then? from the amorous hares' pens. Oh, quite far in most regards! but then this lower similarly then. Still a higher lover in humanity, no matter how fast asleep, in the advancèd brain and spine, consciousness' keep. Brutus making rounds, and with the most muscle, attempts to flail in angst the road-blocking populace trapped within his swathing girth; but to the credit of the meat, the future of a race preserved, and just maybe in the dawn of mind, a conscious higher, truer love is birthed, trembling upon the dust beneath the wide-eyed fair-goers' feet, some dampness of the mists of night's time cakes, with the beginning and the end of what Life makes. At a sharp angled reflection of a neon glimmering shining brightly perfection, in the corner of her dampened eye, the crowning maiden beauty queen, sees a dimming in the brilliant scene; desire fulfilled at the fair, late, late, night 'till early, early dawn. Howling all the while, the Brutus fiend, out from the spinning, whirling machine.

In a Moment

Some Force, wearing faces exchanging places, crying out in silence, Ultimate Voice, from moment to moment. In fluidity, the speeding motion of all, as if some constant television scene, never ceasing changing—until at last peering out thru you, in eyes' radiance—can for a single moment all motion stop. It seems as if one eye, some signatory song, plays thru the radially long, the fanning iris blue, then brown, and black, and green. As if to empty that television scene, of eternal differences, and moving, moving, moving, the One beguiling end to elusive, hiding Friend; from a hundred thousand faces in flight, thru eternal night. The gently falling shade of light, illumines just an iris: the splashing elongation that determines singularity of identity, and, yet, in that distinction, still the Common Cause created, from a whole to parcels; and, so, in truth, despite the rainbow coloration, still no differentiation. So in the musical eyes, the symphony of individuation! The flight connected faces, in that quietude of instant recognition, what is perceived to be in you, is in actuality, the common You. The delicate feminine, in the flowering parade, of the hundred thousand faces, in iris eyes identification is made. But so, in suspicious beauty known, the peeling away of what is seen, the enchanting, sacred One Reality, dispels as unique souls sailing from the Sole Origination. Sweet belle, the tolling in the iron spell, cast from moment to moment, until, at last, freezing in a moment as You in your iris.

Marys

Awesome fate, to walk into, the gateway keystone of perspective shimmering light, cast adrift atop the sea. Blueness from the iris eye, spilt onto the magic sky, seems to be a reverie, of some past Summer high, or elegy for the Spirit in the sea. All about, the Marys calling out, or gulls' cries, at the saturation point of beauty. *No more ends to Summer, please!* Nature Mother humours as no other, and despite the pleas of August lovers, She tilts the world with a cooling breeze, brings fall to the water-washed sands at the edge of land. If, in a spurt, some substance may be eked of noumena, a proof of eternity may at last be had; perhaps only, in belief? beyond the finger's touch, or the ear's detection of music rough, must some feeling lay, such that knowing is a precision brain hidden in the belly! How much heavier the sight of gore to the gut, than is lead. Surpassing in speed electricity, the brilliance of knowledge in feeling. All about, in receptive hanging out, tentacles of aerie octopi grasping at the light, squeezing tightly, as if to hold rightly, though in abstraction against impending night. Every particle composing earth, sweetly a heavenly mother of the Christ, giving birth, bearing witness to and sustaining mirth, descended from above, buried in the dust, resurrected in the bust of the mortal mother, suckling babes and passing vision then into men, who grow and spill their love into a whole new mother. Nature nurtures life with the gift of 'Begin, again!' The proclamation of the Mother. All the sea, the finite infinity, in water cells resembles in humanity, and, so, save light, is the mother of all others.

DRIVER ON THE NIGHT

Half a world off darkness, seeing some being in the ink, miraculous mover, from point to point, on the night. Silence of the early new day without proper light, seems Stillness prefers the predawn, and invites and welcomes the driver on the night. See some amber tail lights, then red, brake lights stopping vehicles in strange areas, beneath the sulphur glow of a half-moon forgotten by those who just might know, living beneath the pseudo sun. Who looks up on the run? Quiet atmosphere, when a cigarette glows against the silver-speckled sky of black, seems a nature calmed for rest, minor expectation, that day may not come back, just for once and first; how long the dusk and after! for the driver on the night. *Hear a certain music, dear: some muted strings, and brushes on a tympani, in a seductive melody, but purely in support, of the foremost imagery—passenger with a driver on the night, face aglow in the sulphur half-moon light.* A gentle breeze blew your hair softly, slowly, seeming as if underwater goddess for an evening, ready a smile and a nod, then a head-thrown-back laughter, to mock the defeat of light—though tomorrow will never come, still flourishes the driver on the night. In backdrop, you disappear, save for the blocked stars that interfere with your stealth—for among the bespeckled expanse, your silhouette defines the darkness amongst the black! where stars do not shine. Until you giggle at the find of you, in that undercover moment before, you were one with Evermore. Then motion caught you caving in, and laughter betrayed your invisibility. Feminine nakedness revealed, the darting sprite in the sulphur half-moon light, and where you had only just stood, the stars residing in your silhouette, were returned to their glow. One stop along the way, in the black but sulphur half-moonlit early day. Your laughter echoes thru the strangeness of the scene—an unknown urban forest of the wildest mortal dream, a mixture of sleeping shopping malls, tail lights, and trees. *Hear yet the certain music, dear? some muted strings, and brushes on a tympani, in a seductive melody.* Passenger with a driver on the night.

Beauty Mistress Faire

In disconnection, the darkest days no mere reflection, of nighttimes without end, but outright rejection by the Light. In hopeless squeeze of identity, at two inches from the end, the fading party knows, the Source from which flows the soul, and calling out by name, from behind the Brilliant Star in the murky blue afar, a stranger to although and at last reacquaint. And not yet at paradise's gate, but forayed out more than half-way from home, there can be no turning back, and a remedy sole remains—trudge on in patience, due diligence, and wait....And in the deep of desert night, black has surrounded and choked the bright, only the beauty of the mistress face, may provide the wings necessary to circumscribe that night, provide the will and direction, a borrowed second sight, to be and go beyond the fear of loss of personal welfare—it is the love of the Beauty Mistress Faire, that gives the wounded soldier air, to advance beyond despair, to distinguish the living from lack of life, to provide motion when bad dreams, nightmares deny the feet their motive power to, beneath the cloudless desert sky, carry to water the parched and weary, once ambitious, enough to have ever made the attempt at crossing, even the desert, in the day, so immediate the goal. Under spell of sun hallucinations, a gold-ringed nation offers invitation, and rainbowlike, a singular coloration, arcs between day and night, and carries lost souls thru and beyond, the window set in darkness. Protrudes the face of Beauty Mistress Faire, and gives poesy to the bard, such that the wit of music and writ, exudes those astral colors golden, violet, silver-white; clever sound transmuted to color—and from the mistress face of gracefulness, the lover under the spell, feels the touch of all the brilliant, remnant rainbow others! added upon, for attainment of the initial three: It is the delight of the Mistress Beauty Faire that carries thru the night, one whom made myth of a factual life postponed, stalled upon the high desert sands far from journey's destination, even further from home. Beauty Mistress Faire, burning hotly in almond eyes, fierce fire for consummation, purification of one who desires too much of thee, or fails to project, your opposite image higher. And it is in that fractious heat, that is forged the shimmering vision of beauty whole. All this summarized: from behind the earthly lies, a flash of hidden heavenly truths revealed in the sparkling almond eyes, in the sparkling almond eyes, of a split-second serendipitous mistress meet.

Twelve Monarch

The walk may be perceive, in the faerie realm, at edges of the sea, failing then in flight, the butterflies collect to cease to be? In the hollow of one footprint, delicacy and beauty lay, with damaged and partial wings, in its haven for a day. Cold sea laps at the portal to infinity, where still somethingness attracts the meeting twixt the massive. The face of a bug, but when added wings and color, a floating mini-mural held high by the skies. Yet the monarch no longer flies. Sleeping time in early Fall, the quiet monarch contemplates the wave. With barely a flutter, Nature Mother mutters, then sputters, for along the shore way lay eleven others, neither in nor out of the condition of sin—or awareness of the body. What if to teach? what heaven out of reach? that a progression of such gentle beasts, may alitter the beach, as if some aetherial messenger dozen, fallen angels, or gulls yet to be arisen, in some future beginning; perhaps a spilt saint's piece, or portion; or spark of brilliant fiery infinity—but most definite a lighted thing, by a glow beyond the condition of having to have wings. To stare into you, thru eyes dark, to find there a remnant soul, left behind within, to switch off the lamp at final departure. A mute voice, from behind which sings, songs of eternal Spring. And so in Fall, and true to the word, twelve monarch fell upon the seashore. The subtle warmth, from a human palm, may extend, postpone, for just a slightly long, defray cold death beneath waters' reach. Cruel dance, to approach then recede, upon the shallow's thin glass, that wetly supports yet captures thee. When a will has withdrawn, and color drains from butterfly wings, bleached in a blue lake wash, a superior vision may then entertain; twelve monarch gone.

CAVALCADE OF SCALLOPS

Love said, 'West!' Into a setting sun, the marriage of the sea to the land beneath impending stars of day's ending—Who owns the dusk? be it the greedy night, or the daily age of light. Rare the balance of woof to warp, and seeding then, the on-or-off way of men. Blown from the disturbèd west, wind from the sun, pushes wave after wave of the sea, breaking, mixing in with a mellow dulling yellow, until then the cavalcade of scallops portends a quickened end. A certain weightlessness, descends of the sea, as if to cause a recollection of a high field of ripened wheat, standing windswept upon a mountain steppe, and with the sweeping, the Hand of God by human eyes is met, and seen to caress in vast strokes. And so with the sea's top, and its cavalcade of scallops alive—the Hand of God, or a hundred thousand great, white dolphins' leaps and tucks, or the rolling surf! Eked from some two-ended ray, at this end of which spills forth today; at the other, the invention of tomorrow? lay, beyond and yet to become the first sights beneath the rising sun. Fall's breath is breathed in the rumbling chest of Divinity. From Nature Mother's full breasts, the children of Eve suckle the milk, or the sea. Crying out, staring into that West, the gulls announce this scene, with muted voice, lacking the intensity, meaning Nature Mother held a secret too big to be kept by the sea; betraying gulls, then tickle her ribs with chuckles—it took a thousand gulls' chattering to one clever kingfisher, to induce them to divulge the secret: The end is the beginning; the setting sun, only a few hours shy of the rise.

TISIPHONE

Sound turned into colors red; the robin stood proud, breast puffed, pushed out, as if in anger; grounded yet longing for the clouds, steely sweet, the feisty Beauty Maiden Youth, took aim at stubborn sooth. A standard raven face, coal Night collected in warring eyes, thin lips and woman's thighs, all intent on loving woman, making real her self, projecting from the mirror she held, all the warrior she had dreamt of. What passing fancy? the woman who admired manly, and wished to be He that controlled brute forces, here beneath eternity. Fury, but a Diana she, with quiver still, raised though with potentiality, an arrow razored on edge, to buy, if need be, her manly season, from the dread other sex, so pounding inside her head—having entered true the admiration of said, stored within her eyes, from what observed of the fighting, killing men. *Why, Beauty Maiden Youth? do you wish to condescend, when loveliness and perfumery, set fires to earthly seas of mundanaeity. For instance, you drew for others, in your image drawn, the prospect of an English flower garden, and one strolling upon a cobbled path along, from which to gander, gaze at constant beauty in a rush; the thicket gathering of the nearby bush, from thru which peer toward yesteryear, future lovers who'd outlived each other, managing to escape, those razored arrows edges' cuts the fiery Beauty Maiden makes!* The darkness descends her, and painted in to her flowing hair and eyes, the twinkling shimmering, glistening stars, wavering—the little children of waves—as if seen thru a rising heat on edge, such that delusive, magician's handiwork of tricks upon the eye, transforming, made to disappear, all beauty from the seer. Errant locks of her nightish hair, draped across her blackest eye, and though relaxed, a timing beat in feet tapping, madly tapping, out an inner score, furious praise, devotion, to the Evermore. And if He she huntress sought, momentarily He would balk, being charmed to an instant paralysis, by the blinding light collected from all those stars of her night, focused, redirected, shot with laser-perfected sight, into His heart, where ne'r He expected, the fiery Beauty Maiden Youth, to speak with the voice of a hundred thousand angels. Some power borrowed from a hidden inner place, mysteriously larger-by-far than its confining outer space, she tapped when she laughed. *Have you ever traveled, Fury? to a land beyond your own, far from the pounding lakeshore industry, that He pronounced your home, to play the cosmopolitan you were observed to misplaced be. Your fire dance, Maiden Youth, you used against the burning truth, a record run across the surface of the sun, and now came to earth to display.* The fiery lover Maiden, a major part in His play. *But on dispatch, you, would not suffice to do, the duty of any wife of man. That arrow finally aimed at the skies within, let fly, left at the flick of your finger thin. You sighed, for mortally wounded in the side;* her creator He, fell from the skies. Possessed now of her quarry, thus, the fury drew a bust, a trophy given He, in award for His defeat. How the Lover divine, in admiration, of the fiery Beauty Maiden Youth, had been dethroned, had seceded His seat. *Your voice the sweetest tone, musical, as said, to the weary traveler in hearing range, is home. You, the fury who, made heaven such an uncomfortable place, for the manly God in love with your face;* whence He withdrew from His infinite selves, to be alone as only two. This is the story of the slewing fury, Tisiphone, the Beauty Maiden Youth.

PASSING OF DAY

Extraordinary events, adding to a life, what lay in the balance? then, when the mundane seems all. Some gift for the small. Surprises at times, for the laughter, high spirits, to initiate some goal to be sought. What high watermark? to tie in the attempts in life, to some life's work that had already been. A mountain of past deeds, were the planted seeds, that in the present grew, to pain the best. Some skating upon fate, ever present aware of the thinning ice, seem a bird with wings. What harm befalls a child of Light? save extended associations with the Dark. Cool moon of Fall, seems to hold in its grasp of mellow light, the world below the night, such that the walkers on the world, navigating by the dim, are thankful for the inextinguishable candle in the highs. But how bright the guru light, to burn into the tragic past, life after life out of sight. The contents of a day, the helping or hurting thoughts, the acts right or wrong, make up the humble song, the breathing play thrust onto the shores of eternity. Passing but once, the tour up, makes space to fit the individual love given a soul by an entertainment-seeking God. For fun, lovers meet, then the patter of tiny feet, and the drama of the scrambling cash; one considers what became of abundance, prosperity. Can a lover's touch sustain? the needs of a world gone insane. Beginning again and again and again. The losing party, who sees a sunset, raging across the age. The fighting ceases only when, the bodies are too many more than, those old enough to hold a gun. Sleepiness, a period between lives, for rest, reconsideration, of how the buying of the many lies, had induced the fallen to yet another sleep. And it is the dream of the lover, that brings eternal Spring, and reawakening in the eyes of babes, with all too poor a memory, of what went on before.

FLOWER PARTIAL OPEN

Would it be fatigue? or some goal yet to be perceived? and trudging thru the expansive black, vast abyssal plane, between the acknowledgement of pain, and the far-off end of it. This flower seeming past bloom, on the surface of any moment's choice. Full and unfaded crowning hair, mocks somewhat the creases in her face, deep-set lines around the mouth and eyes, some near-future call to a slowing, some downhill tour of a roadside nature flower showing. And then she laughed, and some light spirited out from within, thru her eyes. She brightened up, and suddenly, sassy lady, she! with all the reason to care to be. A childlike giggle, a nose that wiggled, yet the darkness of her complicity, added up to covert hostility. From behind the forced smile at times, she wonders about those goals not met....and the stickiness of the life beneath her feet. The desire to flee and the partial bewilderingly affected image in the mirror. How cuts the whip of time upon the bard face. But catching coalescent eyes, turned up when thru the opened window, she sighs to have met a lover in an instant, and in surprise, who takes her close, to place a kiss upon her lips, observing then her eyes two closed; spanning inside, from above blue earthen skies to astral heights, she soars beyond the human Night! How quickly then she becomes a girl, again. No feignèd happiness as giggle does complete, as the hot kisses, the warmèd hand upon her cheek, a stranger's thumb and forefinger grasping her left earlobe, as if for keeps. From beneath her mundane life, emerges a bird in flight, flashing brightly, her incandescent light; then, laughter again, squeezed out from the beholding tight. The certain musicality, fallen from Andromeda, condescended in the whispers in her ears, played smoothly, strung out long, the celebrated angels' song. What such affection in the broad of day transforms of barely more than walking clay! In truth, and truly, she knew the living, what freedom feels the birds up in the wingèd blue. And electrocution sweet.

STUMBLED INTO

One of Jason's men, sent on mission just then, to find the water. Searching thru the forest, stumbled then into, the nymphs who held the view, and guarded the water against the men. In that clearing where lay the pool, the bathing feminine collected the falling light, redirected, reflected heaven's height, which flashed as though a bursting candescent lamp. Catching fire, the forest around the pool, burning in consuming desire, was Hylus the fool. But how to withstand such flamework, unscorchèd, when the magnetism deludes the eyes, and draws closer and closer the highly combustible to the fire! The maiden's two reached up to Hylus from the pool. But having burnt a'ready in the eyes, the loss of orientation to North and South, up and down, their enchantment fell complete—not even a man of Jason's mighty fleet, could determine which end was up—the head or the feet. Bedazzling muses harped, with angelic voices, away the ability of Hylus to pull away to safety—or to at least escape. What violent deals the peaceful beauty makes; steals what otherwise would pass unbeknownst, unaware, untouched by memory's make. In sufficient heat, even wetness is burned from water, and then how deep the void, where once had been a sea. This, then, the fate that befell the men, of Jason's fleet....Hylus, falling down, distant past recalling in her lovely, strange yet familiar face, at the instant of recalling even a name, burned to death before he drowned, not in the battled death with men, Elysium's reward eluded him, but from heaven's whiteness he found the recognition in her eye—and in that instant that he passed, alighted in flame, and wet—he knew she also knew him. Drawn white with beauty loaned from paradise—her flowing hair and shining face, the brilliant eyes and kindly smile. Yet Hylus held in a deathless mind the wisdom that surpasses the earthly Night—the maiden nymphs, Jason, and the voyage on the Sea of Life—all a trick of light.

TORRENT

The Southwest winds begin again, and whip the sea into foment. Constant bursts from infinity, make divine recompense. Quiet life on sandy shore, mediates the Evermore, gives birth and living; hence, the waters lend talents to those who admire, the mini oceans with countless spires; shrinking, growing, having hire, to gulls and floating butterflies, all the soaring water-loving things with wings. Halcyon or Kingfisher, sings of a far-off Spring, as near not at all, the ghost of all Summer's going leaves in Fall. Footprints in the shore, mottled by the breeze, near erased for tomorrow's clean slate; hard to prove then that any souls did move across the bounty of sea, seeing less than more from the shore. Seated at a vacant picnic table, yet bedecked with past images of a banquet, brought to return when the warmth gave way to chill. Haunting freighter passes low on the horizon, headed for port, fat with coals against the snows yet to come. Fantastic Summer on the run! Souls of bathers still stand in the sand, raised hands against a mourning sun, squinting salute familiar to many an artist's eye. What purpose such blue vistas? save to anew the old, already viewed, *déjà vu*. What breath of life inhabits the great waters? save the respirations of Nature Mother fine. The Beauty Human tends to melt, and the sea is want to freeze, when the two doth meet—one begins to resemble the other. And so she disappeared, Madame Beauty, into the seaside. The white, and the tan, and the blue, now spoke of the former you. Whence has gone the admirer of late Summer beach? She is in the wind, the waters, the sand.

FOOTFALL

She stomped once before a kneeling eye, though delicate foot and small, sheathed within the calfskin pump, attached to a leggy tall; the waif out of place, seen sideways disappears, still featuring the recently departed California glow. Now entrenched in gulag snows, the tragedy in travesty. The beauty who stayed too long, drowning in environment wrong, still drawing a smile, with song; slender, graceful bird in flight, she soared too low in the sky of Night. A kindly smile in the face of assault, once perpetual dream had halted; stalled then in the overrun situation, that which had fueled a future of energy, occupying the identical space—a bypass in the race—with the decrepit maul, now hammering her face. Pulling up the weight of earth, the Beauty Maiden Youth nonetheless stood tall in truth, and with that stomping foot, raged out to end it all. Only just begun to fight, the maiden youth in the second decade of life, firmly attached to her dream, spinning in a world. Too ornate for the darkness of this place, wanted to cry out to you, 'Run for your life!' Too difficult to witness the slaughter of the dutiful, unconnected lamb, noble strider in a materialistic land, who stacked up tall ideals against the smallness created by men. Feminine fury in a hurry! *How do you do?* That rumbling shook a shelf beneath the soil, where your footfall disrupted the globe's magnetic coil, surrounding everything of mass, such that plates began to dissipate energy, electron orbits abated, beams of light slid from the earth's crust into the dark night. The ensuing shaking quake, result in the footfall's wake, brought the walls of the dread gulag down, melted its snows into rain. Heaven's rays shone down upon their child at play, among the sad of the incarcerated, turning them if but brief, glad. The ceiling of the gulag prison break, revealing the twinkling midnight lights above, but no moon closer to heaven, thus sadness escaped in a rush of backdraft wind pouring in, and your angel hair was the first to declare that Night was caving in. As the surf retreats into an oncoming wave it meets, in a brief moment of equilibrium, stands—trading places—you and the stars, or the end of the world to begin. Your hair stood upon end, then your frame, becoming aetherial, elongated, as you grew tall and taller and taller, to drown into the falling collected light, of all the descending stars of night. Your footfall in protest to a dream under duress, found the sound of it landing upon the ears of stingy gods of light, at first reluctant, then agreeing, to allow their stars to secede the night, accept in their place, the furious Beauty Maiden Youth, whose footfall in protest, conscripted the heaven's stars into a serviceful demise. Slightly shocked to have departed so abrupt, your brown eyes draining into tan, it was your attempt in desperation to never die, or compromise. You were a child of the Eternally Brave. Of course all night's stars assembling in one place, the roofless gulag, your stomping place, caused quite a stir in cosmic order. The pursuant black hole, had not been scheduled, and from one furious stomp of the Beauty Maiden Youth, a galactic neighborhood was rearranged!

GLAMOURING

Clamouring for the one Thing, that makes a love not small. Given the endless trails of aways, that hearts take in the day-to-day—what pleases the ears and eyes, and the resultant infinitude of made-dies, passing thru electric skies, of the charged particles, floating free, from start to eternity. What blessing then lies in the eyes of the golden maiden? if the million subsequent cries, pull the terrors off the dies and loose them upon the men living in chains, acting insane, for the gentlest touch and the errant but electric glance, of the lovers freezing trance. Golden maiden from chemistry's set, thinking thoughts confused in the matured-not-yet, beaten down by academia's constant rounding off and grounding out, so that rote memory gets supplanted for wisdom's tree, and then the ended trend of sincerity, originality, spirituality. Outdistancing her age, the golden maiden lived into tomorrow, and, out of phase, tasked—or was baked—by the light of not-yet days. Time traveler nonchalant, Fates' child relieved of wont', gifted of mercies mild, to behave for the future days, in exemplary ways, the bestowal of the golden maiden time traveler under control. Volitional, feeling the zest of heaven's sent, exuberant-coloured complexion, as if painted by the Dutch master of Drenthe. So preoccupied on glamour yet so individualized by her intelligence, that the conundrum causes her to, at any moment's regard, don wings, take flight. But, held tight for a second's sake, searching the irises of her eyes, for the acknowledging grant, to conscript one soft kiss upon the lips!

Summer Day of Night

In the Summer day of night, full moon looking on, quick, catch a glimpse of silver fire upon the lawn. The silent rite of absent sight, propose to blindness in that night. The silver seal, the burning zeal, the flaming light, all the silver sights of the Summer day of night....Seeing not, the vision begins, Divinity appears in the mists in the lowlands. Striding thru, riding upon gentle feet of the pre-dawn dew, the lovely silver you. Kindly electric feminine, collected, tall and strong, slight lank wiry, with generous bosom for your young—you feed more than the babes of Spring—how precious this youthful mother goes about stealing the beast from men, in a delicate operation whereby the power of the sex reveals, that woman conceals the truth. In such possession, no covetous thing, her flowing hair and sparkling eyes, the spilling of the spring waters, that fountain of withheld sooths. How heavily she comes down upon the ground; faint curiosity per the weightlessness you construct—must be some massive power in the inner workings of your mind—imaginings of Himalayan mountain snows—the outer world a reflection of an interior look. Rumbling thru the silver mist the dainty, massive, young mother missed, the kiss having been thrown before her way. Therefore unphased and rolling on, thru the silver fire upon the lawn. Unburnt and surpassing lovely, she met in the waning moonlight, an earnest appeal from Dawn. Hand back to the earth so much of your weight; too massive you've become for the mortal man on the run, pursuing you thru the silver fire upon the lawn, with the moon looking on, this Summer day of night.

LATE SEPTEMBER

A thousand times, this photo has come to mind: A view of you, in late September wine of reverie, the coed walking quietly thru the leaves, books clutched to breast, head bowed in remembrance or future thoughts; a heart's desire with coal flowing locks, in late September of university youth. The Maple leaf journeyed to a fall, from treetop tall. The timing exquisite, and fortunate leaf, at whose death you do bequeath, the vision golden upon that silent Mt. Pleasant street....As you fell, leaf, in your demise, you alighted upon the shoulder of the passing prize beauty beneath. Love looked up and on that leaf, so delicately balanced now upon your shoulder, upon you upon that leaf-covered street. Recognized the face from afar that had heretofore occupied so much memory for so long. Even now, you remain only twenty, and then as again you did not see, the one who loved thee. But such is life in relativity....The stride of you, then, smiling at the leaf, which you took between pinched fingers, and placed in a pocket near, perhaps to perform, in some later year, such a memory exercise as this, pressing between heated wax paper, this fortunate leaf. In such a way, the future you lived in the present late September day. And with what surprise you met, the beholden roses with eyes wet, for near not-so-distant past, reunited with a lover lost. And like the hummingbird who briefly lit for licks, so you cried to find a lover lost, but to then forget, in late September. A talk in confidence with you went well—and to have you if but briefly as a wife, to live a whole life that was never to be—in one night—is a dream come true for posterity. *What greed overcomes? such that the beauty a lover holds from all others, so that to great distress, the grasp kills and gives wings, to make of Love a Phoenix being.* Your laughter a music score, beneath the starry skies of Evermore. That single eternal night, in late

September. To describe the chimery of its tone: a giggle that became a music score, which tickled some heart of joy, some blissful center, ecstatic core, and in then a full ring-out of cello play, and light accompaniment in glistening almond eyes, for the lover seeing a sunrise five hours early. Perfumery of angelry, your heaven scent made of impending deathy spring, the glorious florals of Spring out of order; confusing, thus, the Southern-headed geese, who turned at this sight beneath, to head into their coldest Winter in some movèd Northern South! But who could tell them the truth? when below, a lover wooed away their snow, for but a brief but convincing Summer, in condensed day, in late September. And as you talked away the evening, your silent listening lover took delight, in your lifetime's symphony spent in just that night. Tragic dawn, for forty years long, found you standing in its morning light, wearing sleeplessness as hair and form, from disheveled dreams to haunt morn, only just forget; but lingering effects, found you saddened, and only slightly gladdened, to know your lover could no longer hold back the snow, as it had come time to go. Your silhouette before the streaming light of kitchen window bright, you prepared a traveling lunch—the kindest act for a lover ever performed. The bittersweet taste of intention removed from its initial place—the food partaken in the absence of the loving hand that made...the saddest breakfast. The kiss upon your lips forbade the future from prying into the gaze, of two pairs of eyes reflecting souls who had borne love from some long-forgot height. Although never met again, there remains two lovers who lived a lifetime in one late September night.

FRIEND

Vast friendship now broken into the Night. Who? What? resigns into the Right. What identity answers to a name? other than a soul that is beckoned. Silver points break the black of night, all that remains of the Eternal on High. Collective coalescent, accretion disk universal, some vast toy borne for future naughty girls and boys. The descension from the Source of light, in cosmic instance—Joy's overnight—when who flew from the beloved few? save You; yet from every inch of space is pinched the truth and endlessness. Further borne, a planet formed, and memento to the night—a hanging moon— shining bright. A burning sun at day, further wicks away, what Higher Love had supplanted in the cosmic dust. All that is awake in Nature's shake, puts to sleep the Maker in Her keep, the gentle human beings, at once godlets and a terror. Divorced of Spirit with a name, a coallike soul hides in flesh remains, and though dead awake and dying with a smile, in proclamation its happiness; the lost and buried soul, prays for one great quake, some divine friend to bar the escaping memory, of what firelight within transacted all the Night without; holy kin—the Dream's dreamers dreamt—of a simple place to being. Seeming chance meeting, the guru burst upon, the broken singer of a terrible song. Bright awake and bearing down upon, to milk the deepest mind and heart, for what promising part to play to bring beginning to this End. Oh, Divine Friend, make haste to the forgetful.

CAMPFIRE IN THE CORRIDOR

The seat of love in some above, condescends to play upon, the bottoms of all lovers! The blessed face of admiration chaste, the beauty who became another, in exchange of deepest affections, escapes the wrath of consequent transgressions. The splining in the central spine, compressed in place by Mother Divine, as the intricate touch introduced the rush, that turned all human loveliness to gray; shot slipshod for the skies, the opalescent rise, left far behind, the reason for the rhyme, the song of which surpasses the hearts of two who never sang. And back on earth, in valleys low, the bodies of the lovers play out without their souls, the drama of ages. Whence has flown to the Evermore? North of that Campfire in the Corridor, save the sacred names inscribed on each beloved soul conceived. What name shall she call her lover? when before she answered to another, most definite a he! at some point in earth's history. Poke a finger in the flesh, and, sure, firmity attests—but peel away the bone and blood, and peer then at the underlight! Confessed by the soul from behind its door, to warming lovers' hearts by the Campfire in the Corridor. No lovely lips or face or hair, worn not humbly by the maiden fair, ever made truth of the lies she lived out thru her lover's eyes....on some dark night, take those lovers past the light, grand discovery tour, see what of the Timeless More, the Campfire in the Corridor. Then has she gone insane? to declare her lover has another name.

WILLOW FIELD

With the heavy Southern heading sun, sinking into the end of day, the half-turned ginkgo leaves, flip on their trees, from green to yellow, and yellow to green, in flux between tomorrow, and the already seen. Shine feebly down upon a meadow's spine—the arching back, a hill, and the dipping-down sides, lay silent in its selves, of flowers and grasses, to listen to the chorus of dusk, of cricket, cicada, locust, and grasshopper giving voice to Mother Divine, Who comprises the All of what takes up space. In syncopation absolute, these holy little players' flutes, toot Her will with perfection—in that a tiny will combined with Hers portrays the state of grace—the humble beings no less than pure, stare, constantly without boast, Divine Mother in the face, and, as such, may be the envy of a higher race. In the fall breeze, and muting colors, purplish coneflower sways in time. Queen Anne knits her lace in a pungent aire, pulsating, lofting. Darting larks fold wings and pinch split tails to inherit this perfumery in the cells; it has some secret memory jog value for them. What do they recall? but some enormity in being small. Late-cast ragweed frowns at its deeds, for having to play the role that makes so many weep. Cypress sprigs bend with envy toward the lowland wet, where the always-seeking waters let, to sate the thirsty cattails, which enjoy looking *up* on life, but which keep company with the willow grass, always reaching toward the sky, for what remains to be seen beneath the heaven's high, of some exuberant evolution toward consciousness more profound, for, loh, fingers and hands for which to hold, the hand of Madame Beauty Human. She stands tall and straight, and as if some honeyed flowered bush, monarchs flit about her, dreaming of the delicate landing. Flowing white hair and dress, seems Mother Divine took a human hand this time, in the willow field. Madame Beauty turned, if for but an instant, to recognize a distant friend, a former love, long lost. With the weight of a full moon's pull upon the earth, Love gave birth to this magnetism twixt two souls, in willow field, in late Summer. The beginning and ending, and beginning and ending, the cycles of life produced anew, an old husband and wife. In willow field, with quiet kindness and royal poise, Madame Beauty moved about the meadow flowers, reunited with an hitherto undiscovered heart: How the past may cascade upon the fore, and drown an ignorant mind, in the instant when two lovers lost, again, catch each other's eyes. In soft recognition, of what two once had been, she gained new meaning of loneliness and hopefulness, and took on a mellow glow. In willow field.

LITTLE HOUSE AT THE STILL-LIGHT EDGE OF NIGHT

She stood, back toward, at kitchen sink, facing toward, approaching dusk beyond the window. Manifestation of silence all surround, as sleeping Nature cast the day to remembrance in alteration of its dreams. The Western downslope along Ridge Road, and stringy cloudglow across the horizon, made frame for the still-light edge of night. Only crickets remained awake, to begin the day of night, and with merry chorus, summoned hiding Darkness to come out to play. Attendant deer, now brave at the hour, moved about as if man gave them nothing to fear. Chasing the set sun, with increasing speed, the also-steeling stars, appearing in increasing number with the advance of their cause. The quiet, rolling hills, and pocket meadows, had retired beneath sheets of dew, not feeling in their depths of slumber the pointed hooves of the deer, and not hearing that cricket chorus to the night. All color had fled the meadow flowers—the blue from the bells, the butter from the cups, the red from the clover, the green from the grass—stored away to prepare for the morning fair all pigments and hue, which they present each day, brand new. All of Mother Divine's colorful show, had faded into blackness....and yet, in the impending night, the day had just begun, in a way. Madame Beauty, through her window on this night, gazed into the sound plus ways of second sight, conjuring a peaceful silver world forever in starlight. At the sink, she peeled carrots for the coming day, and chose choice fruit, an apple and an orange, a handful of nuts, a slice of bread. Her coal black eyes administered the traffic of the night beyond, to the cosmos of her inner light. Tall and lean, with shoulders square, flowing black hair, a full bosom to nurture her infants into tomorrow, into a peaceful silver world in starlight—all of her self confined within a simple cotton dress—put Lovely to the test—which to treasure best? In full chorus now the crickets, as black Night had all out to play about; the deer, with no man to fear, grazed easily in the sleeping meadow, where the flowers' minds tossed in their deepest dreams of astral colors. Madame Beauty took a kiss upon her lips, before she turned out her kitchen light, searched within, switched on another; decided to meet in their dreams, the flowers.

HIGH POINT ON RIDGE ROAD

In the quiet country best, where heaven had come to rest, in the golden setting sun, a high point on Ridge Road put paradise to a test. A covenant of the arch of the bending rays, says peace is silence for as far as one sees. Set here to describe, below collecting dusk, beside the golden already: A quiet, elevated road, the backbone spanning the county, ancient ridge left misplaced by retreating glaciers from long-gone, nearby lakes; running North to South, Ridge Road pouts—blessed Shiva had fits, bouts of mercy, and engendering gifts, shared the Himalayas of India in tiny bits! to otherwheres of the West; thus, handed down from Eastern heights, Shiva's baby teeth for the distinct American bite; pocketed meadows aflowered, blazoned colored—afallen rainbow, divested of eternity—spilled onto the grassy green of the rolling highs and lows. And mind the golden sunset glow! Oak and Maple trees, as if waves of an on-land sea, break to and fro and form the headlands and the hedges of the adjacent seeded fields. Flowing down the Western face—the plot of land upon which sits the humble place, small home with the sunset porch, where nightly Apollo of the Sky is observed to extinguish His torch, after which He yet works on but unseen thru the night. The mischievous deer dart in and out of this tree-lined spout of Nature Mother's finest pouring out; twirling squirrels hurl about in preparation for Winter's furl; the sickly sweet tinge of Fall dusting the tips of the trees' leaves, confirms—the squirrels are the best preparers of all. After sunset, when Night lights its body with stars to forgo the fright of loneliness that humankind is still a long way off, confined to the land of a distant planet; where from a miniscule stand or humble home porch—man reaches out to frightened, lonely Night, with prayers of awe and with the faculty of sight. Ambient crickets' chorus offers consolation, and in further support of Night's plight, they vow to wear black until humankind reaches the stars, at which time their wardrobe dark exchanges with white, for the wedding vast of mankind and Light, and for the happy funeral of Night's sorrows.

THE RELIGIOUS EDUCATION
OF VERONICA

Deep within the reflection of introspection, eyes upturned. Scanning inner skies, palms outstretched in reception, the lower whites of her eyes become her eyes, shiny seas of milk, upon which sailed a cathedral image mirrored. She stood in personage sans mind, before the wooden doors. Up high, the stained glass Christ stood by, peering down, staff in hand, he sought to make addition to the flock. Already fled to within, the corpse of Veronica yet stood still. The seeking, sought, with the truth she fought, and, loh, no longer remained without knowing, the normal from the sane. Rapture on the Cathedral grounds, just outside the wooden doors; breathless, cold Veronica, a Catholic barely ten days old, in womanhood of latter days than the babies who get wet heads by the hands of priests, but youth enough at twenty, to hold within a vision of blessed change. What driven blast of will to cause a young woman to thrill, to find the soul within. Bright stars in the dark of night, she gazed upon within, with coal black eyes aimed up thru her forehead. In that single eye from two, a natural without the taught, she of heaven's grace and beauty already knew Los Angeles, Los Angeles standing by, less than inches away; lovely maiden and angel-in-the-make. Veronica quickly died in the Cathedral yard, at first sight of the stained-glass Christ. Last whisper on her lips, in the sunset beyond Los Angeles, *I lived before I died.* Hope you made it home; you seemed to be so well, best fit, to the sacred Catholic writ. Many flew to thee, just outside, before the wooden doors. Smiling radiance, caught a glow from somewhere on Sunset, near a sacred bowl, a pond not far from the sea, cupped in the little mountains of Santa Monica. Divine swan blessed, the waters were the test. Holding light, passing it to you, in passing. How close and yet how far, from the Masters, in your car, on Sunset. Thanking you for driving by, Mary brought you home. Birthright to Catholicism, yet you must have traded for some other tricks—until now. The wooden doors opened; the cathedral inhaled; the flickering candles in the entry danced. Veronica, pale, came home at last. *Addendum: Upon the lips of Veronica, placed a kiss and cigarette. Saintly yet pragmatic she smoked down the business in the town. In the starry black of night, of coal for two dark eyes, wore dreams of innocence toward the morrow's many mores. Some speculation, that life's dream had an origination, she backtracked down Sunset. The Pacific spilled onto Sunset, and Sunset borne escapes from the sea. Driving away up Sunset, she rediscovered its birth purpose. The well-traveled route brought the seer from the sea. Veronica at the wheel, black hair fanciful upon the air, blowing thru the open windows. In peace, and right, Veronica left the sea, up Sunset. You smiled, and you laughed as you drove up Sunset toward your cathedral. Friendly with the Heavenly Host, admired by your beau who once watched you smoke and drive, but faded, lost. Who loved you most before you died?*

LIGHTHOUSE

Remake of a memorable day: The top half of a fully cocked head, hinged from hear to ear. The white hot firelight blazing in the eyes, burning holes in the dark of night; crying down the walls of heaven. Illumined sage, crowned in intelligence with the wisdom of the age, the upper mind seated in the highest head, still the pulsar turns in the heart, trending the end and the subsequent start—the cycle of days of ways. Oh, what blackness makes a mark of earth, where wantingness and struggle toward paradise, taxes the additional lives yet to be lead. And how many births, deaths, must just you postpone? defeat? with the kindness, love, placed at the feet of one beloved! You saved all. Count the stars of ephemerality, tucked inside some universe berth, palmed to the pocket of a great god; assignee fettered to toil beneath the One Designee, absent to beyond the Beyond. This sprite spark set to a midnight march, traverse to time, the race thru space. And, loh, here in the heights of the Himalayan snows. The reflected lore of the Evermore, in thine eye; reflected then to the eyes, protracting from the conduit Endlessness in pupil black, spilled to bluish explosion of galactic iris, tempered and cooled to white light or cornea, the manifested right—upon which grows the wheat and cattle, the firmity under foot. That purity in white, the beacon bright, rested now upon the shores of night; pulsar fed, and rotating round, is it the lighthouse in midnight? or the brilliant eyes of the half-cocked head? Open, open, spill a lotus to the floor; dabble then in that Evermore. Collect true souls from this, thine thus—long about a Noon, in beyond that reflected door—flip side of somethingness—no less yet landed here—sent from formless Spirit, in time to slay all gods, for the death of lesser heaven. Set softly on the common path, shout quiet with actions as opposed the spoken word, this Himalayan yogi came down, with total platitude for a minus life—sum of the two differences you made—or did not make—in one life. *Crying down the walls of heaven, your white hot light, burning holes in the dark of night.*

Introduction to the
Diaries of Veranda

Endless breeze batting thru the open window, buffeting the reader at the wheel of the parked automobile, Beauty Maiden Youth; strands of hair, dancing in the air. Light beams seeing what seems, emanating as the eyes; she pours over some written word, the contents of a notebook. Clarity in her visuality, enervates as if some grand mistake, that some one other should see, her moments alone with eternity. A brave song, for such a picturesque wrong, as the Beauty Maiden Youth, torn between two apparent truths: One clamouring at the senses' door, one so silent, even soundlessness is cast ashamed aside. Aloof, beset, she finds the Transcendental Sleuth resides quite close; intimate, at hand with One she values most. The secrecy of discretion, unwarranted and so, depression; for some other would not betray such a sacred way to pray. *Please, into your world admit three; not so distant and different as you would suspect—can't you see into he? Beyond regret this chance meeting is the doorway, first step, of the all-consuming tet.* Hand-in-hand, you enter a brand new land—vast brightness surround; concentric worlds spinning, spinning, spinning, rolling, rolling, rolling, in your Eye. Then, one by one, locking into their coordinated place; rocket fuel for the handicapped to attempt the race, this vision not only you knew, as he observed the Gold Ring with thee....rumbling accompanied the matter crumbling; great arc's of lightning produced the disappearance of the car, leaving you hanging, dangling in this storm, as earlier had your hair in the air, suspended from some other where. From beyond a Brilliant Star, a Great Gull came alighting, breathing out, in, the thunder. When all Beauty cast asunder, paling to the wailing, the crying from the Violet Skies, brought back to life what hitherto had died, transcended to the air, remaining in essence there. This potential of life the Great Gull ignites; the Violet Skies—plural in that overlapping—approved the Beauty Maiden Youth, for admission to its aerie Ocean Truth, now supporting the maiden and the Gull. From no reference for time, disassociated from the land, the maiden took his hand, and pulling, falling then, the Great Gull led them in, to the Whiteness of the Stars' Brightness, an ending true, for two to begin anew. She dropped the notebook, it's pages filled with her past life, fluttered back to the earth, landing in what had been her spot in the parking lot. *How often she had sought, fought unbeknownst, for that dearest friend.* That story is told in the Diaries of Veranda.

Dazzling Brightness of Place

A gentle breeze if common stance, plasters minds to a circumscribed perimeter. For all the world to one who never travels far, is a tiny place, mysterious. And the death-tongue of identification, with what lay before the eyes, the consecration of mesmerization. The tricky little satanics of interests and desires, account for keeping and holding the otherwise brave in some mire, a step from the grave. What rockets launch beyond the walls of the enclave? carrying man to some better place, may flight unheeded—unknown—from the small cell of the microverse of one's own creation. What red light stops and keeps comfortable? the world journeyor, vast problem solver, mass portrayor of the beautiful. The essence of smallness infects the unadventurous—death ensues at the very point where one refuses to risk death in an intelligent manner, for some noble cause. The trying time when light appears black; and black, in truth, is light beyond its feign, when living is life in a tent in a tornado's eye—gleefully at peace with all. How safe is safety? *Must you gain your worth in the eyes of someone who holds you as object?* What is being free in verse? than blind to the murderous axe of practicality—spending time, at length, admiring the lovely flower, until the flower becomes you; a saturation of consciousness to the extent of identification: One man became his large car; one woman became her child; neither obeyed any longer, sanctity, sufficient to seek out the other for clarity, as is intended, leaving both blinded, stumbling, lost. Beyond the wall, if they could but envision, were vacant seats in the rocket launch—someone once identified, by sustaining long, sole concentrated thoughts, with joy, until joy became in an aesthetic plane, tangible and sensible. All else of reality, so called, his toy—at play, abroad, the great god of man, sharing with other bedazzleds, his escape plan of discrimination of identification; careful where you aim. What you see is what you'll be—time to divest of the neighborhood.

LEARNING TO JUGGLE IN FARO

As the setting sun, reluctant on a run, took need of the stillness of dusk, in that deserted waterfront of Portugali Mediterranean waters. Seeming part abandoned rail yard, part rustic alleyway, the lonesomeness of paradise by the bay, no less charmed away the hovering lifelessness of the place, laying in stark contrast to the natural splendor, and the quietness of the natives; fair maidens, dark tanned and slow tongued, silkily moved about in day, as a fog descends the night. And a kindness unmatched in its unspoken presence; unsurpassed elsewhere in peoples of different climes—as if a secret homemade jelly had spilled onto the mass' floors, streets, flowing beneath their feet with mouths, sipping, tasting in the stuff, thereby becoming into; caféd by the sugar of the sweet life by the sea of eternal Summer, at whose other end lay Greece, and the portals to other blissful places, upon her island life and continuation of this sea. The ferry to the seaside, from golden to across the Faro bay, would be a while. Okay, for it was a Summer's eve in June, near the lovely sea abroad, majestic portrait, golden skyway West, putting heaven on earth to the test. Picking up stones with time; what better way to let it pass? than by learning to juggle. Faulty at first, suspending one, two, stones in air, passing hand to hand to air, then three at last, three. Young maidens approached, and in the musical voice of the mysterious tongued, with pointing—the ferry, at last, it seemed, would run. Approaching pinpoint on the horizon at the bay, then prominent figure pressing to the fore, a tiny fishing boat appeared in all fine detail. The ferry? Indeed, Hylus and the siren nymphs did board—atop, on deck—no within! The burdened craft set sail, with the joyous passengers wavering in the Mediterranean breeze, labouring for the open sea, in the June Eve.

DEER-WOMAN-DEER:
EVOLUTION THRU THE NIGHT

At dusk, fleeting magic, rust at sky, the graceful deer appeared to die, in meadow flowers and shadowy grasses; she took to task, blessing passes, for the living among the dead, shining lights who sat in Darkness' stead, thru the night....Gentle deer, she strolled among meadow hilly green, and colored flowers; rolling hills implanted thrills, for the looker-on....The coming and going, of the slender creature, dashing to and fro, with some energy unknown. Pausing near, to press an eye so dear—where Night itself hung in right—within the darkness of her eye. Fixed loose in frozen statuette, she gazed thru this way—all potentiality or the future of motion—for an instant dynamically at rest. The globule of the coal black eye, reflected the setting sun, so that three orbs concentricated thus: the solar, the earth, her eye, unifying into one. The image of a man in her mirror, standing by, so that at a future's behest, past many cycles of time, one lover may recall and know another. In the recesses of a countenanced thrust, she withdrew the photo to her soul…. Later that night, deep in Darkness' delight, the spritely woman flit about beneath the moonlit sky, leggy and dashingly, the Beauty Maiden Youth, slew with sight. The looker-on, admiring the fleet resemblance of the deer in flight. All will in essence, spill from the point between the eyes, with some madness, she whipped her form across the meadow. Encircuited route, the Beauty Maiden Youth, disappeared beyond a hill, then reappeared, and headed toward, increasing her flowing loveliness still, coming to, from the darkness beyond that hill, so that in instantaneous rush, having flown across the meadow floor, and now standing stopped before. Liquid hair pouring down to shoulders bare—the cascading of the fair—without a moment's dare, she gazed into a looker-on, with deep, bottomless night for eyes. Searching an ancient memory, for the template of a lover's intensity; finding thus, managing yet to hold her gaze unbroken, she quickened as if a quake, to know she was looking at her matching fate, in the looker-on. And now the three orbs with joyous ignite—the moon, her eye, the earth—conceded a fourth, and addition to Evermore, one for the looker-on. With maddest sense of shyness, her nakedness became known before the love that was her throne—that upon which sat her elevated heart. She turned and fled into the night. Losing Love, the face of the moon above, waned, drained....Later that night, heavy on the horizon, the sliver moon, loh, grew, for in the wood below the bedroom window looking on, a twig snapped, in anticipation of the dawn? but then, again, a startle within the overgrowth, gave away the hide and seek....*Is it you, dear? in the wooded near, calling upon that distant song, sung, and so familiar....* The snapping twigs moved left to right, across the bedroom window's sight, yet without the moment's revelation of the form of you. Finding identification, the darkness covered your motion, but the footfall that caused it all, in the silent light of night, could not be found to be the imprint sound of the woman or the deer. What fear? checking in on love, below the open bedroom window and the waxing sliver moon, so that in the solitude of invisibility, you stealth traversed the land, crying out unheard, for that template love—found, lost, found, fled—exiled from heart to suspended animation in the head.

ITALY BY MOON

The moon of late June spilled into the rail train cabin room, through a window beyond which passed Cypress spindles in the early Summer night, whizzing before the light, creating a flickering zoetrope, starring occupants within the train cabin. You half reclined in uncomfortable sleep, half facing the window, the light, bared arms crossed to hold you tight in dreams, your skin took the hue of cream, in this, some surreal scene. Face and arms aglow, a radiant spectacle of a timeless maidenhood, perfection in the dim hush before dawn, in the fully grown woman, a preserved angel hiding in you, revealing only in the dark safety, in sleep. Brown hair pinned behind right ear, the unbroken rail of silver illumined trail, from the near forehead, brow, cheek, chin, neck— all expressionless in rest, fading back into neutral between the days' behest. And the South speeding train rocked gently the two adult infants, in Her far reaching arms, cradling in a cabin bosom against harm, barely a stranger in Italy, wanting to be home together in Rome, ancient familiars found on the lam, invaders of a foreign land, new lovers long overdue, but old friends from *déjà vu*. The difficulty determining your breath coming and going, for the rocking motion; you may well have left unspirited the goddess image for the company while your You flew about brand new, in some distant dimension within. Entertaining in dollike fashion, you began to create a worry, that Life may never return to pick up where last left off, reanimating, as is the habit of a player on every new stage of the daily age. When just about to check, the chest heaved to breathe, cognizable only in the sudden calmness of the slowing speed of the train—Venus was alive in sleep, or temporarily checking her dream? The great fortune of the divine gift of traveling with a mate, to some heretofore undiscovered place; to be with you in a world brand new.

The paled stars, having lost their competition with the moon, all together failed to outshine with their collective bright, the moon that magic night. Softly turning to, opening eyes heavily, the emerald reflections two, captured, took prisoner that once-victorious moon. You half smiled, turned back away, disappeared into tomorrow's Rome.

In Ships of Light, Passing High above the Night

In culinary dread, of the fast of consciousness, overhead, with telescopic beam, cutting open a window on this scene, among the clouds, to observe as a witness, the foreign faces of pilots in ships of light, passing high above the night. In alter-dimension, some nightmarish tale come real, was the horror of the visionary pale, for mismatched in will and strength, as darkness descended upon this valley place, the speed and stealth and power of great magician ships, on dispatch to some provincial galactic outpost, in attempt to secure for the overlord of a universal empire. In contrast to the pastoral nation below, subjugated by farmers and cattle and fields and flowers, in motion how very slow—when, like lightning flashes, these astral ships cut across the day beyond the night, far from ordinary sight. The sense of fear would source from the insignificance of the Cow People compared to the intelligence of what Mind vast, capable of spanning the interstellar gaps, while apparently ignoring what fertile Earth may offer. Not ignored, but perhaps unseen, was blue and white and green home. In the tiny window of the fore ship, strained enough to find detail upon the pilot's face, of one ship among so many, intent upon another world, or perhaps buried deep in thought or calculations, the blankness of detachment to details. The chilling concept of the High Command in control of such a fleet, thrilled, shocked, spilled the courage at the feet. On a whim, an errant soldiership may come in, annihilate the human from the sin, then return to the stream of light and light-filled ships, circumscribing the night beyond the day above the night—to stand safe upon the firmity of earth, while visions of potential doom passed up and across, and to be the only one to see, made rearrangement to the aims on eternity. Not alone in a grand scheme, an ultimate visitation once must come, and hopefully in some peace not heretofore seen. *And what most dooming constraint to the human outlook, that it must at first fear, as if no gods were or ever near.*

Radiator Thine

Remarried in a moment reclaimed, she filled the room with her smiling warmth. At first glance, she embraced with no hint of actor—family long lost but then reunited. In an instant a lover long foregone in past, remembered all asudden—for a brief once let, as if Time's condominium on lease momentarily, a glad heart to see such a golden beauty meet at the door, at a day's long haste or work, end. How clearly then, with early afternoon Spring light flooding in your office window, the minute spent with you would be the only that eternity would spare. Rare and delicate flower, you—the yellow tulip of first the season of warmth. And in a slow turn of the head, you shook off the small talk of a stranger, in passing, so that an aerie profile fit just with this scene. The locks flowing down to shoulder length, and a drape of it tucked behind an ear, lent a lovely casualty to one already so dear. In pastel blouse unwrinkled, kempt as if first day, with accomplice khakied slacks to accent the carved steel of your person. Why the pretense of clothing? as if a bared arm or face with lips exposed, is not enough nakedness to confuse the eye of Beauty looking on...and in, within. And there Mother Divine makes her works work, shining out with individual stamp, thru you, and you, and you, and you. To truly smile sincere, in the midst of a business conduction, is a thing to behold most dear. No smile ordinaire, but with a simple parting of the lips, though silent truthfully, music yet still poured forth. There can a symphony be if played within a chuckle's length; and when a former lover giggles, an infinite composition of aurora drops tingling upon the tin lid of sin, always ushers out a type of love that lifts higher what acts of affection that may have elsewise dwelt lower. To have sight of you, wife, after so longly lost from life, berefts in the thought—when the experience is cast abroad—who is not kin! Because a view so precious as you, eked in, that which had been shattered and scattered, that no longer mattered, repaired, recollected, and auto-caused to begin anew again. What foreign electricity invoked in that room with you, so that the flooding-in sun, your shining face, the seeming separate loves withheld, all combined to overwhelm. Turning to leave, the business end, looking back when you had looked away, gave fright and disrepair, to the otherwise exuberant air, for no sooner had the exit occurred, when your radiant face fell from glad to sad—the shocking revelation when your innocence no longer felt pressed to pretend to happiness? But maybe you were simply free, when the demands of day took less than every moment of your mind away from a beloved one, another husband, other children. Unknown, but that blank, expressionless fall that had happened to once only a second prior gave beams, was a perch to have to see, no less. One doubts the cause of justice, when the mirth that may light the stars in eyes of lovers long lost and then reunited, that abides sadness in place of joy continuous, despair so closely upon the heel of laughter, the comfort and affirmation of an unspoken request to be held, after so many millennia forgot the meaning of a lover's touch, warmth. To see one adored awoken from the depth of the sleeping ages, and shine to only then return quick to the unconsciousness of the day's motion, is to be shaken to the core, to sustain breaks in the solidity of the Infinite More, the Dramatic Perpetuator of stories retold, resold. There can be only weeping, to lose you again this way, that gives sympathy and value to the life of the blind, who had never to gain and lose, images so tender and lovely to the heart's eye.

MAIDEN YOUTH AND THE NOBLEMAN OF CALUMET

By the end off Time it would matter not what form stood between, or what reasons determined scene, for the excavation of bones might tell, how a life was lived well. In ageless days, what onus must just be put upon? such that you would be nothing but beautiful and right. That the years might interfere with an appropriateness of smiles based upon so gross a material plan. Would you not laugh without condition? on that which you felt humor. In spite of the years, that beaming favor of brightness in your eyes, still charms as though a child chiding a child of an own league. Maiden, Youth contracted some pact with thee, granting powers, in payment, of immortality. What slippery footing, steering from the rear, accounting of control by the reaction of the face, the actions of the object you hold dear? Naught wont of admiration, fair maiden, spry move about with finessing catlike clout, whose lethalist weapon is the desire within the eye of your hire; payment exchanged with even one estranged, never-having-met your nobleman of Calumet, who possessed the wisdom to know his weakness was that desire. From the mountains near the seas, he descends to find in thee, the subtraction of what the years cost his madame. Seeing, thus, in comparison to a flower, how gently thy scant demand of days has pressed thee. The mysterious effects the circulation of the sun-in-reverse have upon one! to your machination of the age; conspire to defeat what Youth finds dire. Marry to the merry state, all the wisdom of your senior better? to behold the angle in presence. Not the flight path of the soaring human bird? to ponder than steal such a victory from the Fates—arguments of

Right unheard! Perhaps the boldness of the lightening strike, and the intrusion of its accompanying subsequent thunder clap, carve into stone a destiny of two such actors indivisible, at war with Time, as the Maiden Youth in love with her life, and the Nobleman of Calumet.

Snows of June

In the green of June, with the waters looking on, the Cottonwoods flew by the sea. Astrolling joy along a path in this scene, may in some regard appear as the cold February Winter, drear—but only in moment's effort....The frozen gale a mere balmy breeze; the clouded pregnant skies the burning sun of light, shining down to the cupping wavelets nearby, happy to have the business of almost Summer-deep heat, to offset the cold, cold sleep. In a magical scurry, the flurries were Cottonwood flowers in flight. Landing upon the grasses, the fading green to white, made the June into a February firm-convincing sight. Giving way to the dabbling white, pushing out the might of light, fighting for command of the sky, the clouds and the sun, both lost out to the Pure White; spilling then upon the waters, the drinking, cupping wavelets wore paint; splashing onto the shore, the Purity wanted more. Kissing in mind the flying cotton, all was then decorated in the white: the sky, the sea, the sandy beach, the grasses of the peninsula. This sacred storm raged, unnoticed by the maiden youth, a writer upon a page, curled upon the sands, pen in hand, working. She gazed up to find an emphatic touch, displaying the perfection of feminine sculpture; sea nymph at rest. Staring at but thru, she, blinded to the interloping admiration, displayed a forced smile of having-to, for politeness—but mostly leaving residue irritation at the interruption of some holy writ yet half bit! She conversed in a kindly glare, mostly withdrawn within to another Where, fishing the seas of inspiration. The startling dichotomy of Beauty Maiden Youth and fire, burnt all illusion lending Winter to the white, except for a coldness she harbored in her eyes, belying the smile. *What could angels find so troubling here, dear? beyond the problems of wearing human flesh!* A giggle to you, sweet nymph, and though your mass lay defended in some misunderstood appearance that none see more than the fair young woman in distress, know your true identity has not gone undetected.

WORLD OF WOMAN

It was hoped that you might lead the resistance. The steel in your gaze, commingled oddly with the innate nature of compassion that is woman. At any moment, a gleaming sword may reveal a razor edge, as you calmly, gently, eased back the tunic covering it, and your own swordlike frame. Twice, twins, for a moment in acumen and business. The remarkable ability to manage numbers so that a practical practice results—you are a doctor of numbers, and another was known as well. A mother, by the two photos upon your desk. Wondered at the frail happiness supporting the smiles on the faces of your two daughters. The fragility of that thin layer of joy that supports all things physical; metaphysical thin ice. How easily a stray bullet from Life's gun—stirs the waters beneath that ice. How insidiously, and how often sensationally—the cracks appear; how frigid those waters to the fallen thru. How on God's earth can there live any smiles for long! Indeed—the comedies of youth; the tragedies of the elder years. Winced at whatever coldness numbed reason to let passion cloud—the mating season—to bring a babe into the line of fire on earth. There—in the gray tinge of the crystal clear iris of your—coldness. Fascinating faculty that woman makes love—that coldness may transmute to warmth—the frost of the moon's dark side, melted by the heat of a miraculous sun, having found the shadow regions, long lost in the minutes of the business administration feminine. Would you gut, as if a man, a pig in the day? and yet a kindly lover, mother be, at dusk? Men have no such ability, due to fixity. You tap dance, wisp, to and fro, from cut to cure, as though a human jet. Reaching out, to sweep back the shoulder-length hair, to delicately secure it behind your ear. Could you acknowledge a sea of wonder? in some admirer, of you. The slight accent, betraying a region that circumscribed, made a chuckling fancy—your twin to the East, led quite an apposite life, due to environmental influences—of urbania—but how similar in form and behavior had you not been separated at birth. You were too tan for the season, not unattractive at a glance, but the effect was unnatural and out of place—unnecessary for you, more than anything—you were a natural creature, and the artificially whitened teeth disappointed—what of what birth gave you? No need for a flower to dress up—a drop of Beauty from some other Where may not be improved upon in a lesser Here—come as you are—be as you are—but glimpsing that arching flail at your side—won't hold it against you. Wouldn't want to lay cold at your feet, the cut pig of the day.…Two diplomas on the wall gave some history on you, but only brief, and incomplete. It was work to coax a smile, from those thin, professional lips, set apart an inch—a mile—from where it came, that smile, it engulfed the room and occupants; then wondered at the trials that perhaps occluded the sector of the soul reacted, thus enacted the expression of joy—you said, 'This part of the day I work and frown; you made me take me out of context. I appreciate that, but work is work. And you are the pig of the day. And I'm sorry about that.' With a slender hand, featuring French manicured nails, she surgically brushed back her tunic and drew the flail, in a single fluid movement. The smile on the faces of your two girls faded into rapidly descending darkness. Can't be proven but swear, if the sense of touch is the last to go—that felt the surprising warmth of your thin steely lips upon own.

MILLION-YEAR CONTRACT

On the deck afore, wind fluttering thru the years of yore, the cutter on the high seas blue, beckons like the call of you. The lonesomeness of the stillness of the landlessness—how simple the environment at sea. A hundred thousand astralnauts, spiffying up the uniforms, standing at attention against the breeze in the bay. The dozen cutters left the open seas, having returned home to port, to rest from salvation's hearty task. The microblue of water dust, scattered across the skies, accounts for the shared time outs, taken by missionaries mesmerized in the sub-aether regions of earth—the cosmic hypnosis initiated by the wave function of firmity, the *Power in the House*. Respite for that taxed, less-than-Spirit, must-be-renewed form, commences, engages the soul sailors of the seas. Mysterious navy, without guns or bombs, clears mind mines from the peoples of earth—crystal clarity results. Thinkingness, rippling upon inkiness, waylaid no more in darkness, transmuting to invisible ink! if at all. To be standing among the brave, on deck, that breezy day, is to be living a forfeited life, for the charge to sail the blue, en mission, en route, en toto, is a signature upon a million-year contract. How many lifetimes hence? must be lived to accumulate a payoff. What shall hold the world from fragmenting in future? if not the glue of such a navy true. And now to port and rest and relaxation.

Butterflies and Angel Wings, and the Maidens of Aetheria

The ghost of you hangs above the sands that gird the shores of Big Blue. Beckoning thoughts of the Infinite, the waters and skies are wont to speak with your voice of silent thunder, hitting the viscera as if a cannon shot, leaving for blooding and breathing naught heart nor lungs. A spirit, then, left to dance in your world, skirting the proper Bifrost bridge to the lighted realm now called home. Beneath the blue of Big Blue, behind the air of the sky, within the white of the clouds, the rambling ghosts congregate according to some unknown timeline, very difficult to ascertain, with meaning or understanding, even when introduced to, in conception. So with some sense of divinity, now, the thought of the One Mother who bothered to entertain Her children with earth. Granting blood and breath, She weights down the soulets, sets them ablaze with passions for bright colors and shiny things, distinguishes within them a preference for feeling or reason, prays for their timely return, and lets fly the drama for the aeons, the world cycle. One trick is the implantation of a memory for Aetheria—a hunger for the unseen and untouchable, and the never-distant suspicion that the real is unreal. Bumping into ghosts, Aetheria boasts with Holy Hosts, then the argument for reality becomes somewhat of a joke, with the ebbing of the slowly flow of the streaming rainbow amorphous. Such lightness and weightlessness and gently moving thoughts, combine to annihilate time; the Neither-Here-Nor-Where? strikes sharply the face of space, so that purpose lets loose to seek realignment to some task, but no work is felt to exist, despite efforts? to wear it thus. With the same pleasant shock as Hylus, who stooped to supp from the crystal pool in the deep wood, the beautiful maidens of Aetheria melted the boundaries of singularity, with the sheer curiosity of having met for the first time with their own selves in mirror image, which looked nothing like what they knew to be familiar. The bizarre new wholeness, as of the light sticking to the globe's other half during night in this, then coming 'round with the spin of morn—and staying for a permanent day. The wisp and chortle of the music of Aetheria, the echoes of the rumbling tides of earth's seas, the shrill sound of the sunrays reverberating with feedback home to their source; alternating in current, the rainbows travel to and fro, 'tween earth and heavens. Maidens of Aetheria travel in such ways, only by day, daughters of the misty light, citizens of the rainbows. The jokestresses, they, and endowed with compassion, like the feminine way, supplant, when wars and death distract, butterflies to the Summer meadows, and fragile filleted seashells meekly hinged by a remnant ligament, or angel wings, to the shores, for proof of a life possible here beneath heaven, where Truth to rule the mind, and Love to comprise the heart. When the soldiers paused their fight, long enough to take in, breathe the mysterious watery breath blowing across the sparkling seas, it begins.

Madonna with Child and the Maiden

Your silent love you gave unacknowledged. Strangers, passing days in proximity, and therefore intimacy, but the silence kept the distance finite, made a reality of the mysticality, that you glimmered so near, yet so far. The child you carried within would feel it, too—the closeness, the warmth, of two dancing around one, a participation of some higher Force of Conglomeration, specializing in accretion of the scattered dust of existence, the experiences that make a body human—yet never meeting, really, as a sole soul. This individuality from the duality, the separation, an arbitrary unitization of a substance so amorphous and liquid as the invisible Light cast in a quanta called you. You, child, will never really know your mother dear. You interfere with the Shining Light that gifted holy sight, cutting out of Night, illumined lives such as yours; the shadow cast your presence, and, where do dancing shadows touch? Only admiring the Source of existence, in union, may the experience touch be felt. God bless you, Madonna, for the reflection of your shining face. The wholeness with which you beam, smiling with the body entire. A happy thought ignites the dark, so that the sun shines upon you well before dawn, and triggering the cascade of falling stars you collect in your eyes, so that the infinite deep of space need be no further removed than your pupils. The golden thread that light wove lay upon your head, flowing down into locks and waves upon your shoulders bare, playing with a Spring breeze, as though a million joyous strings harping musique divine, from some long forgotten time. You looked *at* but somehow thru, and longing for the touch of you, for you to gently rest your face upon this hand, so that holding you may in a way retain indirect the essence of fire uniquely your flame; the capture, to have, and in that instant lost. Machinations of Time assault the lovely happy as if a sea of pins pouring down upon the naked flesh. The impossibility of cupping the moment of the sight of you, to sip for the lonely old years ahead; the futility of the oddity! Though the nature of light, despite the convincing earthly mandates, decries laws and rules, and declares such a miracle may be....But for now, until angels' secrets reveal, that magic must play out and hold in the facility of memory. In the astral music of the moment's sight, the maiden came to bask. Another shining love, placing her hand upon the child, forayed into the beauty of the moment all the failure that would meet all other hands in their attempt to contact you. Only in the larger Self, would the child and the maiden and Madonna meet the admirer—as the dancing shadow possessed all hands, and yet none. What vision would leave bereft, is the unconscious mirth of you, of which your admirers, the attendant maiden and your child within, and others, were aware. *You don't know the power of your shining light; the Beauty asleep in joy; how bright you make all other faces. You are the sun. Joy is your laughter. Love created you. No small wonder, the retinue you drew. Thank you, Madonna, oh, thank you.*

The Green Plain:
Song of Spring

Spreading out before, down the sloping shore, of the highland mountain plain, emerald directionless green, canvassing the scene, near the sea. Provided that none are left to oppose, what sanctity's best doth propose, the peaceful island life, on the British Isles, might defeat the Night, of rampant undelight, of warring tribes of earth. Watering from skies, from seas, keeps the greenery plush. How, or might, must, find joy in a look around, a visitation from another nation, guest most bested in this hyper-literary land; what more may compose? from clouds and sun, and mounts, and sea, and islandness. Circumscription of the walk, leads to round and round and round, for want of an allowance of an unbroken straight line. Until humankind finds walking on the water an option, the stronghold upon arts and letters remains. The stunted travels gives birth to the journey of the mind, a propensity for new sanity, and a sense for a delicious laugh: *I know where to find the funny.* Emboldened by the familiar—every inch's been covered a thousand times— and thus the resultant boredom, from the downside of the sloping plain, the lovers lay to observe the sea, and its endless unfamiliarity. No rote procedures in patterns far, in waves, or eyes' irises. Birthing and deathing, the start and finish beneath the distant horizon upon the surface of broken waters, and in the sparkling color of the eyes, reclining in gaze, upon the green plain.

LET ALONE

If, in Beginning's momènt, the hearty Heart of heaven spent, time enough to defy a section of Its own mind, forgotten to autonomy, though tethered back to autocracy's source. Knocking on the door of...whom at home to answer? What became of fun? Where hath gone the sun? The Mother's on the run. Though in all probability, this starlike red shift, may only be in apparency, and in the loneliness of the abyssal plane, in darkness, in silence; even emptiness must be a product of some maker. And when angrily shout at, the Mother keeps Her peace withheld, and hears—nonetheless—because unspoken retorts appear, decorating the walls of hopelessness, and cracking the facade of separation, by twinkling in the eye of some divine friend, an heretofore stranger, expressing kindness uninvited. And then it is clear what great ship's bow towers above Her populated seas below, a beacon on high, that craft sailing by, as seen from below, in the waters; for the mere existence of such a thing as a seaworthy monster—manmade—inspires in that that creationary backing Hand belongs to some Other? To simply *be*, in greatness, on patrol, though parked, speaks a shouting, crying scream that the Mother had her children, and then set them free. The merely sight of the Shining Light in Night, evokes images of eternal Day. What good reason to have faith in joy? to see the Self above a cosmic toy? to take part in belief of a greater Good, when so scattered, shattered, a One must be, to take up residence in even the littlest of souls, building nests in trees, floating on the skies of high, far above even the great boats of the seas. And so Ma Divinity has a long memory, and some vast love, to cast out but then to recollect, and recount, welcome home a human child, one as far lost once as that tiny sparrow. And all the while, since its beginning of sentience there, with feathers, the singular collection of glimmers gathered one-by-one in time, became a thousand thousand years hence the transformation illumination that lit the white and the gold and the blue of the astral portal thru.

Abyss

Warring heavens took aim, and a pursuant onslaught upon one found out—couldn't reverse the memories of the Unforgetful; wingèd ones in crystal clarity of mind and insight, and, therefore, very dangerous to those and that arousing interest. It is a sport, there. A pantheon of such shooters hides away, for safety's keep—the targets, of course—until a gaming moment presents. Typically, the Beauty Youth, in maiden, collides with shiny Love, and what hath presupposed to Joy, begins a stressful test. Electric-handled frost, accretes upon a will, and, as the galactic night begets of dust the day—in anciency, birthing stars alighted in Her might, Hera having touched her torch—borne the sun, the day, that first morn—so a soul is born. Appealèd glow, given self and affections, builds a life around, to then beset upon a human task of some planetary moment—and with this singular goal at heart—the bows of Apollo and Daphne are strung and pulled, fed then with arrows flung, and an unsuspecting mark must create philosophies to account for his blood. What climate, then, for love? How many deaths can a glowing one hold? before the day disappears for good. The maiden and the youth then stand, before an abyss at hand, and peering into the Unseen's land. But the human eyes are black, and Darkness occluded day. But as the so-called 'dark side of the moon' is not overlooked by a meticulous sun, shining in supposed night, from earth's sight; so the Unseen land comes to view in the telescopic forehead of the earthly blind. Even the gods fall short in the aim, to sportly hit those there. The gods then err where the humans fight fair.

INCENDIARY DEVICE BURNS
MAN ALIVE IN GREEKTOWN

During the tide of night, the frantic fast of earthbound life, and madness dash away, crashed at last upon the floor of Greektown. For an instant, the wave of fear froze, since no water found the nose; near, only a distant river that had run dry long before. In the night of early day, the vacant streets buffeted the desire for populace, and oddity be sincerity, for the night was Friday. If only one souvenir be had, one encompassing symbol of the place be found, then electric connectricity may a light, ignite; incendiary fall of right. Ensuing angels, pursuing charms on men, hiding in some corner alley dark, peer out unseen though sensed. This cascade of starlighted souls, hovering invisible, with perspectives of droplets in space as earth, enigmatically collect visions through pinholes on universes; fixed in mirth, untouched by the horror of mass, and its bloody afterburn, post touch. This horror of the damnèd worlds beyond, seeing cracks everywhere, through which it leaked, portention to spill within the matter plane. How could the discussion of resolution take? when even only one saving souvenir would not appear. Bereft of touchstone advanced, the amulet life, the livor in perpetual Night, had not hope of being found, in the eternity surround, beyond the Beyond. Then the rabble of the roused appeared through sound, hiding underground in illumined caves, spinning and pulling and rolling their way, in gambler's bliss. The populous, forever awake in chance, raised prayers to Hellas, so that a di might dance, happenstance upon BINGO! Hmmmph. What may pose? to so simple reduce the godly bent to the dream of a deuce! What let the sin in? Entombed in this captivation, this preoccupation estranged an Indian nation, from a land its own, pre-owned! In perpetual delight, a single light in a skyscraper; shone, a beacon above the deserted plaka. Following a silent command, entraining for that light, on foot. Entering into the base, looking up, arising into the inner core, then fell thru the opened door. An aetherial woman met and beckoned in, testing, analyzing, then, the curious femininity masculating her mission. On the surface of her self, this whippet beneath a crown of hair, in articulation, cut aires. Self-possessed, then possessing thus, perched with her delicate frame, she innocently lead with the bust. This womanhood in command, wrote upon papers, penning mysterious thoughts. Beneath her manly beauty, as such only on account of drive, not form! a Mother Divine seemed near. Often wondered how She slivered self, adopting out Her kin, so that to dazzle the eyes of men. She hoodwinks into setting afore the intoxicating reflection of the flesh. The proportion and symmetry of this manifested femininity, elicited a music of perfection. Were it not for matter's mess, the glimmer of her inner shimmer, would blind. And as it was a'ready noticed no electric lights, holding back the Night! T'was the lovely general's Self, that blazed in that office height. An odd kindness, reservedness, humility, even once, a blush, mixed all to inform her breeding in God fearing, or respecting. What graceful art of being, must the feminine continuous play. Nearly dollike she flit about, but never without intention. She had agenda. And yet perhaps most curious, she seemed detached into from her truer Self, as if the truth of her beauty lay known yet concealed away from what Force must just requested this role for her to play. For each two thoughts of her work before, another four were of some Evermore. So personal that even she bade hesitate to dwell—lest the performance of the work at hand become too weighty to wear to move about, or intolerable. How very close she seemed to igniting then, catching the fires of hell in her brown irises. Lying was not her way, and so the truth that she must bear, pulled down upon her play, the curtain of Beginning or Ending, whichever most appropriate. With intimacy, she sat to discuss, leaning forward to quietly whisper what she required, and with each breath in every mouthed word, she became more and more and more a friend. The initial strangeness of a stranger's meet, dissolving rapidly into decay, as birthing in subsequent moments, a budding love. And so, in short order one may be found—but then hopelessly lost, having fallen down. There seemed no fear in her eyes, and her confident countenance, gained from the infinite repetitions of her duties, gave no hint that she paid consequence to the empty streets below, to where the missing populous had gone; that the walls of Greektown were coming down, under the burning flames of desire.

Looking in, she merely looked back out, with whatever satisfaction she had gleaned from the inner scene. She was victorious, somehow, without even participating in the fight she saw raging below. Were it not that she was its product, she would be pronounced 'untouched,' 'above it,' as literally she ruled from the heights. *Souvenir? Greece is in flames, and you...appear to be burning, too. But dowsèd dream of what seems, cannot apply to you, in your sky high.* She touched a hand, and the Beyond came in; through the multiplying cracks, licks of fires, the countless brilliant angels standing by, aloof, all at once took interest in Greektown, and came in, and manifested, took form, fell down in the burning.

MUSIC

Hovering over a library, you played an inner tune. Dressed sharply in skirt and blouse, your youth gave proof to outlook; hair brushed back, as if to expect the deeply bristled aires of opportunity, to carry into futurity the best of you, in effort. Then, with strangest end, peeling away from beneath the young face, some alter you took its place. Peering out thru hazeled eyes, an ancient miracled musician who would take command of instrumentation of some novel work, and present a masterpiece to this world anew, unheard but not unrecognizable of ilk; ones master so convened beyond Time's apparent finity, loses not in possibility the momènt, to bridge the past, bore thru space, connecting time to one who lived before. Ignore not that loveliness is but temporal; to see beyond is to be beyond, though where the single eye goes, the flesh is reluctant to travel with, which leaves standing before, a displaced opus, out of time and space, barred from exigency's erase, and here, and here, and here, limited in icy, frozen, heavy minutes, flowing, oh, too slow, to reach escape. Wanted, then, in present and presence, you towered, still smiling despite, hovering in full knowledge of some infinite delight, that played out in music, magical, and mysterious; a wanton lost disagreement bereft you to keeper of others' tunes, when the soundless wand of original genius lay silenced within your hand. A foreign grid of iron, imprisoned you where you stand. But the beauty of the Eternal Youth shone in you, one who gifted fresh lives with the strength and patience to gather the pieces of failure, and to reassemble the truth in glory, whole, if for but a millennium's share of eternity misplaced.

In Motion:
Constituency of Starlight

Steady to the fore, the vector of the flowing floor, stretched into horizon at peace and at one with finity, the nomads disperse on mission; dispatched from eternity, a rosary of blessed beingness descends upon. Free peoples crawling out enpopulate beneath the heavens' gate, until the end, before beginning, again. Swamping earth, circular-minded souls, appearing, disappearing, so that the aliveness of earth remonstrates, and can be measured in will-units, abounding in grace. Season of the waylaid, having frozen in place, Death ensued this harmonious place. But not; just jest! True, would have this retinue, vibrant, flourished, pulsating in light—in motion—separating yet cohesivating, individuals with single-pointed thinking, laser beam cutting thru worlds' difficulties, firing dreams, hiring visions and facts, recreating reality, moment by moment. Kindness, a servant be, portal transfixed in remembrance: One calls out, *Viola! Viola!* in the voice of a master shipwrecked by earth, galactic carnage in little stars' berth; light bumping into matter, spilling onto form, then sticks, coalesces into *planetes*, moving, moving, across the skies of temporality, choosing the shortest route, least resistance, loveliest scenery, flanked by greenery, and flowers of all colors. Wondrous, beautiful, *Viola!* awaits at roadside nature overlook, for traveling permission, to ride with. No longer alone.

Blue Lake Mystery

Midnight found you outright....but before then, North Coast lay flat upon, her host; blue waters, Blue Lake, blue noumena. The magic of a landèd stretch, pulled between East and West, hung beneath heaven's nest, perched upon a sandy rest, 'tis paradise's best. In amusement, echoes of you, facing sunset upon a bay, waited for you by the bridge. In Time's focus harsh, memories blur, but in Blue Lake all come clear to fore. Gently lapping waves upon shore, by day, mix with blue sky, white clouds, a fluid all around. In feminine peace, non-violent Nature nurtured. In disbelief, so joyous the grand effect on you, environmental hue of blue. So at best was peace there, that Beauty shook upon look. Oh, soul, how you are missed, eaten whole in Space's remnant stole. In day, golden peoples populate the surf, hands raised to shield eyes against the rays. In the reflecting glimmer of the wavelets, you smiled; face there, you. All your self, a million times reflected in blue. Crying out against fate, you would not die. Yet, to revisit this seeming lie, *for Space's jesting hast, tucked 'way Time, and you, in attempt*, spilled no less upon this plane, providing footing for the past's insane lovers, relegated to the prison of the bygone. Though, in the revisit, the startling glimmer of the trip-wires made, faultless light is encouraged to milk into sight the personages that once held hands here, in perfect harmony with this world, at home.

LOOP

Saw you in the passing round, faces displacing spaces, though yearèd worn, clarity comes to fore, looking evermore like infinite you. Smiling, glowing one, turn the corner of time, run round. Yet here is the original moment seen. Prosperity beckons, glowing one, from that sea, blue, deep. In the end, there, you, before the next beginning. Blessed marvel, how handy the man you date; therein lay the thing you hate, the hidden from the never-to-be-found. Glowing one, sure smiling, ever smiling, lighting up a place. Glant light, slanted out yet in, the tour-of-the-globe, such a radiance within. Single-sighted Night, one-sided fight. *For a remarkable year: crass underside, terse around the mouth, the Holy Hell chewed up the human grouse.*

Silent Light

Grace met another. Soundless vision, two women in the read—one is grace, the other only shows her back. Unmistakable moment; and how they move around an invisible pole, to which they are tethered, individually less than whole. Grace's shining face, shares cosmic secrets with the woman showing her back, who must wear a friendly face upon her alterside. In animation's triumph, two characters in caricature, perform a Saturday cartoon for the deaf; stationed as such, behind plate glass storefront, all action took place, as if sound turned down. Communication thus began, by the writing of the soundless face, and the movement of that backèd woman. By the glowing smile, seeming slow motion warmth, the nodding and turning head, the receptive air manifested. Some story interest, some conversation of depth, the sudden downcast look—a reference to the bereft? What glue could hold this two to such an unexpected rendezvous? In the storefront meets the seller and the sold, made way for the clearance of a situation droll, within. This happenstance horticulture of the heart, something active and reactive, had reached into them both. The pasted remuneration, evidenced conversation with That beyond creation. The clothing of the spirit, shining though worn, bespoke a jagged edge of life exposed, and pursuant cuts—the bicyclic spokes of the soul—though painful, when shared between another, upheld as would two wheels one vehicle made whole.

SOLDIER AND THE SICK: A WINTER SEA REQUIEM

Decided to carry you into heaven; at season's end, feary Neptune fought to defend, the pearly ramparts barring entrance. Along the frozen footpath-pisteway beach, pinched between a Winter sea to the West, towering cliffs to the East, and darkness. Held you in arms. Sparkling stars on high looked down to twinkle upon, communicating with silent light, voices unheard but seen to affirm the right of a child of earth, though beckoned proper in His good time, to steal home nonetheless. The symphonic crash of Neptune's might, upon the frosted breakers of February's make, handed to the first of March. The fury of a divine appointment, made known within the malevolent waves, crashing only feet away, each a trident strewn astray; whom may assume to approach? what the Father protected most. Sheer cliffs upon which dwellors chose to sit, in cantilevered houses with windows bearing pasted faces of lookers-on, who see two dim specks, inching into the Northern night, along the snowy beach below; a would-be-overtaken pair—soldier and the sick—advancing upon the opalescent glow of eternity. Your failure created the need, and cause for heart's content, for soldier to see you safely where no mortal must can go. Cacophony of musicality, icy watery lair of Neptune in motion—vast arctic sea, to bar in perpetuity, such a flight of a dying soul. Excellent employee of Divinity, what chance the few with mammal vulnerabilities? to steal unharmed into timeless, spaceless infinity. Against a numbing cold, the polar gale of the King of the Sea, would suffice to set such suitors free, of the binding chains of physicality; as if flanking violent oceans entrapping upon the lowlands shore, could not do the job complete! Might the progress reports by those strange cliff dwellors above be sent ahead? to the Keeper of the Gate, telling of a stalling, trundling effort, of the antlike soldier and his tiny kept-protectorate. The message would be to retire early: only another failing, foolish expedition, held fast at the mercy of the sea, of icy guardian Neptune's success. And even invited, none have ever marched into heaven....But interior incandescent atomic warmth, birthright of all children of earth, first preserved, and then promised proof against impossibility—cause for the comfortable to quake. Flowered Summer gardens, the Berber carpet green of grass, the company of pure hearts, the blissful sight of flying things, a gentle stroke upon the back, the warmth of a coo—were all that mattered to the simple you. But complex faults—the arrogance, the urge to pounce upon a mouse, or to pee where it was forbidden—are among such things that you'd overcome, won against your nature by meditation upon the Lamb. You, in the last days, achieved perfection, and accordingly'd been gifted a key to paradise's kitty door, by an angel on the Lamb, here-to-fore unknown and unsuspected by heaven's main gatekeeper man, Saint Peter. And so, unannounced, as the cliff dwellors' lights went out, and they to bed—soldier and the sick stole past Neptune's best defense, arriving off to the side of Peter's gate. Then distracting by a lunatic dance, soldier lowered the sick down and thru her now unlocked kitty door. Soldier watched long enough to ensure that kitty was safe within; as she sprinted toward a catnip bed she transformed into light, like had all the inhabitants there. Waving goodbye, nodding to defeated Peter and Neptune, soldier about-faced for the long walk home alone, head hung slight, despite the consoling company of the chimerical stars of night.

Vulnerable Knight and Beauty's Forgetful Child

In a slow and religious atmosphere, situated out radially from any metropolitan whirl, the sleepiness produced such a girl....Faint recollection, when examined in the eye, she was a beauty caught in momentary cosmic forgetfulness of Self. Even still, Diana had spilled a partial goddess to her huntress devotees; and Time, with collaboration's fame in Space, conspired to alter fates, of devotion-spent attendees. The mask of grace be upon her face, so entirety naught be lost to the past race. Rapturous cut, she stood beside a fellow. In countless such a circumstance, she'd surveyed, parlayed, been invited to the dance, such that reverie bit fatally, and grooved into the mind of a god, a great rut, within which history's ghostesses became maidens, each new life. In a world of delusionary carefully built, no detail left out to distract from the truth, that even and every real, a mere manufactured bit from light—a trick of illusory sight. Statuesque, at poise, vertically aligned, oriented to star signs in outer reaches—to the trained observer, she revealed to be a goddess, no longer lost. Stranded in Finity's fix, stranger long lost to her soul: how to make believed what had been stole? which identity was truth? that that loveliness in the lying mirror presented the ultimate betrayal. Conjuring attention to fall upon the flesh, the Satans guided her eye, so that blinded, unable to see, this once child of eternity fell from Olympus, into a human woman. Repeated again and again, at death ascending back to the Mount, where Diana would warm embrace, deprogram the turmoil and falseness of that earthly place. But when endlessness ceased to charm, the rainbow circumscribing the Olympian dawn, she followed for new adventure. And here, in a second upon this sphere, the actor in this merry-go-round was spotted! In the irises of hazeled eyes, printed in holographic tan, confirmation that royalty *might* die in exile. With sacred duty conscripting, Olympian other fellow with spare recollection, suffice to take on the role of knight, inner armour shining. Gallant mission of the cavalier: whisper in the maiden's ear, sweet somethings, to combat that abstract night, occluding her truthful, original soul of light, that the prodigal Diana's girl was missed back home on the Mount, that Zeus and Company had tired of her constant 'goings out'*! Tall order for a steely knight to remain in control of his personal Night, weighing heavy upon his own impending, vigilant Dawn.* Symmetry that hallmarks beauty, added up in twos: eyes, ears, lips, breasts, and limbs. Two—Delusion's favored digit! If for but an instant the one eye of the knight became two, destructive forces of forgetfulness, would bereft the magnetically summed incorrect. A knight might fall for love, in a complex, lethal play. He observed as she flowed across the public space, then seated with her beau. Inching ever closer, in intimacy's range, it turned out to be gaze, not whisper, that delivered the fatal blow to her false memory. Igniting interest with a bellowed toss of irresistibly unusual conversation, she abandoned the dullness of the boring snore who across from her did sit; cocking her head, turning just slight, so that one doe-eyed met. Locked in trance, as the crowded room froze still, she received the bridging beam from the eye of the reminding knight. Enrapturous divine, of the feminine line, a daughter of Diana soundlessly cried out. Cascading ruminations of Self long lost, reunited at the center of her infinite mind. Just before the invisible bridge collapsed, the knight, in her eye, witnessed the supernova blast, as transcendental Beauty made manifest—if but to pass only a momentary test—a near spit image of Diana broadcast. A knight reveled in her likeness to Mother Divine; bared, nude, quiver in hand—she gasped at the instantaneous destruction of her histories past. Merely the effect of awe, rested upon her countenance, as her pail-sized vessel expanded to receive the banished sea of Infinity. Struggling to remain in her human form, she gently, ever so delicately, turned away. Having relearned the rules in the cosmic game, the old knight and newly goddess bade goodbyes imperceptible to ruling parties that accompanied—sacred actors at work in a near-miss love affair.

SILVER WINTER NIGHT

Angels arriving with descended snow; two towns connected by a road. Tumultuous ocean, and hazardous nearby, deep in the quiet silver Winter night, a lone traveler regards the illumined snowfall beyond, laying in fields between sleeping homes. Those nuclei of advancèd beings, warmth as if a fire at hearth; radiations beaming bright, hidden wings, and awfully human by sight, disinherit the earth. Renunciation at the end, they haunt the hearts of seeking men. Strange flyer before the moon, outlined in black, made Darkness assault what little day is sometimes in the night. Turning to watch the creature pass, zooming before the eye, the night owl of Winter flew by. Pandemonium for a split second, as a demon seemed to scream, pouring from this mouth of owl, destructive, murderous cries, piercing the armour of the heart and feeling, these sounds took a bullet turn. Death for a moment, hands let loose the wheel; careering unattended, the auto sped beyond control, against the vibrational, catastrophic force pulling out the soul. Chest cavity fought the gravity, as flesh began to part; bumping into a pounding heart, a signal was sent to the angels standing by. On dispatch, the shining stars of hope, sacred remedial agents of worlds above, instantaneous gave chase, intercepting and slaying that flying harbinger of doom. Snapping back to a body's keep, the grasping of the wheel. Explosive cataclysm, the Satanic met its end. For a moment, black feathers mingled with the falling snow, each flake a brilliant face, eradicating gloom. Deadly gest aside, salvation never requested; yet having won, the last free soul sped on, thru the silver Winter night.

Magic Flower

Comparing to a flower, steely stem to uphold beauty cups, staunchly brazen in strength, the midst is where the fire grows, Light glows. Petals so familiar, though strange in that never known, a portion of a flower to remain always in mystery. Nervous in lying wait, for the flood to overtake, what gentle roots' firmly hold may make. Portions only revealed to a lighted day, incomplete color scheme, then, though presence of a rainbow in entirety not in doubt. Hidden, then mystery. Lack of revelation, obscured and postponèd be, woman. Darkness feeds upon the Light, where she stands in perpetual Night—the lit-by-Day damage done to the eyes by Evening's violence, she remains sustained between seen-in-partial-phase, and occluded. Gifted only first sight, any second belongs only to another species, men! Incomplete, the partial spouse, treads within a lacking house. Cold captive by blind spots, she must reach to he to see. Admirer, as the whole to missing parts attracts, shines quaint and delicate luminescence upon a darkened self; far out within, a landscape begins again, populated by florals never catalogued, she works miracles in he. A magnetical union of twirling power, to spin the worlds inside the stem—orbitals, tiny specks of space, attached at different levels, whirl around the micro-galactic center, with an infinite reach within, so that poking out thru an alterworld beyond time, place: a flipside life, all together different in form and apperarance; related to constantly anew, another life heretofore withheld from view.

Orange Blossoms

The bespeckled air, shimmering in the morning sun, cresting just the mountaintop tips, so that horizontal rays flattened the new day, as though a sea surface; microscopic waves, in the masses of backlit particles aloft, make indistinguishable the life, from one lived, perhaps, in a paradise lost, when the orange blossoms loft. Leaving your love alone, when the borrowed home, is a place all its own, that is all two lovers have, where true love may roam, freely, about. Tall Pampas grasses wave, whisper; magical morning, *a new day*. Palm of mountain bowl, the Conejo Valley-hand, hold with deep affection the resonating perfection of this portrait that lay beneath the Palm tree. In an instant the scene stands still, when the heartbeat of the lover spills, onto the orange blossom Spring. The blood the lust had heated-bring, the Second Coming: the opening of the lotus heart, the rapture of becoming, in the perfumèd orange breeze, the greater Self that permeates all that heaven makes, *is* the Light that projects the Show; all the knowledge that is the knowing. In momentary oneness, then the other had become another; though two selves, where hid a single lover? Dark morning in your eyes, sun of heart, rise, mourning for the green in the hills, that would part with the Spring, and in turn, the lifeless Life ever after such, when parted the twain ones, dissolved in a dream that had given too much. Yet, still, at home beneath the stars—no difference between the night sky and the surface of your eyes; the sparkle, the stars, and the black pupil-iris, the Far. Awaiting dawn, together, and release of the orange blossoms' sweet, from the trees of the Valley below. Remains in perpetuity.

HURRICANE

...with a specific gravity, madonna approached, a dark storm of *intention*, whirling, twirling, convecting; lightening shot from her black eyes, destroying all that might oppose her own—*intention*. Naught a spoken word lost to an aside; each utterance a razor-tipped arrow, fired in precision at a mark specific—*bull's-eye!* Another dead enemy. And with a beautiful smile, extreme poise, she blew across the open space, of ordinary days near the sea. Oriental gaze—light of other days—Eastern invasion on the West, puts the lover to the test: What is *other?* What is *best?* What remains to discover of the *known?* The exacting strain of effortlessness, with which speech directs the power and the energy that is the composition of the cyclone. The white flesh of her lower back, the bright earth peeking out from the night of her tunic pulled down tight; a catholic mass of elevation climbing her spine, within which six worlds lead to a seventh heaven. Dissolution of the constituency there, with a dispersal of the atomic lights, dropping them at the gate. What flies thru the skies in storm? that is not the makeup of the days of a life at norm. And, with amusement, all in motion about the eye of the hurricane, in a fantastic, miraculous way: flying cows, autos driving as if planes, houses aloft and tossing as ships on a sea of black clouds, and people mysteriously appearing and descending into infinite dark; human magicians or odd invertebrate sharks? But most remarkable were the intentioned words that she evenly spoke: not one ever tossed aside, said in haste, without consideration of its mark. Madonna never babbled.

SITTING

As grace may have it put, madonna, poised to conduct, smiled brightly up, at the arrival of her new chair. Beaming, she sat softly, seeming—eyes closed—in blissful heaven, spinning 'round in place—the girl at carnivale—peeking out thru the professional woman in her paces. Still, frozen in a moment's chill, she the picture of humanity, when asking for approval, from the seeming-lesser he. Then, the nodding affirmation that she sought, and then her final receipt, with delight. Spreading arms wide to receive—a flower to the sunny skies, some petals peeled open; rains from no apparent clouds, to water, her soul soil of joy: to she, the potted plant of happiness, a soft kiss upon the lips, had bade farewell to what a lover misses. Feeling the heat upon the cheeks, and the lingering breath passing between, to sustain the dream that naught else is all but One. And with the stopping breathing, the ending ceased deceiving, that Life is upheld by water and bread. Nay, there is a light in Love, which shines thru all that is true. Madonna, then, suspended in Joy, Light, Truth, had little to do but be happy in possession, smiling ever wider, she spun 'round—Sufi bliss rider, ascending on her chair, arms surrounding the air, higher and higher and higher, pulling down the highest heaven, with the corkscrew hook motion—exactly what it took, to first broach the brook, that is the fluid lowest heaven, aether. Eyes, of brown, rolled up and back, she lifted off from earth; storming the Gates of Pearl, Saint Peter took note that she had stored purity in the whites of her eyes, which were, in the day of the Lord, the very gates of pearl....

SOUL FLARE

Madonna sat, statuesque, listener of all the rest. She held out her hand, offering an accompaniment to the dance of digging in, to the troubles of the mental self. *Voyage to Nowhere. Voyage to Everywhere.* Eyes asampling of outer space, far from a bright sun, such that the twinkling stars of deep night, the sparkling on the surface of her sight, the *shining.* And in this a way, the universe she held in her gaze. What tumbling occurs within? that had led to ejected pain, enough to lay claim and hands to sane. The glorious courage she possessed; the willingness to identify and to slay the barriers to her spiritual way. Perhaps the genetic collision of Hungarian and Dominican, had produced a maiden supersleuth? such that applying the hard-soft intelligence to the lover of warm ocean breezes and vast expanses was the proper and exact combination to expressly open the safe-lock on the desire for safety—soaring, then, fearlessly close to the sun of her soul, and nearing its orbit, the illumination of her face—no *reflection* of the soul-sun, but identification of what she had become. *Burning brilliantly bright, flare star on the edge of night.* Spring day, Madonna a flower in her flowing dress, picture of a morning meadow, colorful, rolling green, with darting larks and buzzing bees, butterflies of an astral eternity, passing thru the scene for a day. Madonna breathes; her breast heaves. She accepts a kiss from her admirer's lips, and rests her head upon that shoulder.

ADVERSARY

The maiden feisty, at the rear of reach, hand held out, as if to teach; soft, long fingers brushing, touching, representing the contents of the heart; tremendous energies, raising, rushing, stilling hushing explosions trying to be. From, the East end of Night, to the West end of morning—the Darkness at its blackest. And so the beautiful stars, shine ne'r so bright, as in the lacking light; pinpricks aglow, stellar snow! storm struck without warn, a soul surrender in a nod; harshness melds to softness, then, as the love entrains—recognizable to two, who, blinded a moment afore, to vast histories together as one, to endless mysteries—losses forgotten to destinies—for the misbegotten. Remembrance golden, in the face beholden. Would a kingdom be recalled? for the jarring in a kiss, or the themes that had mist, imbued. Crying, a misery of longing to be near, she flared at the smiling sight of the enemy thief who had, in the Night of day, stolen her heart. Bright light, sun of soul sight, burning, with the yearning for expansion, expression of passion, the melting—and then a storm of ice, as the head turned forward the expression back to neutral—a desire no longer of fire! A want satisfied. A return to heaven's lowest higher. The shining dims, firmament of the soul-surround caving in, a *stark sky* falling. And, asudden no longer recognizable, no longer noticed; beautiful strangers, again. Bright stars twirling, whirling about, falling, falling, falling, into your eyes, for the remainder.

Approaching Storm

Passing storm; as the aging, the days go faster, so storms moving in and out faster. The thumb screws turn. *How hotly the fires of tests burn!* Storm clouds gather across a distant horizon, upon a vast sea, doubling in apparent tenacity, in waves' reflection. Time stands still—in youth—for the lacking sooth, and the ratio of days spent versus those awaiting future rent. With fixated gaze upon the setting sun, enter fast the ancient mind machine—annihilator of space, manipulator of time. Watch, asuddenly the scenery: trees, flowers, *those seas*, melting, growing, altering, in a flash-flash moment. So, a life of horror must be transformed in such a waiting, magical way. 'If you don't like the karmic weather, wait a minute,' said the fool. Dizzying earthly experience: what powerful glue, desire. To be at the mercy of the fire, is to step off the time machine, upon which the trees green, and the faces mean, melt, decay away, and then instants later, all is replaced, regrown, resewn. Brilliant races rise to, evolutionarily, take the places of those that had become ashes. *Wait a minute, travel far, safe within the cosmic car.* Enormity of Time's wand, waved in fronts of humans' foreheads, telescope to view into eternity—the spiritual eye—true meaning of the unicorn. Galloping to that sunset, subset human, remarkable horse, to the oncoming nite, flanked by the approaching storm. But safety's, immunity's in that magical horn.

Harvest Flower

Upon the shelf to orange down, a looker on to those and that of the Fall sun.
Madonna shines, a radiant find; luminous face beaming the warmth of
wisdom, love, to the chilled, dry, anxious for the harvest nigh. Dearest heart
of auburn, exposed to frost; frozen at the edges, but always intent upon the
Spring; the garrison of heat within to sustain, survive, though Winter's sleep
complete assaults to steep, creep into the animation of life. Counter that;
repository, the Beauty incandescent burn, against that Night, to warm in
the absence of the Light. She waves in the winds, the gale of sins that merit
not ins, for the bestubbled afflicted, the put upon. Smiling at the sight of
love, she receives the wounded doves alighting home. The transformation
of the face—Summer sun out of place!—the harvest flower blooms in Fall.
The All of Mother Divine, Madonna Fine, petalled lips to accept the kisses
of affection; hair gently tucked behind the ear, to hear readily the sweet
whispers of admiration, sans interfere; Love asking back, as at the harvest,
feeling lack, so much had been given....The home of Fall, the bounty, that
call; the gleaning the reason for the season. Standing tall, and waving, the
harvest flower hazing, at her round eyes of brown, at the giving up of love,
and the fulfillment of the cycle of life, that she had served so sweetly; Beauty
she had become so completely.